The Practical Prophet

Sheng Kung Hui: Historical Studies of Anglican Christianity in China

Series Editor: Philip L. Wickeri

The Anglican (and Episcopal) tradition has been present in China for almost two hundred years. The purpose of this series is to publish scholarly, well-researched, and authoritative volumes on the history of the Sheng Kung Hui ("Holy Catholic Church"), with an emphasis on its life and work in Chinese society. Sponsored by the Hong Kong Sheng Kung Hui, separate volumes in this series will include studies of particular people and institutions, as well as studies of the broader social significance of Anglican involvement in Chinese history.

Also in the series:

Christian Encounters with Chinese Culture: Essays on Anglican and Episcopal History in China
Edited by Philip L. Wickeri

Imperial to International: A History of St John's Cathedral, Hong Kong
Stuart Wolfendale

The Practical Prophet

Bishop Ronald O. Hall of Hong Kong
and His Legacies

Moira M. W. Chan-Yeung

Hong Kong University Press
The University of Hong Kong
Pokfulam Road
Hong Kong
www.hkupress.org

© 2015 Hong Kong University Press

ISBN 978-988-8208-77-7 (*Hardback*)

All rights reserved. No portion of this publication may be reproduced or transmitted in any form or by any means, electronic or mechanical, including photocopy, recording, or any information storage or retrieval system, without prior permission in writing from the publisher.

British Library Cataloguing-in-Publication Data
A catalogue record for this book is available from the British Library.

10 9 8 7 6 5 4 3 2 1

Printed and bound by Paramount Printing Co., Ltd. in Hong Kong, China

To the love which made Ronald Owen Hall's life work a reality

One wonders how far the past influences the present. How far "now" is a result of "then." Perhaps they have this in common that they are both the result of that intangible part of one which is one's character, one's soul, one's self, whatever you like to call it. I mean that the "self," which acted in a certain way "then," is likely to act in the same way "now" and in the future. For that reason we have some right to know people's pasts. We can only really know what they are "now," if we know what they were "then."

R. O. Hall to N. Baron
June 2, 1919

Contents

Series Introduction   xi
   Philip L. Wickeri

Foreword   xiii
   Paul Kwong

Preface   xv

Acknowledgments   xix

Chapter 1   Sowing the Seeds: Early Encounters with China   1

Chapter 2   The Making of a Bishop: Bishop R. O. Hall's Early Years (1895–1932)   19

Chapter 3   Working under the Threat of the Japanese: The Diocese of South China and Hong Kong (1932–45)   47

Chapter 4   Managing the Diocese under Political Turmoil: The Diocese of South China and Hong Kong (1946–51)   85

Chapter 5   Shepherding His Flock in God's Beloved City: The Diocese of Hong Kong (1951–56)   111

Chapter 6   Consolidating and Expanding His Work: The Diocese of Hong Kong (1957–66)   149

Chapter 7   His Humanity and His Legacies in Hong Kong   185

Appendix 1   Transcript of Bishop R. O. Hall's Tape Recordings Made after His Retirement   207

Appendix 2   Bishop R. O. Hall's Life Events   213

Appendix 3   Bishops Consecrated, Deans Installed, Archdeacons Appointed, and Clergy Ordained by Bishop R. O. Hall   219

Appendix 4   Churches and Schools in Hong Kong during Bishop R. O. Hall's Episcopate   223

Appendix 5   Names of Places, People, and Terms in English and Chinese   231

Appendix 6   Sources of Information   237

Index   243

Series Introduction

Sheng Kung Hui: Historical Studies of Anglican Christianity in China

The purpose of the series Sheng Kung Hui: Historical Studies of Anglican Christianity in China is to publish well-researched and authoritative volumes on the history of Anglican-Episcopal Christianity as a contribution to the intellectual, cultural, and religious history of modern China. With an in-depth focus on one particular denominational tradition, which has been in China for almost 200 years, the series presents an interdisciplinary perspective that will also contribute to the history of Christianity in China. The emphasis throughout is on the life and work of the Church in society. Individual volumes are written for an educated audience and a general readership, with some titles more academic in character and others of more general interest.

The spirit of Anglicanism is expressed by the Chinese term Chung Hua Sheng Kung Hui, meaning the "Holy Catholic Church of China," the national church that was founded in Shanghai in 1912 and the first non-Roman church body in China. Anglicans stand between Protestants and Catholics in their approaches to Christian tradition and church order, but they are usually regarded as part of the Protestant movement in China. Since the nineteenth century, the Sheng Kung Hui has been involved in a wide range of educational, medical, and social welfare work alongside efforts to spread the Christian message and establish the church. In the first decades of the twentieth century, Chinese Sheng Kung Hui leaders began taking the lead. The Sheng Kung Hui has also played an important role in cultural exchange between China and the West.

Copublished by Hong Kong University Press and the Hong Kong Sheng Kung Hui (Anglican Church), the first volume in the series was Stuart Wolfendale's *Imperial to International: A History of St. John's Cathedral, Hong Kong* (2013). This was followed by *Christian Encounters with Chinese Culture: Essays on the Anglican and Episcopal Tradition in China* (2015). Subsequent volumes will include biographical studies, a book of essays on Anglican women's history, and a volume of historical photographs. It is hoped that the series will encourage further dialog on the place of Christianity in the history of modern China.

Philip L. Wickeri, PhD, DD
Series Editor

Foreword

R. O. Hall was the longest serving bishop we have had in Hong Kong, with an episcopacy lasting from 1932 to 1966. We are grateful for all that Bishop Hall did for our church and our city. His time with us was a turning point, for Hong Kong itself, for the Hong Kong Sheng Kung Hui, and for Bishop Hall himself. Within our church, we stand in his shadow, but we also move forward in new ways.

This new biography of Bishop Hall is long overdue. It is based on personal and archival materials that have not been used before. Unlike earlier studies, this book lays special emphasis on his contributions to Hong Kong in the decades following the end of World War II. It was during this time that Bishop Hall worked tirelessly establishing parishes, setting up schools, and attending to the social welfare and housing needs of Hong Kong people.

In all that he did, theology was very important for Bishop Hall and his ministry. He was neither a liberal Protestant nor a conservative evangelical, but a catholic Christian, humanized by his work with the poor and his encounter with China, and deeply involved in the social and political issues of his day. His catholic Anglicanism may be understood as "that way of regarding Christianity which would see in it not merely or primarily a doctrine of salvation to be apprehended by individuals, but the establishment of a visible society as the divinely constituted home of the great salvation, held together not only by the inward spirit, but also by certain manifest and external institutions,"[1] to borrow the words of Michael Ramsey, the 100th archbishop of Canterbury. For Bishop Hall, this understanding combined the sacramental sense of Anglican theology and churchmanship with a strong involvement in social and political issues.

Bishop Hall's view of Hong Kong and China was a great deal more than a product of a particular theology and church, however. There was a concreteness about his life and work that found expression in a pastoral approach to the priests with whom he worked, as well as with the laity, and a sympathy for the poor and the outcast wherever he found them. From his first encounter with China in 1922, he was drawn to an appreciation of Chinese culture and work with Chinese people. This stayed with him all his life. In relationships with others, he could sometimes be short-tempered, I am told, but he would reach out afterward in a spirit of friendship. His involvement with people and the problems they faced helped to humanize him and make his work as bishop more passionate and real for others. It is no wonder, then, that R. O. Hall was profoundly shaped by his friendships with people, friendships that extended far beyond the usual circle of English "old boys" from a certain time and place and class. This is part of what enabled R. O. Hall to be such an effective and inspiring bishop in Hong Kong.

It is important to note Bishop Hall's continuing relationship with the People's Republic of China after 1949, in light of the return of Hong Kong to the Mainland in 1997. He and his wife were invited for a visit to China in 1956. This was a relatively liberal time in pre–Cultural Revolution China. The Halls visited Canton, Shanghai, Beijing, Hankow (Wuhan), and they met with many Anglicans and leaders of the Chinese Christian Three-Self Patriotic Movement Committee. In Beijing, R. O. and Mrs. Hall were also invited to dinner with Premier Zhou Enlai.

Bishop Hall was the only church leader from Hong Kong to visit the Mainland in the 1950s. Many people criticized him for being too close to the Communists after his trip, even some in his own church. But he went to China because he believed that maintaining personal and public links with Chinese church leaders and government officials was important for Hong Kong. This has been important in our church ever since, as we have sought to develop relationships with the Mainland based on friendship and mutual respect.

The Practical Prophet: Bishop Ronald O. Hall and His Legacies by Dr. Moira Chan-Yeung will help readers become acquainted with Bishop Hall and all that he did for Hong Kong and China and for the Hong Kong Sheng Kung Hui. It will be of great interest to people in our church, and to those who themselves knew Bishop Hall. More broadly, this meticulously researched study will be interesting to readers who want a better understanding of the recent history of Hong Kong and Greater China. It shows the importance of the church's involvement in society for all people, centering on the life of an extraordinary individual.

Paul Kwong
Archbishop of the Hong Kong Sheng Kung Hui
August 2015

Note

1. As quoted in A. Michael Ramsey, *From Gore to Temple: The Development of Anglican Theology between Lux Mundi and the Second World War, 1889–1939* (London: Longmans, 1960).

Preface

Unlike some of my friends, I did not know Bishop Ronald Owen Hall (ROH, as he signed his name) personally. The only time I met ROH was at my confirmation when I was a teenager, and he placed his hand gently on my head in blessing. Who was to know that, as a grandmother in retirement from my work as a physician-researcher in academic medicine in Canada and Hong Kong, I would be gripped by his story, working on it for ten hours a day for more than three years?

My first intention of writing about ROH was simple: to find out more about the bishop who dared to defy the Anglican tradition seventy years ago by ordaining the first woman priest, Li Tim Oi, in the Anglican Communion. Yet, as I carried on with my research, I found myself utterly absorbed by a project I first thought would take only about a year. In these past three years of living with ROH's story, my appreciation of him has only deepened. I have come to see him not only as a practical visionary who served the Divine by serving the Chinese people of Hong Kong at a crucial time in our history, but also as a complex human being, full of longings, questions, and those inner contradictions that we all share.

ROH was the longest-serving, most influential, and perhaps most controversial bishop in the Hong Kong Anglican Church. His episcopacy, from 1932 to 1966, covered the most tumultuous period in the history of Hong Kong and China.

Although ROH was British to his core, he gave his heart to China. After the May 30 incident in 1925, when Chinese students were killed by British officers, ROH was invited to work in Shanghai on a difficult mission to improve the relationship between the British and Chinese. He developed such a strong affinity with the Chinese people and Chinese culture, that when he became the bishop of Victoria, he adopted a Chinese name he wished to be remembered by: Ho Ming Hua—one who spreads the light of the gospel in China.

On visiting the tomb of Confucius, ROH was so overwhelmed by its harmony and beauty that he did something that would have shocked other Anglicans at the time. He bowed three times in front of it. Few Europeans, especially those with an illustrious clergy lineage, would ever show such a sign of respect to a Chinese sage. ROH came to believe that God, who must have inspired the Chinese to build such a wonderful structure to commemorate a learned scholar, had always been in China—a pivotal belief for his future ministry in Hong Kong and China.

In 1936, instead of baptizing his own son, he asked a Chinese bishop to baptize him in Hong Kong, a British colonial outpost. ROH wanted to make a political and theological statement that Chinese and British are equal in the sight of God.

His ordination of the first female priest in 1944 caused great furor at the time and almost split the Anglican Communion. Many did not know that this radical step cost him his chance to return to England as a bishop. It also cost him personally, separating him from his family for many years and exacting a tremendous toll on his marriage.

At a time when communism was branded a godless and evil ideology in the West, ROH recognized the spirit of personal sacrifice and dedication to the welfare of Chinese people in the early communist movements in China. ROH's relief work and his contributions as chairman of the International Committee for the Promotion of Chinese Industrial Cooperatives, or Gong He, in raising funds internationally and distributing them successfully proved crucial to keeping light industry going in different parts of Free China during the Second Sino-Japanese War. He was recognized by both Mao Zedong and Chiang Kai-shek. He rejoiced at the founding of the People's Republic of China in 1949, sincerely believing that communism could provide the Chinese people with better lives after centuries of poverty and misery. His involvement with the workers' children's schools in Hong Kong and his controversial visit to China in 1956 had even earned him the nickname "the Pink or Red Bishop."

ROH was pre-eminently a social activist who advocated low-cost public housing to accommodate the massive number of refugees in postwar Hong Kong, creating a number of imaginative social welfare agencies that looked after the needs of underprivileged people, especially orphans, juvenile delinquents, and children of workers. His influence led to the development of the Social Welfare Department in Hong Kong in 1958. A visionary in education, ROH helped expand primary and secondary school places for the refugees and the growing population in Hong Kong, and pioneered a form of modern secondary education that emphasized training young people in trades rather than academic work. He founded Chung Chi College and played an important role in the establishment of the Chinese University of Hong Kong. Many in Hong Kong believed that his work contributed indirectly to the eventual economic take-off of Hong Kong in the 1970s.

ROH also foresaw that Hong Kong would return to China in the not-too-distant future, contrary to many others who said this would never happen. He planted deep roots for the Chinese churches by expanding them to the extent that they would not only survive, but flourish after the political change. He understood the importance of having an indigenous church that could withstand drastic political changes in China and Hong Kong. When so many in Hong Kong were rushing to learn English after World War II, ROH advocated the value of preserving Chinese language, history, and culture.

There is no doubt that ROH, as a human being, had faults. Impatient by nature and hating red tape, he consistently tried to cut corners to avoid bureaucracy, and his impetuous nature often led him to rush things in ways he may have regretted later. This pattern of doing what was expedient to move his projects forward no doubt was also a key to his success, helping him bring these pivotal projects in postwar Hong Kong to fruition. It is true that he did become more authoritarian, and less consultative, as he grew older.

ROH drew people to him through his love, spirituality, leadership, and charisma. Most people who had had contact with ROH or worked with him felt loved by him, and were inspired to do their very best. He used his earthly power as an Anglican bishop in a British colony, but also a power drawn from spiritual depths: the power of an inner authority.

This book focuses mainly on the ministry of ROH from 1932 to 1966, because information about him and his ministry before and after that period is limited. It is also known that, before he left Hong Kong, ROH burned almost all his personal correspondence and documents, bringing very little with him back to Lewknor, Oxfordshire. Fortunately, the personal letters that he sent to his family in England were kept.

Thus, what I have learned about ROH—the man, the activist, the bishop—has come from the following sources. The primary sources include: (1) personal letters made available to me by his son, Canon Christopher Hall, including those between ROH and his wife, Nora, during their period of separation from 1941 to 1954, and some of his unpublished sermons. I have spent countless hours using a magnifying glass, poring over hundreds of letters written in very tiny handwriting and narrowly spaced on very thin paper; (2) personal letters located in the Chung Chi Divinity School Archive, from ROH to his sons: to Christopher, between 1954 and 1958, and to Joc, likely written in the early 1940s; (3) Bishop's House Archive, from which I obtained information about the Diocese of Victoria and South China, as well as all institutions of Hong Kong Sheng Kung Hui, including the churches, colleges, schools, social welfare institutions, and medical clinics covering the period between 1932 and 1966; (4) Hong Kong Public Records Office, which has volumes of "bishops' scrap books" containing newspaper clippings of news of the Church from 1932 to 1966; (5) Church Missionary Society Archive, found in the Hong Kong University Library Special Collection; (6) National Archives, London, England, which provided many of the official documents related to the history of Hong Kong and the Church, covering the period of ROH's episcopacy; and, (7) Lambeth Palace Library, England, which supplied the official communications between ROH and the archbishops of Canterbury.

To help fill in the historical context for ROH and his work during the postwar years in Hong Kong, I have also drawn upon David Paton's research materials and his biography of ROH in the Chung Chi Divinity School Archive, *Outpost*, the official journal of the Victoria Diocesan Association (1929–67);

St. John's Review, the official publication of St. John's Cathedral (1930–67); and *South China* and *Fragrant Stream*, which were published for short periods during ROH's episcopacy. For the political and social background covering ROH's episcopacy, I have consulted many books that are detailed in Appendix 6 (Sources of Information).

This book is different from David Paton's biography of Bishop Hall in the following aspects: (1) its extensive use of primary documents as mentioned above, some of which have been made available to the public only recently. It covers ROH's contributions and the development of ROH's attitudes, philosophy, and theological ideas before he was consecrated as bishop of Victoria more extensively; (2) in deference to Mrs. Hall, Paton did not write anything about ROH's marriage. It was a difficult marriage. This book highlights not only ROH's public life, but also his struggle with the pain of prolonged separation from his wife between 1940 and 1954 and the stresses and strains on their marriage; (3) this book also discusses his visit to China in 1956 and his attempted interpretation of Communist China.

The book has seven chapters: The first two chapters describe ROH's life before he became the bishop of Victoria and South China and trace the factors and events that influenced his theology, his attitudes, and policies. Chapters 3 and 4 provide a chronological account of his ministry in the Diocese of Victoria (South China and Hong Kong). Chapters 5 and 6 discuss his ministry in the Diocese of Hong Kong. The last chapter analyzes ROH as a person as well as his contributions to the Church and to the society of Hong Kong.

Although my professional training is in medicine and science rather than theology, I have tried my utmost to present ROH's theological beliefs and philosophical outlook with accuracy, especially his ideas on integrating faith in the modern world and what it means to be a Christian, which were central features of his life, his vision, and his legacy.

I earnestly believe that Bishop R. O. Hall, or ROH, as we will refer to him, deserves a place of honor as a pioneer and a visionary who contributed greatly to the Hong Kong Anglican Church, the Anglican Communion, and Hong Kong society.

Moira M. W. Chan-Yeung
September 16, 2013

Acknowledgments

I wish to register my deep gratitude to Canon Christopher Hall, for access to his father's letters to his mother from 1941 to 1954, as well as photographs and other data. I am also grateful to him for his careful reading of the manuscript to ensure the accuracy of information.

I am beholden to my three advisors, the Reverend Dr. Philip Wickeri, senior advisor to Archbishop Paul Kwong of Hong Kong Sheng Kung Hui, Professor David Faure of the Chinese University of Hong Kong, and Professor Bernard Luk of York University, Toronto; and to Dean Matthias Der and Dr. Christopher Munn, former associate publisher of Hong Kong University Press, for their guidance and insightful comments.

My sincere appreciation goes to Archbishop Paul Kwong, for permission to use the Bishop's House Archive; Michelle Lin, who was tireless in getting old, dusty files from the basement of the Bishop's House for me; Professor Lo Lung Kwong of Chung Chi Divinity School, for his generous consent to use the Bishop R. O. Hall Archive; and Natalie Wai of Chung Chi Divinity School, for her diligence in copying some of the documents.

I owe irredeemable debt to many friends who have given me a great deal of help in the preparation of this book: Dr. Samuel and Mrs. Ellen Lam, for their encouragement in starting the project; Dr. Sue Ann Cairns, for her editing, which has improved the manuscript immeasurably; the Reverend William R. Crockett of Christ Church Cathedral, Vancouver, and emeritus professor, Vancouver School of Theology, for teaching me the importance of traditional Anglican socialist tradition and other aspects that shaped ROH's theology; Mr. Hanson Huang, a lawyer, historian, and computer expert, for selecting files for me to review in the Hong Kong Public Records Office, the National Archives in London, and Lambeth Palace Library, and for providing interesting historical tidbits and advice throughout the project; and Mr. Y. W. Fung, an educator who coauthored with me the history of the Diocesan Boys' School, for his invaluable advice on education in Hong Kong and his critical review of the whole manuscript on several occasions to weed out excessive details. My gratitude to them is beyond words.

My heartfelt thanks go to Mr. Timothy Ha, for his helpful advice and for the use of his office in the Bishop's House; Canon Alan Chan, the Reverend Paul Tong, and Mr. Michael Lai, for their generosity in granting interviews; the Reverend Lewis Leung, for arranging some interviews; and the Reverend Louis Ha, archivist of the Catholic Church in Hong Kong, for supplying statistics of the Catholic Church; Dr. Kenneth Suen and Angela Kaan, for their invaluable suggestions; and Miranda Ho, Stanley Yeung, and Anne DyBuncio, for their secretarial and technical assistance.

Lastly, I thank my husband, Dr. David Yeung, a psychiatrist, for his insights into Nora Hall's psychological problems. His enthusiastic support and encouragement throughout this lengthy project has been most profound.

Chapter 1

Sowing the Seeds

Early Encounters with China

God moves in mysterious ways
His wonders to perform . . .

How could the death of one laborer trigger massive protests throughout China, with severe repercussions for the international community? How did Ronald Owen Hall (ROH) then get charged with the near impossible task of promoting understanding between people with different histories, different interests, and different goals in the British and Chinese communities?

On Saturday afternoon, May 30, 1925, the international recreation grounds of Shanghai at the west end of the Nanjing Station were eerily empty. Expatriates usually congregated to play cricket, tennis, and baseball, but there was no laughter, no hum of conversation, no plonk of tennis balls, no thwacking of balls on cricket bats.

Nearby, however, just outside the police station on Louza Road, a large group of Chinese students was protesting loudly. In an attempt to crack down on trade union workers, Japanese foremen had beaten a Chinese laborer to death. Members of the Chinese Communist Party had displayed bloodstained clothes at schools and factories, incensing both the students and workers. Slogans were plastered on the walls: "Down with Imperialism!" "Down with Unequal Treaties!"[1]

The police of the International Settlement under British officers had arrested around 60 students and their ringleaders and charged them with breaking the municipality law which forbade unauthorized political meetings and agitation.[2] By 2:45 p.m. a much larger throng had gathered in Nanjing Road outside the Louza police station, demanding the release of the arrested students.[3]

Just minutes later the protest heated up even more. An angry chant began: "Kill the foreigners!" "Kill the foreigners!" "Kill the foreigners!"

The British station commander, Inspector Edward Everson, was called out. As the crowd surged forward, he felt nervously for his revolver, yelling in Chinese: "STOP! If you do not stop, I will shoot!"

As the waves of anger rolled toward him, he fired into the crowd.

Other police officers followed his lead. According to a Chinese report, 32 died and 89 were wounded.[4] Among the dead were four students, all members of the Student Christian Movement in China.[5] This incident galvanized the nation. That evening, students and workers in Shanghai gathered at a mass meeting and declared a general strike. As more and more workers went on strike, Shanghai came to a standstill. The strikes, coupled with violent demonstrations and riots, spread like wildfire across China, resulting in many more Chinese being wounded or killed.

The foreign settlements were thrown into a state of emergency. Hoping to defuse the volatile situation, the Diplomatic Body[6] in Beijing immediately dispatched representatives of various nationalities to Shanghai to investigate the incident. After determining the facts that had culminated in the mayhem, the Diplomatic Body concluded that the municipal and police authorities at Shanghai were "to no small extent to blame for the tragic events of the May 30th and were deserving of censure accordingly."[7]

In a judicial enquiry carried out by the British, American, and Japanese judges, the British and Japanese judges exonerated the police and the municipal authorities. Only the American judge faulted the police for letting the situation deteriorate so far that a fatal shooting resulted. In the end, even as the police officer responsible for the incident was forced to resign, he was recognized for his past services.[8]

The Chinese were enraged by this judgment.

Given a series of humiliating events that foreign powers had inflicted on a weak China, the above incident in 1925, known as the May 30 incident, was a tragedy that had been waiting to happen.[9] In the 1920s, May had been the month of intense political activities for students across China—May 1, Labor Day; May 4, Student Movement Day; and May 9, National Humiliation Day. Dr. Sun Yat-sen had died earlier that year and China was still mourning its first revolutionary leader. With political fervor and emotional tension running at fever pitch among students, the May 30 incident further electrified the nation at a time when the anti-British, anti-foreigner, and anti-imperialist feelings were soaring.[10]

As these sentiments swelled throughout the nation, a different kind of response to the May 30 incident came from the YMCA (Young Men's Christian Association) and the YWCA (Young Women's Christian Association) which, because of their popularity among young people, were influential to the public life in China.[11] On the day following the May 30 incident, David Yui, the first Chinese national secretary of the YMCA, called an emergency meeting with several of his associates—both Chinese and American. In a room where the sorrow was palpable, Yui spoke somberly: "Dark and difficult days lie ahead in China's relations with Britain and in the relationships of Chinese and Britons in China. We have tried hard to get R. O. Hall to join us and to help us deal with these problems as Christians should. We have felt it was important. Now it is plainly imperative we have him with us, and that without delay."[12]

David Yui and his colleagues had met ROH during the World Student Christian Federation Conference in Beijing in 1922 and had been deeply impressed with his humility, sensitivity, knowledge, and leadership.

T. Z. Koo (Gu Ziren), a friend of ROH's from earlier days, who was in charge of the Student Department of the YMCA and a key player in the Chinese Student Volunteer Movement for the Ministry (Chinese Student Christian Movement),[13] sent ROH an urgent cable, asking him to come to Shanghai with his family, to "bring some healing to the bitter hearts of the Chinese students."[14] Koo and the other Christian leaders wanted to do what they could to bridge this "no man's land," to bring "responsible leaders of the Chinese and foreign communities" together for face-to-face conversations regarding the unhappy situation, and to promote good relationships among the nations to prevent future wars.

In November 1925, ROH, his wife Nora, and their newborn son, Joc, arrived in Shanghai, the financial center of East Asia which then handled half of the imports and exports of China. ROH's most important mandate was to act as a reconciler between the people of China and Britain, at a time when large numbers of foreigners were leaving because of the anti-foreigner and anti-Christian movements.

It had become difficult for Christians to participate in national affairs and public service, as they were continually regarded with suspicion and even hatred. Membership in the YMCA was declining. The educated Christian community, the YMCA and YWCA, were beginning to say that they belonged to the "Christian Movement" rather than to churches which were perceived as far too Western in style, far too dominated by missionaries, and far too disinterested in national affairs.[15]

Missionaries and the churches were unpopular among the Christian community for good reasons. Christianity had not taken root in a significant way until after the First Opium War in 1842. Under the protection of Western powers, missionary activity from many Protestant denominations as well as the Roman Catholic Church increased dramatically, with the missionaries establishing not only churches, but also medical clinics, hospitals and founded numerous educational institutions from the primary to the university level. Yet the good works of missionaries were inevitably linked with Western imperialism, unequal treaties, and foreigners' privileges of extraterritoriality—not to mention the patronizing attitude of some missionaries that they had taken up the "White Man's Burden"[16] and could not counter the anti-Christian feeling among most Chinese.[17]

It was into such a politically fraught environment, with its tensions boiling just under the surface, that ROH arrived in Shanghai. The YMCA had a staff of over 300 Chinese secretaries, 60 Americans, three Canadians, and three Scandinavians and one Scotsman—but there had been no English over the years.[18] ROH was to be the first.

ROH and his family settled in an apartment building in the "French Concession"—under "American Law in French Territory in China." The apartment was no more than one spacious room with a bathroom and a sort of pantry/kitchen, although the family could, if they wish, share communal meals. They divided the room with a blue striped curtain. They also bought some good Chinese furniture, which they intended to take home with them.[19] As they settled into their apartment, Nora had a maid to help her out and she was able to decorate their apartment to make their life more comfortable. ROH held discussion groups and talks in their flat and Nora became a most gracious hostess on these social occasions. According to Nora, ROH was kept extremely busy and was hardly home except to sleep, weekdays and weekends alike.[20]

First Encounter with China: Beijing Conference and Shanghai Conference in 1922

ROH was not a total stranger to China when he arrived in Shanghai with his family in November 1925. He had visited China in April 1922 as a British delegate of the Student Christian Movement in Britain,[21] to attend the World Student Christian Federation Conference in Beijing. He set off for this conference shortly before Christmas 1921, taking a train from Paris to Marseilles, where he embarked on the Royal Mail ship *Kaiser-i-Hind* to Bombay on his first trip to the world outside Europe. Like many who travel, he was tempted to compare the unfamiliar with what he already knew, but he quickly realized the importance of accepting and appreciating different customs.[22]

> Two things stand out . . . People are wanted here, a thousand times more than the greatest need at home, but they must be very pro-Indian—almost anti-British. I mean anti-British customs. It's much harder than I thought it would be—I've found that in a week—not to be continually contrasting Indian ways unfavorably with our ways. It is a different way, sometimes a little worse, often (when one gets there) a lot better than our way. What matters though is that it is different—like French sanitation—and you have to lump it and learn to like it.

After traveling for a while in India, he arrived in Hong Kong sometime in March before sailing to Shanghai on the S.S. *Empire*.[23] Years later, in 1962, he revealed how even as a young man in the early 1920s, he had questioned colonial condescension toward other religions and cultures. In his address to the World Council of Churches in New Delhi on Christian Unity, he sounds critical when he refers to what the "grand old Oxford Mission fathers" taught regarding Hinduism:[24]

> Forty years ago when I was first in India those grand old Oxford Mission fathers told me they had come to the conclusion in spite of theological theory, that Hinduism was wholly evil. But when I asked the question of

Figure 1.1 The apartment block, 1331 Fuxing Zhong Lu, Shanghai, where ROH and Nora lived in 1925–26. It is now regarded as a heritage building as shown by the plaque in front of the building. Photographs taken in 2012 by Robin O. Hall, grandson of ROH.

Father Manu Chakkravarti, their leading Indian colleague, he replied, "Had there been no light in Hinduism, how could I have found the True Light?"

Of course, a certain colonial imprint still shows through here, as ROH views Hinduism as not on its own terms as a religion equal with Christianity, but as a valid entry point to discovery of the true faith.

Still, something seemed to call ROH from Asia—especially from Hong Kong. While in Hong Kong, he spoke to the students in St. Paul's College and St. Stephen's Boys' College and met the respective headmasters. He met Dr. Katherine (Katie) Woo, the headmistress of St. Paul's Girls' School,[25] who would be leading the delegates from Hong Kong to attend the National Christian Conference in Shanghai in May that year. He also took a short trip to Guangzhou and visited the YMCA where he felt the tremendous American influence on the organization. When the boat for his onward journey to Shanghai was delayed again and again, he wrote to his parents, "There seems to be a fate against my getting away from Hong Kong."[26] Little did he then realize that just ten years later Hong Kong would become his home for 34 years.

After a tour of Hangzhou, Nanjing, Jinan, Zhangzhou, and Tianjin, he eventually reached Beijing.[27] There, instead of banners of welcome, anti-Christian demonstrations greeted him.

This first World Student Christian Federation Conference in Asia was also the first international religious conference in China, a significant event for the country. But even before the conference, many Chinese students had demonstrated against it. Although missionaries in the eighteenth century were driven by love, compassion and solidarity, toward the end of the nineteenth and the beginning of the twentieth century the motives had shifted and been replaced by pity and condescension. The attitude was adopted not only toward non-Christians but also toward members of the younger churches, the "fruits" of the West's missionary labors.[28] A missionary atlas entitled *The Christian Conquest of China*, in which different parts of the country had been assigned to various foreign missionary agencies, enraged the students.[29] They chanted slogans against the Christians and wrote many critical articles, accusing Christianity of being an enemy of science and free-thinking, and the willing ally of "Western imperialism." They demanded the missionaries give up their control of the universities and schools. The anti-Christian movement was inspired by some Chinese intellectuals in response to the World Student Christian Federation Beijing Conference amid rising nationalism. These intellectuals saw that Western science offered the exciting vision of a new society and a powerful weapon in the education and mobilization of youth and the masses, but waved off religion with defiance. While attacks on the conference attracted a great deal of public attention, there were no ugly scenes or attempts to disrupt the meeting.[30]

The World Student Christian Federation Conference in Beijing

The Beijing Conference marked a watershed in the history of the World Student Christian Federation, signaling the worldwide mobilization of Christian students reaching out in faith and fellowship.[31]

Tsinghua College, the venue of the conference, was built in 1911 partly financed by the Boxer indemnity fund that the United States government returned to China. T. Z. Koo, the main organizer of the 1922 Beijing Conference, had approached practically every governor in the country to secure financial support, acquainted schools and colleges with the conference, and brought churches, pastors, and missionaries into sympathy with the purpose of the conference. His impressive organizational abilities were duly recognized by his appointment as the first non-Western secretary of the federation.

The Chinese organizers of the conference, who had worked hard, found their labor rewarded with the attendance of 850 delegates from 32 countries. China contributed 500 delegates from colleges and high schools. At the entrance to the college hall, ROH found a huge banner displaying an old Confucian saying "One Family Under Heaven," both in Chinese and in English, in line with the Federation's motto, *Ut omnes unum sint*—"That they may all be one." Despite the differing nationalities and former enmities, and the strife and warfare which had existed between scores of delegates only months before, a sense of common purpose quickly descended on the conference.

The topics of the open forum at the conference covered a wide range of issues related to Christianity, international and inter-racial problems, and social and industrial reconstruction. Many sessions focused on issues that emerged from World War I, especially war and peace. Several important points of agreement emerged from lively debates in the forum and in the general committee meeting.

First, students from all parts of the world avowed their belief in the fundamental equality of all races and nations, and considered it part of their Christian vocation to express this reality in all their relationships with others. Secondly, the students considered it their absolute duty to do all within their power to fight the causes leading to war. Thirdly, despite a lack of consensus about what should happen in the event of war, there was determination that each would follow the teaching of Jesus Christ to seek an answer.[32]

As chairman of the Committee on the Missionary Purpose of the Federation, ROH reported that it was vital to have the right type of people to be missionaries. He emphasized that missionaries needed to be humble, willing to learn more about Jesus Christ from the people they served. They must not pose as superior leaders, but must act as partners in the Christian community of the country they serve.[33]

ROH did express concerns, in a letter to the Student Christian Movement in Britain, that differences in theology and racial differences in philosophical thinking were exaggerated during this multinational conference. He urged acceptance, not merely tolerance, of national and cultural differences, and challenged colonial views that some civilizations had progressed through stages of development that left others, such as China, far behind:[34]

> It seems to me we must get out of the way of thinking of degrees or stages of civilization and think instead of differences in kind. Think of China, for instance, rather as one thinks of France or Belgium. Purposely I am exaggerating, for there are differences in degree. BUT IT IS NOT FOR US TO JUDGE THAT. A father sees which one of his sons is the best, but a brother sees only differences in temperament and habits and characteristic. If he goes further, he becomes at once a hopeless prig spending all his time trying to 'improve' his brothers, and make them like himself. It is that sort of elder-brother priggishness which is at present ruining our influence in China. And the word missionary has got hopelessly tied up with that idea.

He concluded the letter on a note that sounds strikingly contemporary: "Unity with diversity; one purpose, many methods; a common goal but countless approaches. How interesting it must all be to God." This idea of balancing the need for unity with appreciation for diversity would be a leitmotif in ROH's approach to ecumenical and interfaith activities throughout his life.

Anti-Christian flare-ups continued after the Beijing Conference, and organizers of the conference arranged for teams of delegates from abroad to visit major student centers in the country in an effort to calm these tensions. In addition to ROH, these teams included scientists, authors, professors and undergraduates from different nations. Many who listened to ROH were so affected that they urged ROH to remain in China, and were greatly disappointed when he did not accept the invitation.

The National Christian Conference in Shanghai

Following the World Student Christian Federation Conference, ROH attended the National Christian Conference in May on behalf of the Reverend William Paton, the British Student Christian Movement Missionary Secretary. Organized by Dr. J. H. Oldham of the International Missionary Council—a body which set up the National Christian Council of China—this conference aimed at passing over responsibility for the control and management of the Chinese Christian Church to the Chinese. Attended by more than 1,000 delegates from over 130 Protestant denominational groups, the conference was preceded by a survey of Christians in many parts of China. The results of the survey were discussed at length during the conference, and reflected important currents of thought among the Chinese Christians.[35]

Dr. T. C. Chao (*Zhao Zichen*), who later became professor of religious philosophy and dean at Yenching University, headed a subcommittee's report on the "The Message of the Church." It focused on reconciling the tensions between acknowledging the contributions of the missionaries and the Chinese desire for autonomy, and contained several key points that pointed toward the organic development of an indigenous church: (1) the Chinese Christians registered their gratitude to the sacrifice and devotion of the missionaries who had helped to build up the Church in China; (2) in acknowledging the Church as their spiritual home, Chinese Christians should not alienate themselves from their racial inheritance. The wholesale uncritical acceptance of the traditions, forms and organizations of the West and the slavish imitation of these were not conducive to the building of a permanent genuine Christian Church in China; (3) the results of past experience and the history of China demanded an indigenous Church as well as an indigenous Christianity, a Christianity which would register the spiritual inheritance of the Chinese race but would not sever its continuity with the historical churches; (4) the Chinese Christians should unite in their efforts to reach the goal of self-support, self-government, and self-propagation.[36]

The call for a "three-self" (self-governing, self-supporting, and self-propagating) church was also loud and clear. Of note was the absence of any attempt to establish ecclesiastical unity.

Dr. Timothy Tingfang Lew, dean of the School of Religion at Yenching University, who gave one of the keynote addresses during the conference, summed up the call for unity in service in his *Message of the Church*: "The Chinese churches agreed to differ, but resolved to love, and united to serve." Upon hearing Lew's speech, ROH was so impressed with the simplicity of the language that he immediately sent it off for publication in the Student Christian Movement journal.

During the two conferences he attended in 1922, ROH made lifelong friends with some Chinese. These included T. Z. Koo, whose cable impelled ROH's return to China after the May 30 incident and Y. T. Wu (Wu Yaotsung),[37] head of the Association Press, the YMCA Publishing Department, who exhibited an unusual combination of radical politics and deep evangelical Baptist piety. T. C. Chao, an original thinker, became another lifelong friend. During the anti-Christian movement of the 1920s, Chao had advised Chinese Christians to remove the "Western husk" from Christianity in order to discover the true essence of the religion. The indigenous Christianity, Chao argued, would be a useful basis for social reconstruction in China.[38] In an effort to make Christianity a truly indigenous religion in China, Chao later inspired the founding of a Chinese Christian Literature Society to write Chinese hymns and songs and to set Chinese tunes to the words.[39] There was also Dr. Timothy Lew, a poet and hymn writer.[40] These men and others were committed Christians and passionate patriots. They were not only crucial in the formation of the

National Christian Church, but also in the development of Christianity in China in the difficult years ahead.

Second Encounter with China: The Year 1925–26, Annus Mirabilis

From 1925 to 1926, during his second visit to China, ROH was the first English person to work in the Student Department of the YMCA. T. Z. Koo was his chief. In 1950 ROH would describe his first meeting with this sensitive and spiritual man to whom he became so greatly attached.

One sunny day in July 1920 in a World Student Christian Federation meeting in Swanwick, Derbyshire, England, ROH was sitting at the back of the tent when he noticed an unusual Chinese man. He wore an ill-fitting European suit, but when he spoke, his fluent, melodious English left the students spellbound. Later, at the "sing-song" in the lounge, this stranger pulled out a bamboo flute and played a Chinese lullaby called "The Purple Bamboo." The haunting melody mesmerized everyone with its simplicity and beauty, especially ROH. The room became hushed and still. When the very last note drifted to nothingness, there was a pause. Suddenly the room burst into a terrific applause. For ROH, this "little figure with a bamboo flute" was Elijah's still small voice of calm.

Koo's father was an ordained deacon, and Koo was a graduate of St. John's University in Shanghai, founded by his spiritual father, Dr. Francis Lister Hawks Pott. When the World Student Christian Federation decided to hold its first postwar conference in Beijing, David Yui, the general secretary of YMCA, wanted to ensure that other countries would send strong delegations to Beijing. He sent Koo, who was in charge of the Student Department, to speak at other student conferences in Europe and America in 1921. Koo would make another deep impression in England when he attended another World Student Christian Federation Conference in 1924. His eloquence, as he appealed to the audience to join in the work of "building the builders of China," moved thousands of students for the same reason as his music—the clarity and sincerity of tone had spoken through both voice and flute.[41]

Koo wanted to help the leaders of the Chinese Student Christian Movement to "catch something of the British SCM [Student Christian Movement] spirit" and to make it into a much stronger movement outside the YMCA. However, at the beginning of 1926, Koo was asked to organize the Triennial National Conference for all the YMCAs in China and was considered a successor to David Yui as general secretary of the association—a job that he would not accept because he felt that he must be spiritual, not administrative. Koo began to understand that his dream of a Chinese Student Christian Movement fashioned after the British one would never be realized. The leadership of YMCA, which had been infiltrated by members of the Chinese Communist

Figure 1.2 T. Z. Koo (*Fragrant Stream*, December 1953)

Party, strongly discouraged the formation of a separate student organization.[42] Soon afterwards Koo accepted a job working for the World Student Christian Federation and the YMCA in the United States. Without Koo and a separate division for students in the YMCA, the Student Christian Movement in China gradually sank into insignificance.

During this year in China, ROH spent considerable time traveling with Koo to different places in China to meet with students. They came to know each other very well. David Paton, who was the son of William Paton and ROH's biographer, had a photograph of the two of them taken in 1939 and he wrote underneath it "R.O.T.Z." He said, "This was not only because they were known by their initials but also because when one saw them together, it was difficult to tell where the mind of one ended and the mind of the other began."[43]

When ROH arrived in Shanghai at that difficult time in 1925, his major task entailed bridging the gulf between people in the British and the Chinese communities. For that reason he even joined the Shanghai Club, which boasted of having the longest bar in the world. Throughout the year, he spoke tirelessly about Christianity to various groups of people, and even developed a course of devotional readings for the students on God and His purpose in creation. He also organized luncheon parties for the Chinese and the British to discuss ways in which the Sino-British cooperation could be fostered further. The British, surprised that the YMCA had invited ROH to do the bridging, had cause to question their firm belief in the Chinese hatred of foreigners.[44]

Numinous Experiences at Two Chinese Tombs

ROH had two encounters during his year in China that exposed him to a kind of mystical beauty novel to him. These glimpsed experiences seemed, to ROH, to take him from knowing about China to a different kind of "knowledge-knowing" China.

The first one occurred in Shenyang (formerly Mukden) at the tombs of the first emperors of the Manchu dynasty. In an isolated setting, from the vantage point of a pine forest on a hill, ROH drank in the vision of the harmony and simplicity of the architecture before him. He was stirred by the beauty rendered in the perfect proportion and the perfect spacing of every building and every pillar. There was no massive sense of wonder, no tower, no minaret, and no Gothic spire. Yet a distinct sense of harmony was achieved by the proportion and symmetry of each part, the completeness of each part in itself and the perfect concordance of each part with the rest. He wrote to his parents:[45]

> It may have something to do with the fact that for a transcendent God China has a harmonious universe. If it has, their building shows that their sense of harmony is as real a faith, and as much part of their spiritual life as our faith in God.
>
> . . . What can be the secret of genius which makes great architects produce such perfect harmony? What is the inner force of a civilization which expresses its religious feeling in this way?

ROH was awed by a sense of beauty that could not be judged by Western standards. It was an expression of fundamental ideas of life so different from what he had experienced that he could barely describe it. He felt that Westerners could only understand this mode of life expression if they experienced its value and its meaning for life as a whole.

The second experience happened in Qufu, the temple and burial place of Confucius and his descendants. The temple, similar in design to the one in Shenyang, was much more elaborate. In the distance ROH could see court after court, pavilion after pavilion, and paved square after paved square. Seeing this ancient architecture on a grand scale, ROH sensed a deep potent force that must, he thought, influence all life around it. In this moment, as he walked toward the temple, ROH suddenly recognized that this Chinese home with its courts was arranged for descendants of many generations, a home canonized as a vehicle for worship. ROH finally reached the tomb of the sage. Before this tomb—a plain stone slab engraved with four golden characters "Perfect Fulfiller, Master and Teacher,"[46]—ROH bowed three times according to Chinese custom, an act that must have been outrageous and shocking to his contemporary Anglicans. His heart filled with gratitude to God for what this master had meant to men.[47] In his book *China and Britain*, he explained the three bows:[48]

> As I bowed three times in Chinese style in gratitude alike to God and man for what this master man has meant to men, the sense of religious meaning of it all was overwhelming. Here is expressed a warmth of feeling which

breathes life into family ethics, an ethic which before, as I had read about it, had seemed so cold, precise and terribly self-righteous.

These experiences at the Chinese tombs awed ROH so much that he considered them religious. Even though he had always subscribed to the theological tenet that God had created the world, the significance of this truth sank in deeply for the first time. God had made China and its people as He had made other races, but God had revealed Himself to the Chinese people differently from how He had revealed Himself to the Western nations. ROH later wrote: "There was never a time when Christ was not in China, never was a time when China was not in Christ's heart," which became one of his pivotal beliefs.[49]

By September 1926, ROH and his family had left Shanghai for Toronto, Canada where they met up with his younger brother Noel, before returning home. It was with boundless regret mingled with gratitude that his colleagues in the YMCA saw him return to England after a brief but highly significant service with them.

The Halls left Shanghai at the right time because the National Revolutionary Army, led by Chiang Kai-shek, Sun Yat-sen's successor, was pushing toward Shanghai, having fought its way from Guangzhou northward against the warlords. This Northern Expedition to unify the fragmented country was made possible by an alliance (First United Front) between the Guomindang or Nationalists and the Chinese Communist Party under Soviet advisors.[50]

A Bridge between Two Worlds

In his book *China and Britain*, published in April 1927,[51] ROH exhorted the British people to develop a greater receptivity and respect for Chinese values. ROH warned that if the British kept themselves aloof, their insularity would block them from empathy with the Chinese people and from the impartiality needed to administer justice fairly. He hoped that members of the Christian community would be the vanguard that would help all to realize the importance of open and respectful collaboration.

ROH made a plea for mutuality that the Chinese and British work together for the ideals of brotherhood and joint service. Reviewing the history of China and Britain in the past and the Sino-British relations in the present, he acknowledged points of divergence, with tensions arising from the incompatibility of the "commercial" interests of the British merchants and the "political" concerns of the Chinese. Chinese protests of imperialism and exploitation had been scornfully dismissed, and the colonial order defended, on grounds of Chinese corruption and inefficiency. ROH also observed a fundamental contrast in the Chinese and British orientations toward the world, as Chinese were "static" and placed more value on "thought-life" than the British, who emphasized a "dynamic . . . will to achieve." ROH used his personal experiences of visiting the tombs at Mukden and at Qufu to illustrate some differences between Chinese and Western cultural values and expression. He pointed out that Chinese valued harmony and family life above the individual or the state, while the British elevated individualism, personal honor, independence, and achievement over collective or family harmony.

Arguing that China should not be regarded as a market but as a people, ROH suggested that there should be more political, economic, industrial, missionary, intellectual, and cultural contact between the two nations; more understanding; and more brotherliness on both sides. He told his readers about the courageous action of the young Christians of the YMCA, who, despite being regarded by their compatriots as the "Running Dogs of Western Capitalism," had invited him to bridge the two nations after the May 30 incident. He suggested that Britain should respond by sending more men of outstanding intellectual and spiritual gifts to China and invite Chinese Christian leaders and students to visit British universities and churches for cultural exchanges. He then stated that missionary work in China should not aim to create a copy of English or European Christianity, but should support it to find its own expression.

> God does not want us to make the Chinese Vikings. He could have arranged their past differently if that had been his purpose. We are in China to pass on what we have learnt in Christ about God. The Chinese with whom we come in contact, learning in Christ to know the meaning of their own part as we have learnt to know the meaning of our own Viking past, will become Christian Chinese, but Chinese still. They will see their old virtues, special and peculiar as ours are special and peculiar to us, but essentially the gift of the same, one, universal Christ-like God.
>
> But God has also given China a trust for us. In the special and particular virtues which God and His Chinese people have worked out in the past there must be something of universal value, something which God has entrusted to them that they may teach us and the world in general—virtues or values or methods which the world wants and can learn only from China. In the same way there may be similar things in our Viking repertory—virtues, values and methods—of universal application, entrusted to use who first learned them for all mankind.

He concluded, "So may all mankind and all human relations come into the fullness of the measure of the stature of Christ—not only in His divine Sonship, but in His sublime brotherliness."[52]

ROH truly offered himself as a bridge between cultures, between the distant past and the immediate present. His remarks show his ability to detach himself enough from his British training and enculturation to see through to the underlying causes of friction between China and Britain, as well as to appreciate their respective virtues. His reference to the Viking legacy may be seen as a metaphor for ancestral or historical memories that affect the present, and his recommendations for regarding China as a member of the brotherhood of all nations show him as a visionary Christian for his time. Although a year-long experience in such a large, complex, and ancient nation as China may seem a relatively brief time, ROH's experiences of direct contact with Chinese people greatly enlarged his understanding in ways that would affect his actions and policies years later, when he assumed the mantle of bishop of Victoria and South China.

Notes

1. E. E. Barnett, "Letter From America," *Outpost* (February 1957), 38–39.
2. The Shanghai International Settlement (上海公共租界) was situated in Shanghai, one of the original five treaty ports which were established under the terms of the Treaty of Nanking at the end of the First Opium War in the year 1842. It began as a British settlement. Later, American and French settlements were established to the north and south of the British settlement respectively. In 1863, the British and American settlements formally united to become the Shanghai International Settlement. See J. H. Hann, "Origin and Development of the Political System in the Shanghai International Settlement," *JHKBRAS* (22) (1982): 31–64.
3. C. M. Wilbur, "The Nationalist Revolution: from Canton to Nanking, 1923–28," in *The Cambridge History of China: Volume 12, Republican China, Part 1*, edited by J. K. Fairbank (Cambridge: Cambridge University Press, 1983), 527–52.
4. 《外交史主題展：檔案文獻：五卅慘案：調查報告》(http://archwebs.mh.sinica.edu.tw/digital/ArticleShow.asp?ArticleID=126&ArticlePage=7). There is considerable discrepancy among different reports of the number of people who died that day. The Chinese report quoted has a record of the identities of all who were killed.
5. R. O. Hall, *T. Z. Koo: Christianity Speaks to the West* (London: SCM Press, 1950), 19.
6. The Diplomatic Body in Beijing was the foreign establishment in China during the first years of the Republic. It consisted of envoys extraordinary and ministers plenipotentiary from fifteen countries: Portugal, Great Britain, France, the United States, Japan, Russia, Germany, Belgium, Sweden, Denmark, the Netherlands, Spain, Italy, Austria-Hungary, and Brazil.
7. Memorandum on the Shanghai Incident and the Negotiations for Its Settlement by Mr. Teichman, Chinese Secretary to His Majesty's Legation at Beijing. July 11, 1925, CAB 21/286 [F 3055/194/10], The National Archives, London, England.
8. Conference of Ministers, July 15, 1925, CAB 21/286, The National Archives, London, England.
9. The series of humiliating events were: (1) the First Opium War and Hong Kong was ceded to Britain in 1842; (2) the Second Opium War and Kowloon was ceded to the British in 1856; the number of treaty ports had grown from 5 to 80 in 1858 and foreign consulates had jurisdiction over their nationals in China (extraterritoriality); (3) the defeat by the Japanese during the 1894–95 Sino-Japanese War; (4) the Boxer Uprising in 1900 when foreign missionaries and their converts were attacked and killed. The uprising was suppressed by the Eight-Nation Alliance Army. The Qing government paid huge indemnity to these nations; (5) Japan

placed the harsh "21 demands" on China in 1915; (6) even though China entered World War I by sending 100,000 men on the side of the Allies to work in France, the Allies had refused to back China's territorial claims during the Versailles Conference.
10. The backlash of the May 30 incident against the British was severe, resulting in one of the longest strikes in Hong Kong that almost destroyed its economy. In China, the churches lost the right to operate schools and membership of the YMCA in China dropped sharply.
11. History of YMCA Work in China. http://special.lib.umn.edu/findaid/html/ymca, accessed on August 28, 2011. In China, the YMCA movement had been active since the 1890s. In early 1920, it had 30 establishments with 32,000 members and 170 student associations with 14,200 members. It influenced the public life in China considerably because of its popularity among young people (History of YMCA Work in China, http://special.lib.umn.edu/findaid/html/ymca). Its policy of indigenous leadership and control appealed to the nationalistic sentiments of the Chinese. Although the first national secretary was an American, he was followed by C. T. Wang (1915–16) and then David Yui (1916–36). Dr. Sun Yat-sen regarded the YMCA highly since it was progressive, widely based, and had lofty missions. The programs offered were excellent for character building and to prepare young people to become moral and responsible citizens. (民革中央，〈孫中山與基督教青年會關係初探：秦方田衛平以演講為中心的討論〉, September 27, 2008).
12. See note 1.
13. R. O. Hall, *China and Britain* (London: Edinburgh House Press, 1927), 94.
14. The Student Christian Movement (SCM) in China had only a transient existence. In Britain, the SCM and the YMCA were two distinct entities with the former being stronger and more influential. The Chinese SCM was first established in 1910 and organized by the YMCA; it was more successful in middle schools than in the universities. (Xu Yihua, "The Rise and Decline of the Chinese Student Volunteer Movement for the Ministry," *Fudan Journal of Humanities and Social Sciences* [2008] 1:1, 108.) T. Z. Koo was in charge of the SCM of the YMCA. Inspired by the British SCM after his visit to Britain in 1924, Koo had hoped that ROH would be able to help him to make the Chinese SCM after the British pattern. See D. M. Paton, *R. O.: The Life and Times of Bishop R. O. Hall* (Hong Kong: The Dioceses of Hong Kong and Macao and the Hong Kong Diocesan Association, 1985), 46–47.
15. R. O. Hall to parents. December 2, 1925. Chung Chi Divinity School Archive.
16. "The White Man's Burden" is a poem by the English poet Rudyard Kipling, published on March 12, 1899 in the *McClure's Magazine*. The term has been interpreted by some as racist, or as a metaphor for a condescending view of undeveloped national culture and economic traditions. See Stuart Creighton Miller, *Benevolent Assimilation: The American Conquest of the Philippines, 1899–1903* (New Haven: Yale University Press, 1982). An alternative interpretation is the philanthropic view, common in Kipling's formative years, that the rich have a moral duty to help "the poor" "better" themselves whether the poor wanted the help or not.

17. J. G. Lutz, *Chinese Politics and Christian Missions: The Anti-Christian Movement of 1920–1928* (Notre Dame, IN: Cross Cultural Publications, Cross Roads Books Co., 1988), 1–18.
18. Hall, *China and Britain*, 95.
19. R. O. Hall to parents. November 10, 1925. Chung Chi Divinity School Archive.
20. Nora Hall to family. May 11, 1926. Chung Chi Divinity School Archive.
21. The SCM was started in Britain in 1889 to unite students with an interest in overseas mission. It became the Student Volunteer Missionary Union in 1893. The movement originated in 1873, after the successful campaign of the evangelist, Dwight Moody, from the United States. It helped establish the National Union of Students and the World University Service. Its first general secretary was Tissington Tatlow. The SCM played a vital role in the formation of the British and World Council of Churches and became a leading voice on ecumenism.
22. Paton, R. O.: *The Life and Times of Bishop Ronald Hall of Hong Kong*, 34.
23. R. O. Hall to parents. March 17, 1922. Chung Chi Divinity School Archive.
24. R. O. Hall, "An Extemporaneous Address to a Group of Churchmen in a Consultation on Christian Unity Meeting to Discuss the Third Assembly of the World Council of Churches in New Delhi," 1962. Hall Family Archive.
25. St. Paul's Coeducational College after World War II.
26. R. O. Hall to parents. March 12, 1922. Chung Chi Divinity School Archive.
27. R. O. Hall to family and friends. April 26, 1922. Chung Chi Divinity School Archive.
28. D. J. Bosch, *Transforming Mission: Paradigm Shifts in Theology in Mission* (New York: Orbis Books, 2010), 290.
29. P. Potter and T. Wieser, *Seeking and Serving the Truth: The First Hundred Years of the World Student Christian Federation* (Geneva: WCC Publications, 1977), 69.
30. The World's Student Christian Federation Conference, *Annual Report of the Young Men Christian Association of China 1922*, published by the National Committee, 19–23. MFC 247.8.8564, 26, 27, Baptist University Library Special Collection.
31. Potter and Wieser, *Seeking and Serving the Truth*, 72.
32. Ibid., 70–71.
33. Even after practicing as a missionary in China for ten years, in 1942 ROH emphasized this principle again in his book, *The Art of the Missionary*.
34. R. O. Hall, letter to SCM. April 26, 1922, 3.
35. National Christian Conference, *Annual Report of the Young Men Christian Association of China 1922*, 39, MFC 247.8.8564, 26, 27, Baptist University Special Collection.
36. D. D. Rawlinson, H. Thoburn, and D. MacGillivray (editorial committee), "The Chinese Church as Revealed in the National Christian Conference," held in Shanghai, May 2–11, 1922, Oriental Press, Shanghai.
37. In 1951 Wu published the "Christian Manifesto," signed by 400,000 people, in consultation with Premier Zhou Enlai and launched the Three-Self Patriotic Movement.
38. 林愛儀，〈趙紫宸於新中國成立前的本色教會理論與實踐〉，載於《台灣浸信會神學院學術年刊》(2006)。http://www.tbtsf.org.tw/bulletin2006/2-4.pdf. 邢福增，《趙紫宸的宗教經驗》（香港：香港中文大學崇基學院神學院）。

39. *Outpost* (July, 1935): 30 (T. C. Chao's original Chinese hymns). R. O. Hall, "Account of the Confirmation and Ordination of Dr T. C. Chao, Sunday, 20th July, 1941, Saint Paul's College Chapel, Hong Kong." CSCA Chung Hua Sheng Kung Hui Source Documents, http://www.ttc.edu.sg/csca/skh/index.htm.
40. Paton, R. O.: *The Life and Times of Bishop Ronald Hall of Hong Kong*, 47.
41. Hall, *T. Z. Koo*, 16.
42. Wu Qing, "A Study of Bishop RO Hall and His Relationship with China (1922–1966)," PhD thesis (2008), 34. The Chinese University of Hong Kong.
43. D. Paton to P. Smith. May 19, 1975. Chung Chi Divinity School Archive.
44. See note 15.
45. R. O. Hall to parents. July 26, 1926. Chung Chi Divinity School Archive.
46. The original Confucius Stele which ROH saw was 大成至聖文宣王墓 (the grave of perfect fulfiller and master, 文宣王, a title given to Confucius). The word "teacher" (先師) was not there. ROH must have been misled by his translator (a Christian agent) who used the usual appellation (至聖先師) possibly because the translator could not read the seal script (篆字). This original stele, from the Ming dynasty, was broken into pieces during the Cultural Revolution, but restored since. See http://tupian.hudong.com/a3_83_76_01300001145278131295760649521_jpg.html.
47. R. O. Hall to parents. August 26, 1926. Chung Chi Divinity School Archive.
48. R. O. Hall, *China and Britain*, 37.
49. R. O. Hall, "Christ and China," *Fragrant Stream* (1954): 7.
50. J. Spence, *The Search for Modern China* (New York: W. W. Norton and Company, 1990), 330–36.
51. Hall, *China and Britain*, 32–34.
52. Ibid., 170–71.

Chapter 2
The Making of a Bishop
Bishop R. O. Hall's Early Years (1895–1932)

Lord, make us instruments of thy peace,
Where there is hatred, let us sow love;
where there is injury, pardon;
where there is discord, union;
where there is doubt, faith;
where there is despair, hope;
where there is darkness, light;
where there is sadness, joy;
For thy mercy and for thy truth's sake.

Attributed to St. Francis of Assisi

The Formative Years

What was the path that led Ronald Owen Hall to his calling as an "instrument of peace"? Born on July 22, 1895, ROH was the second child and oldest male in a family of nine children. ROH came from a lineage of Anglican clergy that left its mark on him and most of his siblings. Of the eight children who survived to adulthood, three became clergy, three missionaries, one economist, and one farmer in New Zealand.[1]

ROH's ancestry can be traced to Bartholomew Hall, a friend of the chaplain and legal advisor to the famous Puritan, Oliver Cromwell, a military and political leader who overthrew the English monarchy and turned it temporarily into a republican Commonwealth. Bartholomew Hall, who lived in Harpsden, Oxfordshire, received a royal pardon from Charles II. Thomas Owen, ROH's grandfather, sold Harpsden Court, which had been owned by the family since the seventeenth century, and became a country parson in Leicestershire and Rutland. His son, Cecil Gallopine, ROH's father, in turn was vicar of St. Matthew's, Newcastle, a Tractarian (see below) and a High Churchman of the School of Charles Gore, a well-known theologian of that period who became one of the founders of the Christian Social Union, which worked actively to remedy social injustice.

We can better appreciate ROH's later commitment to social justice when we know something of Cecil's (his father) passion for Christian activism. Although he was a scholar with musical talent, Cecil, influenced by Charles Gore, chose to serve a parish in the industrial north and refused to move to other areas more suited to his inclinations.[2]

ROH seldom talked about his parents, but he was a dutiful son who cared deeply for his family. As a small boy who had just been told that another baby brother had been born, he anxiously looked into his father's face and asked, "Can we afford him?" That baby brother, number five in a family of nine, was Humphrey Hall, who wrote that this incident was a hint of ROH's care for the family all his life.[3]

ROH was enlisted on September 4, 1914 in the 21st Service Battalion of the Royal Fusiliers. Three months later he became second lieutenant in the 18th Battalion of the Northumberland Fusiliers. He rose quickly in rank and was appointed staff captain of the 105th Infantry Brigade in January 1916 and brigade major in the 117th Infantry Brigade the following April.[4] As staff captain he found that he was comparatively well-off. Since his clergyman father insisted on serving the poor, ROH used much of his army pay for the schooling of his younger brothers. His younger brother Noel (later Sir Noel) was to gain the equivalent of a scholarship to Brasenose, but not because of any academic attainments of his own. In the words of the principal at his interview, "Brasenose is never too poor not to have some money for the brother of your brother." ROH could even cast a spell on his college principal.

Later ROH would write frequent letters to his parents. He dutifully remembered the birthday of every member of his family and sent gifts or a letter of good wishes to them. Sir Noel commented, "From the age of 15 or 16, he [ROH] was the confidant, the advisor, the Rock of Gibraltar for all the growing members of the family and continued so for many years without in the least undermining the position of his parents."

From early days ROH was an excellent student. At the age of 14 he left the Royal Grammar School in Newcastle-upon-Tyne. In a class of 20 he had come first in 6 out of 14 subjects: divinity, grammar and composition, geography, history, chemistry, and algebra.[5] From the grammar school, he was sent to Bromsgrove School in September 1909, where the housemaster, R. G. Routh, had been at Trinity College Oxford with Cecil Hall. These years spent in Bromsgrove were crucial for his development. ROH was happy, and convinced of God's presence. He was highly popular as the dormitory monitor even though he kept the boys under strict discipline. He was a brilliant scholar, and after five years he walked away laden with prizes and the award of an exhibition at Brasenose College, Oxford to study classics.[6]

His poem, published at the annual commemoration at Bromsgrove in 1919, reveals his affection for his school, already colored by nostalgia for innocent summers of play receding into memory.

How Charford [the cricket field] loves the summer's long caresses
   And whispered memories of happier days!
Mocking the winds which pause to blow her kisses,
   Ere they are hurried on grey worldly ways,
She gazes idly on the mimic strife
   Of bat and ball, and panting hearts—and life.

The last two stanzas of the poem show the grief and loss that he experienced in World War I and the kind of courage needed in the face of duty in a soldier.

The School is peopled only by her Dead
   Who found in duty more than lies in fame.
Who dared with us and suffered . . . and are sped.
   The Chapel whispers each unanswered name
At every corner some remembered face
   Smiles, and is gone . . . and Courage takes its place.

The way is long, we dare not stay to grieve,
   For Hope is Memory divorced from Sorrow,
The Future what the past could not achieve,
   And Courage never hesitates to borrow
What Danger lends, paying interest in pain,
   And, losing all, will gladly dare again.
                R. O. Hall, May 1919, Brasenose College, Oxford

Finding Peace in the Midst of War (1914–18)

Instead of going to Oxford, ROH joined the army in September 1914, after war broke out for reasons that are not clear because conscription was not instituted until January 1916. It is likely that, like other men in England who were lining up to join, he thought that fighting in this war, which people assumed would be "over by Christmas," was the right thing to do.

While fighting in France, ROH was shot in the thigh. Since the wound healed well, ROH was able to return to the trenches in about one month and was awarded the Military Cross and Bar.[7] Although only 23 at the time he was a strict disciplinarian, according to those who served under him: Major Hall was formidable, the German army was less terrifying than the brigade major.[8]

For those who served in the frontline of World War I, death was a constant companion. Even when no raid or attack was launched or defended against, the perpetual enemy shellfire brought random deaths. ROH was carried throughout the war by his faith. He was never absent from a communion service or a prayer meeting held anywhere, even in the corner of a trench. He took refuge in his God from whom he derived tremendous courage. Nevertheless, such horrors must have left their mark in one way or another, and ROH no doubt "paid interest in pain" for his courage. He talked publicly about the anguish of this

Figure 2.1 ROH's Military Cross and Bar, 1914–18 Campaign Medal, and 1918 Victory Medal (Hall Family Archive)

war on two occasions. The first was in his enthronement speech in Hong Kong on December 30, 1932.[9] Years later, in his sermon on Remembrance Sunday in 1949 in St. John's Cathedral, Hong Kong, he recalled his horrifying World War I experience of November 6, 1917. He was in a trench with a wall of mingled German and British corpses and a floor of mud. He saw two young men lying dead, one German and the other English. The two bodies, facing upward, already black and swollen with decay, lay across each other in the form of a cross. As he recalled this moment in his Remembrance Day sermon, his voice reverberated through the cathedral: "From the days of Cain and Abel to the days of Hiroshima and Nagasaki, all war is fratricide! All war crucifies afresh our Elder Brother, the Son of God, who is also Son of Man."

On Armistice Day 1918, ROH went to visit his dying godfather, Canon Carr. While ships' sirens and factory whistles screamed outside, and cheering, sobbing people crammed the streets and pubs, inside the bedroom, peace and stillness reigned. As ROH knelt, Canon Carr gave thanks for his safe return, charged him with his future ministry, laid hands on him, and blessed him.[10]

Oxford (1919–20): A Staging Post on a Longer Journey

In January 1919, as soon as he was demobilized, ROH arrived at Brasenose College, Oxford. Having lost so much time in war service, he decided to shorten the classical course to five terms. For ROH, the university was but a staging post on a journey for which he had long been destined: he knew already who he was, why he was there, and where he was going. While some undergraduates of the day were preparing for a priesthood of tomorrow, he was for all intents and purposes already the priest of tomorrow pausing to be an undergraduate.¹¹ He knew too what were definitely not essentials.

Nevertheless, his focus on the big picture did not prevent him from participating in college life. He shared in a host of indoor and outdoor activities offered by the university and college. He wrote to Nora with whom he had fallen in love a year earlier, "I'm pleasantly tired after about 3 hours tennis and I want to stay and laze about my rooms . . . I have had my first experience of proper rowing, only a ragtime four, went down the river about 3 miles to a dear old pub with a jolly green lawn hugging the river—drank ginger beer & came back again!"¹²

He almost made the rugby team against Cambridge and was always out there cheering and supporting the home team in any game. When he joined the executive of Student Christian Union as social service secretary for Oxford, he remarked to Nora, "I am terribly afraid of making a mess of it. I know practically nothing of what is done and I really ought to do a lot of work." Realizing already the importance of the practical aspect of social service, he added, "However, Social Work is really more important than a good degree."¹³ The activity closest to his heart was his creation of the college branch of the Student Christian Movement.¹⁴

It appeared that he enjoyed the carefree days at Brasenose. He was far from being tidy because he so described his room to Nora: "I generally sit in an armchair and all the various books I look into gradually spread themselves around me in a circle. My mantelpiece is littered with notices of various meetings, or lunches, or tennis parties and with a host of unanswered letters. My gown generally flops around on the sofa, and everything else is thrown hocus-pocus into a big oak table in the corner."¹⁵

When he was elected president of the Junior Common Room, a sure sign of his popularity, he wrote to Nora, "I am rather pleased—honestly speaking I suppose I should be very pleased—tonight because I have been elected President of the JCR [Junior Common Room] . . . It doesn't entail much work, but if one makes right use of the position I imagine one can do a certain amount for the college."¹⁶

When ROH left Oxford with a degree in classics in June 1920, he had not studied long enough for it to be an honors degree. He enjoyed quoting the examiners' comment on his final papers: "Hall's poor scholarship and general illiteracy detracted from his work, but we liked it!"

A Timely Ordination

Since both his father and grandfather were priests, ROH had never really doubted that his vocation would be to carry on the family line. After two terms at Oxford, ROH was elected to membership of the General Council of the Student Christian Movement. In the spring of 1920, the Student Christian

Movement invited him to be the intercollegiate secretary in Newcastle-upon-Tyne, starting in September. The compression of his preparation time, along with the intensity of his focus, proved to be an unforgettable experience. Every morning after breakfast he had nearly one hour's meditation in the chapel, the beginning of his lifelong habit of meditation each morning.[17] Apart from a walk in the afternoon, ROH spent the rest of the day reading in his room and attended only one lecture each week.

By September 26, 1920, this simple and austere regime had prepared him for his ordination. Nominally he was ordained as deacon to St. Nicholas Cathedral, Newcastle, but he would work principally for the Student Christian Movement. On the occasion of his ordination, ROH prepared and completed the documents for ordination himself, which was most unusual and irregular. David Paton, his biographer, did not think that ROH lacked seriousness about the priesthood; rather, he was so serious about it that incidental legalities paled for him into insignificance.

Throughout his ministry people were distressed by his cutting of corners. ROH ordained candidates as priests who had neither studied theology at university nor spent as much as a term at a theological college. When Alan Chan asked him as a student for advice on what subjects to study in the United States for his master's degree in 1964, ROH told him to study anything he wished except theology.[18] It is not because ROH did not respect theology, but because he truly believed in the applied aspects of theology, obtained by practical work in society. He believed that the training of ministers began when they left theological college.

Learning Theology: Ministry in the Student Christian Movement (1920–25)

The disenchantment with Christianity that grew in the trenches during World War I spread to places of higher education in 1920s; in this context, the work of the Student Christian Movement, where ROH was to play a key pastoral role as intercollegiate secretary, was more important than ever.

In 1921, the Student Christian Movement had 28 full-time staff, and a membership of about 10,000, comprising about one-sixth of the university students in Britain. ROH was responsible not only for students in Armstrong College, Newcastle, but also for those in other colleges and universities in Newcastle, Sunderland, and Durham. It was the Student Christian Movement that ROH later regarded as his university more than he did Oxford[19] and where he learned a great deal about theology probably from reading books by F. D. Maurice, Charles Gore, and contemporary writers of religion and philosophy such as H. E. Fosdick and J. H. Oldham.[20] ROH gave talks at different universities, contributed to the journal *Student Movement*, and was at the disposal of the Student Christian Movement committees of the various colleges. His Student

Christian Movement colleagues described him as being "effervescent, contributing a number of brain-waves to the various committees on which they served together."[21]

As one of a new breed of Christians after World War I who called for a reordering of society, ROH helped organize the Glasgow Quadrennial Conference in 1921, targeting three main issues—racial, economic, and political—in the relationship of Europe and the United States with Asia and Africa. In the past, missionaries regarded other parts of the world as "mission fields" focusing on spreading the gospel, but the sentiment of this new breed of Christians was veering toward direct involvement in the political and social movements in these areas.[22] A motion was passed during the Glasgow Quadrennial Conference repudiating the 1919 massacre of unarmed Indian civilians at Jallianwallah Bagh in Amritsar: "We sympathize with your aspirations for a self-governing India, and we earnestly hope that the reforms now initiated may lead surely and rapidly to the attainment of that goal."[23] The Glasgow Quadrennial Conference represented a major shift in the direction of the Student Christian Movement and helped shape ROH's thinking and future policies in China.

The following year, ROH organized a Student Christian Movement conference in the "red brick" or civic universities[24] that concentrated on imparting to their students "real-world" skills such as engineering and business. He insisted that science and industry was "of God" and in the service of God. This conference, which concluded that the universities needed more corporate spirit, the formation of students' unions, and closer staff–student relationships, was rated by Tissington Tatlow, the general secretary of Student Christian Movement, as one of the best ever convened.[25]

ROH succeeded William Paton as the missionary secretary of the British Student Christian Movement in 1921, and in that role he attended the World Student Christian Federation Conference in Beijing and the National Christian Conference in Shanghai as one of the delegates.

In 1922, after he returned to England from the Beijing and Shanghai conferences, ROH took as much opportunity as possible to share his experience and his visions with other people. He was given the task of working with the Church Missionary Society and the London Missionary Society to recruit students for missionary service. As he gave pastoral care and advice to many who had signed up or thought about signing up for the Student Voluntary Missionary Union, he learned how to inspire young people to work as missionaries. He was called the "body snatcher" by his friends from the Student Christian Movement, because he had recruited several energetic, able, devoted young people.[26] These included Gilbert Baker, Geoffrey Allen, Gerald Goodban, Harry Baines, Leonard Wilson, and many other individuals who later worked in his diocese.[27]

In the evaluation of his work in the Student Christian Movement, Tatlow praised ROH most generously: "Not since the days of Donald Fraser nearly 20 years ago have we had in the Student Christian Movement a man with the same gift of vivid speech and the same power of kindling the imagination of students of all kinds. The Student Volunteer Missionary Union has doubled this year, which is symptomatic of a tremendous recovery of missionary zeal since the war. The brilliant and inspiring leadership has come from R. O. Hall more than any other man." While his letters to ROH reprimanding him for cutting corners, or for acting without consulting his colleagues were not rare, they usually began with the salutation "Beloved RO."[28]

Marriage and Family

On April 24, 1923, ROH married the woman with whom he had fallen in love four years earlier. He had known Nora, born Nora Kathleen Suckling-Baron, for a long time, because their families were distantly related. The Barons and the Sucklings also had many clergy in their family trees, some of whom were also Tractarians. ROH and Nora met for the first time in 1914, when ROH was posted in an army camp near Nora's home and was invited to visit.[29]

Figure 2.2   ROH and Nora in the 1920s (Hall Family Archive)

Nora's mother, Mrs. Baron, had no wish to let go of her daughter and opposed the marriage. She ridiculed ROH for his socialism, modernism, and greater interest in foreign countries than in his own, but Nora stood up for him.[30] After their marriage, Mrs. Baron objected to her daughter being taken out of England to be exposed to danger in China while anti-Christian feelings were so strong. It was her demand that ROH bring his family back to England after having worked in Shanghai for only one year.[31] For Nora, the pressures of her overlapping and conflicting responsibilities to her mother, her husband, and their three children—Jocelyn Baron Owen (Joc), born in Newcastle on June 1, 1925; Judith Marion, born in Newcastle on January 13, 1929; and Alfred Christopher, born in Hong Kong on December 10, 1935—were to cause considerable tension and anxiety throughout her life. At the end of World War II, Nora and the children remained in England near her mother until 1954, when the youngest of their three children entered Oxford University and her mother died.

The Return to China (1925–26)

In July 1923, ten weeks after they were married, ROH wrote to Nora: "The itch to go back to China is desperate. I'm beginning to wonder again if God will ever open the way for us to go . . . If he should, you'd love it so—the freedom & and the wonder & peace of it & all the work that is to be done."[32] ROH had thus felt inner promptings to return to China. Despite the offer from the Student Christian Movement to stay until 1929, he wanted to leave by August 1925.[33] And, sure enough, the cable from Koo after the May 30 incident provided the impetus to fulfill this wish.

ROH described the year 1925–26 in China as his *annus mirabilis*, year of miracles. According to David Paton, "Without this miracle year, the love affair with China begun in 1922 might have faded, in spite of his friendship with T. Z. Koo. Then the whole episode would have paled into merely something interesting and exciting that happened to him when he was young. 1925–26 meant that what began in 1922 was deepened and made permanent."[34]

Ministering to Body and Soul: St. Luke's Church, Newcastle (1927–32)

After the unforgettable year in Shanghai, when the Halls returned to Britain, ROH was installed on April 9, 1927, as Vicar of the Tyneside parish of St. Luke's, Spital Tongues, by the bishop of Newcastle.[35] In the wake of the war, and the slackening of overseas demand for many products, the British economy faltered, and Tyneside was affected more than any other region of Britain.

The Great Depression of 1929–32 further reduced the economic output of Britain. By the end of 1930, as exports had fallen by more than half, the unemployment rate soared. The north, home to most of Britain's traditional heavy industries such as coal mining and steel, bore the brunt of the depression. Newcastle-upon-Tyne, a major shipbuilding center, was hit hardest by the collapse in demand for ships. As a result of an unemployment rate as high as 60 percent, many workers and their families were left destitute. Lining up at soup kitchens became a way of life. Many existed on a subsistence diet, and some children showed signs of malnutrition.[36]

As in the past, ROH began his new job with a great deal of zest. He and his friend, Leslie Hunter, a residentiary canon of Newcastle Cathedral, developed social services for the local people. ROH took charge of housing, which in parts of Newcastle was in extremely poor condition. At this time of economic downturn and very high unemployment, people were unwilling to spend on repairs and renovation, leaving their homes in states of dilapidation. To address this problem, ROH established the Newcastle Housing Improvement Trust which would pay 4 percent interest on investments in the trust. The trust converted large Victorian terrace houses into small flats with indoor cooking, washing, and toilet facilities, and provided decent accommodation for working and unemployed families in more congenial surroundings at reasonable rents. As a result, many houses were saved from complete destruction.[37] He sent people to be trained as property managers, following the Octavia Hill principle,[38] so that every rent collector became a friend and advisor to the tenants. Years later he used a similar model to tackle the enormous housing problem in Hong Kong.

ROH was at the forefront of all the work of the Tyneside Council of Social Service, playing a preeminent role in housing and creating centers where unemployed people could meet and occupy themselves to learn something useful for future employment. He set up the Welfare of the Unemployed, the Theological Society, Christian Missions, Student Christian Movement, and built up a very dynamic Christian fellowship at St. Luke's among the younger generation.[39]

As a priest, he knew that it was not enough simply to look after the soul but also the needs of the body and strove to apply himself fully to the everyday life of the community. In a paper he wrote in 1931 on the "Church and Social Problems," ROH stated very clearly that the ultimate aim of the Church is much wider than the proclamation of "a social message":[40]

> It is true that Christianity has a social gospel to proclaim but that gospel is but part of its real objective which is to bring all men to a true vision of God . . .
>
> The Church's aim is not only wider than a social program; it is deeper. The sources of our actions lie much more deeply than we commonly suppose. We see a spring of fresh water making the ground around it green and fertile and enchanted with the effect give no thought to the rain on some distant mountain slope that feeds the spring. No less real and necessary is the mountain rain in spite of seeming remoteness. So does the praise

and worship of God seem to be remote and unconnected with the practical work of altering social conditions. If the rain stopped the spring continues but only for a time. It then runs dry. There are signs today that heavy rains are needed on the mountain of God.

Just as ROH's practical work in the material world was nourished by underground springs of faith, the Church needed to recognize how the vitality and sustenance of faith was connected to the nourishment of people's practical lives. In this 1931 paper, ROH expressed his understanding that the appeal of communism was not just the promise of better living conditions but also the way that it conferred significance and meaning on people's temporary privations. People who saw their suffering as a short-term necessity for a larger goal beyond their individual selves would be drawn by an ennobling dream:

> Our Utopias are too often mere psychological compensation for repressed action. What we need is a philosophy of the next step. It is just at this point that Communism has scored by its refusal to allow contemplation of the perfect to interfere with the achievement of the possible . . .
>
> During that time it has been born upon him that what the unemployed man needs is not primarily more money . . . not more adequate facilities for education and recreation—not even friendship but faith in God and his purposes. That and that alone seems capable of stopping the moral not set up by enforced idleness. The great attraction exercised by Communism lies just here . . . The unemployed communist sees in his own personal suffering a necessity which if rightly dealt with is fraught with great possibilities for the members of his class. In a very real sense he endures as seeing something as yet invisible.

In this way, ROH seems almost to turn the Marxist dictum that "religion is the opiate of the masses" inside out. His realization that the appeal of communism is, in part, its picture of "something as yet invisible" helped clarify his thinking that the Church's social work is infused with a purpose that includes and goes beyond ministering to people's physical needs. Its real purpose is to bring all people to God.

ROH's practical service work in Tyneside and other communities followed from his commitment to the Christ he followed. He and his curates had started a communal kitchen, but found that the Tynesiders were too proud to come. So, they changed their plans. Knowing that on Wednesdays and Thursdays the pitifully meager benefit paid out on Fridays had already been exhausted, they collected a cart and loaded it with soup, minced meat, and rice pudding. ROH pushed the cart around the parish, his curate walking in front, ringing a bell. People came out from their homes and paid the nominal sum of two pence, so that the heaped plates of hot, nourishing food were not received as charity. The story of the soup kitchen was published in Roger Lloyd's "The Church of England in the 20th Century" and illustrates how attuned ROH was to the people he wished to serve, understanding their need for dignity and pride was equally as important as their need for food.[41]

Although ROH was committed to his work in the community and the Church during this period, he also found balance. He enjoyed family life and was often sighted on the Newcastle Town Moor with his family and friends during his day off. He started gardening and grew many flowers on the flat roof of the vicarage. Later he had an allotment of land on which he produced vegetables for the family's consumption.[42] He was loved by his parishioners, both the well-to-do and the economically disadvantaged. His flourishing Sunday school and activities for his parishioners made the parish a very busy one.

He introduced several significant innovations that further reflected his being in tune with his community and his times. Instead of using *Hymns Ancient & Modern*, he proposed using *Songs of Praise*, paving the way for contemporary worship. Rather than relying on endowment and donations from a few rich people, he abolished collections and introduced a Free Will Offering Scheme which made ordinary members of the congregation responsible for maintaining the church building, church activities, and church mission outside the parish. This concept of Christian stewardship became a regular feature in dioceses 50 years later.[43]

He attracted intelligent and able curates such as Francis Gray, Jack Bennitt, and William Greer. The first two worked in China in the 1930s: Gray was later

Figure 2.3   Hall family, 1937 (Hall Family Archive)

recruited to the staff of St. Augustine's in Canterbury; Bennitt, a first-class degree holder from Cambridge, who went to Hong Kong in 1933 and Singapore in 1938, was interned with Bishop Leonard Wilson during the Japanese occupation in World War II. William Greer, who succeeded ROH as vicar of St. Luke's, was in turn the general secretary of the Student Christian Movement, principal of Westcott House, Cambridge, and then the bishop of Manchester.[44]

In Newcastle, ROH spared no efforts in evangelism. With irresistible charm, a beautiful voice, and a gift for vivid and unusual phrases, his alternation of quiet, common-sense speech with passages of fiery eloquence made him a spellbinding speaker. During shows and exhibitions on the Town Moor, ROH—together with Leonard Wilson, William Greer, and a few laymen—often rented a tent, set up a bookstall, and preached to the nonchurchgoers. The clarity, incisiveness, and sincerity of their preaching invariably attracted attention. They were called "The Town Moor Parsons." ROH's loving concern for everyone fostered in the Tyneside residents a sense of belonging to the town.[45]

When the effects of the Great Depression in Britain finally eased in 1931, it was almost as though ROH's training period as a pastor and in social work was over. His work in Tyneside provided an invaluable apprenticeship for the next stage of his life, one in which the challenges would be much more profound, and on a much larger scale.

Becoming the Bishop of Victoria

Ridley C. Duppuy had been the bishop of Victoria since 1920. By 1931 his heart was failing and his wife was in poor health,[46] so he submitted his resignation to the archbishop of Canterbury.[47] Before his departure, Bishop Duppuy had to find a successor who would be acceptable to his diocese.

When the Diocese of Victoria was first established in 1849, its headquarters was in Hong Kong and it was under the Colonial Office. The bishops were appointed by Letters Patent issued by the home government, but from 1870 onward, the practice of appointing colonial bishops by Letters Patent ceased. The appointment of the bishop of Victoria came under the jurisdiction of the archbishop of Canterbury.[48] The diocese initially comprised the whole of China and Japan. As the missionary activities increased and the diocese grew, it was divided into several smaller ones. As one diocese left after another, only South China, which consisted of Guangdong, part of Guangxi, Yunnan, and Guizhou remained in the Diocese of Victoria by 1920 when Bishop Duppuy took over (Figure 2.4).

The Anglican Church of China (Chung Hua Sheng Kung Hui), established in 1912, was recognized in 1930 by the Lambeth Conference as a full-fledged autonomous member of the Anglican Communion.[49] In this new situation, the constitutional position of the Diocese of Victoria became ambiguous. Was the see of Victoria, Hong Kong, primarily a colonial diocese of the Church of

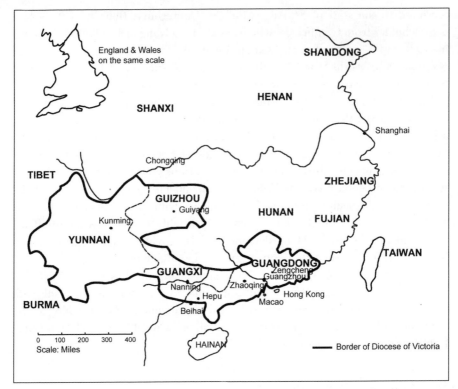

Figure 2.4 Diocese of Victoria in 1932

England, or was it a diocese of the Chung Hua Sheng Kung Hui subject to its constitutions and canons?

With the formation of Chung Hua Sheng Kung Hui, the appointment of a new bishop became a sensitive one. In the selection of Duppuy's successor, Archbishop Cosmo Gordon Lang consulted Bishop Norris, the chairman of the Chung Hua Sheng Kung Hui House of Bishops, who suggested that the appointee should be consecrated in China. Lang also consulted with the general secretary of the Church Missionary Society, Dr. W. Wilson Cash, who recommended that the appointee should be acceptable to both the Chung Hua Sheng Kung Hui and the diocese.[50]

The Search and the Appointment

Several names were put forward to the archbishop for consideration. The Reverend W. T. Featherstone, former headmaster of the Diocesan Boys' School in Hong Kong, recommended the Reverend Arthur Stewart, a Church Missionary Society missionary in Hong Kong and headmaster of St. Paul's College.[51] Ronald Lankester, a Church Missionary Society missionary in Kunming, was also suggested as a possibility to Archbishop Lang.

At a joint meeting of the standing committee of the Diocesan Synod of Chung Hua Sheng Kung Hui in the Diocese of Victoria (representing the Chinese churches) and the executive council of the Victoria Diocesan Conference (representing the English churches), the matter was put to a vote. The result in favor of Stewart was only one out of 19 members of the joint committee, and the reaction to the proposal of Lankester was only lukewarm. At this impasse, Bishop Duppuy brought up the name of Ronald O. Hall, whom he had met. After he spoke glowingly of ROH's work in Tyneside, in the Student Christian Movement and in China, there was considerable enthusiasm from the members of the standing committee. When the motion was put to a vote, it was 18 in favor with one abstention. If ROH was not available, those present in the meeting expressed their desire for the appointment of a man of lively mind, and in touch with modern movements. The ability to speak Chinese was not considered *sine qua non*.[52]

Lang made some enquiries. He received answers from colleagues with whom ROH had worked closely. These letters reflect the perceived virtues—and flaws—in ROH's personality, so some key passages can illuminate our understanding of the man and his character.

Tissington Tatlow, the General Secretary of Student Christian Movement: "He has gift of leadership and enthusiasm. He is good and devoted and attractive to look at and very pleasant manners. The Chinese liked him and I liked him. But he lacks good judgement and I would expect him to be in difficulties with his clergy after a time. He can lead and people will follow him." [53]

Bishop Harold Bilbrough of Newcastle: "Delightful, lovable man, full of ideas and original . . . About half of his ideas are well worth thinking over. He is concerned about social issues, and ways of renewal. He is 'out for souls' all right . . . He will do some odd things and express some odd views but he is certainly a live wire . . . Ronny is a holy man in his own personal life. The only criticism of him is that he often has rather wild ideas (which more thought might modify) but that is much better than having no ideas at all."[54]

Leslie Hunter, ROH's colleague from Northumberland: "He is unusually gifted, full of vitality, enthusiastic, and human kindness, his mind teems with ideas. This is both his strength and his weakness. He is not quite critical enough of the ideas which come with such profusion into his head and is too ready to set them as an equality with those which have been well tried in experience—too ready to 'dogmatize' with equal confidence on subjects of which he knows a little as those on which he is well informed. . . . But his personality is so engaging, his honesty so transparent, his courage so admirable that the harm done will only be of temporary duration . . . He will always have too many irons in the fire. Undoubtedly he has administrative ability. He learns how to set about a job: much of his originality shows in the way he does them."

Leslie Hunter interestingly mentioned Nora in his letter suggesting that the possessiveness of Nora's mother could cause trouble down the road: "His wife may prove a difficulty. She has a bad 'mother complex' and the mother a troublesome human and has given Mrs. Hall a great deal of anxiety. The main reason he only stayed about a year in China was the serious effect on his wife of his mother-in-law's opposition to her daughter being taken out of England. I do not know what has happened during the last 2 to 3 years. . . . The mother's hold on Mrs. Hall caused great strain at times."[55]

In due course, one would see how ROH's strengths and weaknesses affected his ministry in South China and Hong Kong and how his marriage affected his life. On receiving the informal letter of an offer from Lang, ROH, rather insightfully, raised the issue "whether one whose chief weakness is lack of judgement could ever be qualified for such a position" to which Lang replied, "[you] should put curbs of judgement upon your generous impulses and ideas. But there too you may confidently accept that sense of responsibility and the help of the Holy Spirit."[56]

On June 2, Lang sent his formal offer to ROH subject to the approval of the bishops of China. ROH wrote to his mother in June of that year:[57]

> My Dearest Mother,
> I am afraid another son is going abroad after all—to be Bishop of Hong Kong. I hope that will make it easier for you, because you will know how pleased Father will be. It's not going to be easy for Nora and Mrs. Baron and the job itself has its difficulties.
>
> It's not CMS [Church Missionary Society] but a colonial bishopric. Though nearly all the missionary work is CMS and some of it BCMS [Bible Churchmen Missionary Society]![58] This is not yet public . . . The nomination has to be sent to China for confirmation—so it may be another week yet—unless old Norris turns me down completely. He is the chairman of the House of Bishops.

In early July, Lang received a cable from Bishop Norris that there was general approval for the appointment.[59] His Majesty's mandate was then sought for the consecration of ROH to be a bishop, with a view to his succeeding as bishop of Victoria, Hong Kong.[60]

The Consecration

The consecration took place not in China as Bishop Norris would have liked but in St. Paul's Cathedral, London, on October 28, 1932, the feast of St. Simon and St. Jude. A large congregation assembled at 8 a.m. to take part in the celebration of the Holy Communion at the Church of All Hallows, Lombard Street, in the city of London. There were many representatives of the Victoria Diocesan Association (later Hong Kong Diocesan Association) from England and China, and many friends from Newcastle-upon-Tyne. After the service, the party adjourned to breakfast at a quiet neighboring restaurant, and ROH visited them. At 11:30 a.m., a large number of friends filled the choir stalls and the space under the dome in St. Paul's to take part in the beautiful service of consecration conducted by the archbishop of Canterbury. He was assisted by the bishops of London and Newcastle, and it was attended by the bishops of Peterborough, Willesden, and Persia, Bishops Duppuy, Lander, and Wild, the Very Reverend Inge, the canons of St. Paul's Cathedral, and the Reverend C. G. Hall (ROH's father), who preached an eloquent sermon. It was with humble pride that his father spoke of having now given "two sons to China," as ROH's younger brother Giles had gone to Beijing to serve as a medical doctor.[61]

It was a most impressive scene: ROH kneeling before the archbishop, who was seated on his throne in the center of the steps up to the sanctuary and surrounded by the assembled bishops in their scarlet robes. When all those fathers of the church together laid their hands on the head of their new brother, invoking God's blessing upon him, ROH felt awed and excited, yet humbled. He thought of the great task that God had placed on him. He prayed for Christ's presence wherever he would be and that he would accomplish God's will.

In the afternoon, ROH attended the reception held by the Victoria Diocesan Association with Bishop Duppuy in the chair. There were addresses of welcome including those from Dr. T. C. Chao, who was on sabbatical leave in England, and the Reverend Arthur Stewart. The Victoria Diocesan Association was initially set up by Bishop Duppuy in England among friends who had helped him in his work in Britain and in France, before he left Britain for his bishopric in Hong Kong. In 1924, it had a membership of 775. The diocesan branch in Hong Kong had 200 names. The members sent their generous donations for the various projects in China not being covered by the Church Missionary Society, as well as their prayers and blessings. They met twice a year in London and arranged for speakers who worked in East Asia to talk about Hong Kong and China. The Victoria Diocesan Association published *Outpost* two or three times a year, with news of the diocese that they were actively supporting. It played a vital role not only in the ministry of Bishop Duppuy but also that of ROH.

On November 21, after hectic weeks of preparation and excitement, ROH traveled by train through Siberia to China all by himself, to the place of his calling. His family was to join him the following year. On the way, he was planning ahead and began writing to his friends back home inviting them to come to Hong Kong to see what was God's will for them.

The Theological Formation of Bishop R. O. Hall

The man who had been elected bishop of Victoria had very little formal training in theology, because his training at Cuddesdon Theological College had been compressed into a summer term rather than the usual two or three years. Still, he had pieced together a coherent theology from his extensive reading, from working with people in diverse communities, from discussions with colleagues, and from prayer and meditation. Although he was a liberal and progressive thinker for his time, his beliefs were inspired by his conservative Anglican family background as well.

An avid reader of religious and philosophical books throughout his lifetime, he would get secondhand copies of books by writers such as F. D. Maurice, Teilhard de Chardin, Søren Kierkegaard, Simone Weil, and Karl Barth sent to him from England, always carrying one with him when traveling.[62] This eclectic reader, liberal in his thinking, would raise the eyebrows of contemporary Anglican theologians in later years by quoting from John Robinson's book, *Honest to God* (1963).

Basis of Christianity: God's Selfless Love

ROH believed in the doctrine of incarnation as the ultimate key to understanding human history. God is a loving Father who had made himself known to his people in Jesus Christ, who died on the cross and rose from the dead. Through faith, Christians are brought into a relationship with Jesus Christ, a real person with whom it is possible to have a relationship in a sense comparable to that of other human relationships. ROH believed that Jesus' life on earth taught us what life was about and that his death on the cross was a self-giving act of God's love and forgiveness.[63] ROH often spoke of God's self-giving love as that of the love of the father for the prodigal son:[64]

> Prodigal father—the father who gave all he could to the younger son and let him go free with it, and then ran out to welcome him home. He had given all the rest that he had to his elder son, sharing completely with him, keeping nothing to himself, giving himself completely away . . . This is not fatherhood as we know it except the fatherhood of folly, and we know that the folly of God is wiser than men. To give to utterly untrustworthy what you know they are not to be trusted with is the height of folly. But this is the relationship God the Self-giver has with creation.

God's love is also like the warmth of the sun, freely given to all. ROH pointed out that the right attitude of Christians to God is more like "obedience" than "love." But he was inclined to put such obedience in quotation marks because it is a special kind of obedience. It is obedience with one's heart in it; it is an obedience that is like worship.

Christians were called to obey God by showing love for their neighbors, not through mere words but through actions. ROH told his son Joc that the commandment "to love God and our neighbor as ourselves" has a deeper meaning:[65]

Jesus does not "teach us to love." He "loves us into loving." If you want a summary of Jesus' life and teaching parallel to that other summary (Love God and love your neighbor as yourself), here is one: "OBEY GOD AND LOVE ONE ANOTHER AS I HAVE LOVED YOU."

ROH emphasized Jesus' command of "This do and thou shalt live" after the Rabbi recited what was written in the Law to have eternal life. The meaning of Jesus' life was in the words "Do thou likewise."

In his sermons and his ministry, ROH often reminded his flock that Jesus' love is not soft. It is demanding and must be shown through action. On one occasion, ROH wrote, "Jesus trusted action more than words. He healed; he broke bread; he washed feet; he died and God raised him from the dead."[66]

Tractarian Background and Christian Socialism

When he was interviewed by Archbishop Lang for the position of bishop of Victoria, ROH described himself as an "Anglo-Catholic but not beyond the Tractarians." ROH's father had been a member of the Tractarian or Oxford Movement.[67] The Tractarian movement emphasized the Roman Catholic heritage of the Church of England. Above all this meant the centrality of the doctrine of the incarnation and an emphasis on the sacramental life of the church, particularly on the Eucharist as the central act of the church's worship, which ought to be celebrated as the main service every Sunday. The importance of the doctrine of the incarnation for the Tractarians is well illustrated by the subtitle of the volume of essays written by the second generation of Anglo-Catholics, notably Charles Gore and others, entitled *Lux Mundi—A Series of Studies in the Religion of the Incarnation*. The Tractarians believed that God sent Jesus Christ in human form as the mediator for salvation, which was accomplished once and for all through the incarnate life, death, and resurrection of Jesus Christ by incorporating men and women into his risen humanity. The primary means by which this is brought about is by sacramental incorporation into the church, which is the body of Christ. Through baptism, men and women are grafted sacramentally into Christ's humanity and become one body in him. In the Eucharist, this participation in the body of Christ is continually renewed.[68] Throughout his life ROH held on firmly to these beliefs, which in some ways made him feel closer to Roman Catholics than to Protestants. His core Anglican beliefs were traditional, and he adhered to the Anglican tradition of episcopacy, the Anglican liturgy of worship, the Anglican prayer book, and the holy sacraments.

While ROH adhered to core Anglican beliefs, his expression of faith was fundamentally influenced by the tradition of Christian Socialism that he inherited from F. D. Maurice, Charles Gore, and other Christian socialists. God embraced the world in the incarnation, and therefore the world with all its scientific, economic, social, and political life were the arena in which God's mission was to be worked out. The kingdom of God preached by Jesus was not something otherworldly but something that was meant to be realized in the life of society. This is why Maurice's social theology, expressed in his book *The Kingdom of Christ*, meant so much to ROH and was so central to his understanding of how the message of the gospel was to be realized in the life of the world.

F. D. Maurice was the first theologian to develop a social theology after the Industrial Revolution and in response to the changes in society that took place as a result, especially the development of urban slums and the unjust treatment of industrial workers. He perceived the Kingdom of God as a social concept rather than as individual salvation and was concerned with the transformation of life in the world into the Kingdom of God: the creation on earth of a just and peaceable society. Christian theology was therefore a social theology. In 1848, together with Charles Kingsley and John Ludlow, Maurice established Christian Socialism and championed social reforms for the urban and rural poor arising out of the Industrial Revolution, and formed organizations for their defense and support.[69] He focused on education rather than social action as the means of forwarding the work of the kingdom.

Even though Maurice was critical of the selfish and competitive spirit of industrialization, he believed society should be transformed morally through religion and a cooperative spirit, rather than by changing the political or economic structures. Later generations would take the principles of justice and fellowship of Christian Socialism and make something more politically daring than Maurice himself imagined:[70] some leaning in the direction of Fabian Socialism while others of Marxism. This probably prepared the ground for ROH's ability to accept communism in China.

During the late nineteenth century, there was a revival of Christian Socialism, which had ebbed by the mid-1850s. The combination of the High Church tradition of the Tractarian Movement, and the Christian Socialism of Maurice's tradition, led to the founding of Anglican societies devoted to social justice. Charles Gore, another influential theologian at that time who believed that Christianity was a way of life, not an arid philosophy, founded one of these societies: the Christian Social Union. Gore demanded that the Church side with the underprivileged and laboring class. He argued that Christianity must stand for human liberty against the narrowness and materialism of socialistic theory and that the Church is called upon to sympathize with socialism's "overwhelming indictment" of the inequalities and unjust distribution of wealth in society at that time. Both Maurice and Gore rejected Marxist materialism as a basis for social reconstruction.[71] Gore's emphasis on social practice rather than on theological theory influenced ROH's work throughout his life.

For ROH, the consecration and reception of the material elements of bread and wine in the Eucharist was inextricably linked to the transformation of society. The kingdom of heaven that Jesus talked about is not a place to which people were to go after they died but a divine society to be realized in this world.[72] In ROH's view, a Christian needed to apply him or herself to society to help usher in the Kingdom of Christ.[73]

Later, ROH also came under the influence of his friend Archbishop William Temple, author of the 1942 book entitled *Christianity and the Social Order* and whose thinking significantly contributed to the development of the "welfare state" in Britain after World War II. In Newcastle, ROH's advocacy for the weak, the oppressed, the exploited, including orphans, widows, and elderly people, established a template for his work in social reconstruction in Hong Kong after World War II.

His emphasis on a grounded Christianity that expresses love through action meant that he could grow impatient with knotty theological arguments. In 1935, he would express his distrust of theological abstractions: "I thought I could do wonders by proving things logically but I soon realized that all the hair-splitting doctrines that were ever invented would never touch the inner spirit of the men and women who were my neighbors. You could be the finest theologian in England and go on hating your neighbor without any difficulty."[74]

Student Christian Movement's Influence

ROH was deeply imbibed with Student Christian Movement visions and fervor when he began work as vicar of St. Luke's Church, Newcastle, and later in Hong Kong. His attendance at the World Student Christian Federation and the National Christian Council conferences in China in 1922 as a British delegate of the Student Christian Movement greatly influenced him and, to a large extent, determined his future ecumenical and missionary attitudes and policies when he became bishop of Victoria.

God: The Father and Creator of All

ROH, a follower of Maurice who stressed the Fatherhood of God, believed that God is concerned with the lives of human beings as a loving Father with his children. He believed in God's immanence and transcendence, the indwelling character of God in the created world and God as the source of all and above all.

This understanding of God's immanence had deepened considerably during his year in China in 1925–26. After he had absorbed the solemn beauty and harmony of the tombs of ancient emperors and Confucius, ROH saw that China had always been within the molding hands and heart of the God. ROH made two major inferences from this realization. In his book *China and Britain*, he concluded that, since God created all peoples, all nations should live in brotherhood, as "one family under heaven":[75]

> We must, therefore, as a fellowship and as individuals, hold on when others fail in the difficult and costly task of human brotherhood in action . . . And we must endeavor, as a fellowship and as individuals, to be as reckless in or experiments in brotherhood as the spirit of our God indwelling our fellowship has been and is still reckless in His prodigal love of His creation . . . So may all mankind and all human relations come into fullness of the measure of the stature of Christ—not only in His divine sonship, but in His sublime brotherliness.

The natural corollary of the belief that God created all people in different nations and with different religious beliefs is that all should be respected as children of God. ROH's commitment to the principles of "brotherhood in action" directed his footsteps and shaped the direction of his ministry in China.

Lux Mundi *and Articles of Faith*

ROH's commitment to his Christian faith did not keep him from a critical attitude of mind which respected science and critical biblical scholarship. He was familiar with the volume of essays entitled *Lux Mundi*, edited by Charles Gore, which did not deny the Articles of Faith contained in the Creed but welcomed the new light shed on the historic faith of the church, especially in the doctrine of the incarnation, by new developments in science, philosophy, critical biblical scholarship, contemporary social and political developments, and in ethics.[76] In addition, ROH greatly admired Teilhard de Chardin, a Jesuit priest, French scholar, paleontologist and student of history who was passionate about both science and religion and had taken part in the discovery of Peking Man.[77]

ROH's respect for science can be illustrated in a story related by Sir Richard Acland about a lecture Acland had given in China about miracles. The students were interested in what Sir Richard talked about, but the idea of a virgin birth bothered them, because it was something that the Chinese found most difficult to believe. "Well," said the bishop, rising in all his purple panoply, "I don't believe it either. Of course, if you mean that I rejoice to belong to a worshipping community which, for two thousand years, has enshrined in this rather beautiful myth the spiritual truth that in the birth of Jesus humanity was given a unique and unprecedented spiritual opportunity—in that sense I believe it. But if you are asking me, as a fact, whether I believe that Jesus was born without sexual intercourse between his parents, then I don't believe that for a moment."[78]

How did ROH reconcile the tenets of the Apostle's Creed with his scientific education? What, for example, were his views on the Resurrection? In one of his early sermons in 1933, he interpreted the meaning of the Resurrection as spiritual, but no less real for that.[79]

> They saw him as they had known him. They knew him too by the marks of the nails. On several occasions more than one person saw him at the same time. On one occasion one hundred and twenty, and in St. Paul's record in 1 Corinthians, which remember is the earliest written record we have, he claims that over 500 saw him at one time—that most of those men and women were still alive to bear their witness. It was a spiritual resurrection, but by spiritual I mean real. I do not mean that I know, or anyone knows, how it was managed chemically. It was a unique event: a direct act of God, and therefore beyond the scope of science. There must be at least two events of the same kind before scientific thinking can begin.

ROH often told people that he had had a vision of the risen Christ, a vision so real and profound that it became for him the seal of his apostleship. Visions appearing to the mind's eye could have for him an unassailable reality. In 1941, he had been consumed with anxiety about his family's safety when he left them in Singapore and they were returning to England by sea. In his vision, he saw Nora and the two children standing on the sea and behind them was Jesus himself, looking down on them and sheltering them. In a 1942 letter to his son Joc, he reflected that God had used his imagination and mind in order to reveal Himself through this vision.[80] ROH extrapolated further that the Lord used this imagination-and-mind method after the Resurrection to reveal himself to those who were receptive:

> In these days after the Resurrection He only appeared to those who loved Him. This is one of the advantages of using the imagination-and-mind, and not the flesh-and-blood method. If we knew more about it, I think we should probably have to say also that in these appearances He only came for a certain definite purpose. Just as His flesh-and-blood appearance, or rather His whole flesh-and-blood life, was for a certain purpose, so the later appearances, when He used the imagination-and-mind method, were for a definite purpose. The Lord is risen indeed, and hath appeared unto Simon. This appearance to St. Peter is perhaps the clearest example of the special purpose of His appearances.

ROH believed that Christ had risen but that the Resurrection did not have to be a physical one in order to be real. In fact, he sympathized with the view of Victor Gollancz, the author of *From Light to Darkness*, who thought that "it makes a much more complete incarnation if Christ's body shared the corruption that all other bodies share and that we insult God by requiring the physical resurrection." ROH thought that perhaps there are two "Christs." Martha, the practical sister, accepted Jesus' words literally: "I am the resurrection and the life." To the more "spiritual," "personal," and "emotional" sister, Mary, he allowed the outward and visible sign of a physical resurrection that was also deeply spiritual. ROH also found the empty tomb possibly "a little out of line" with what he considered to be the Lord's way of intimating spiritual realities without requiring corporeal evidence at all times.

Instructions for Christian Practices

To ROH, Christianity was a way of life sustained and strengthened by the discipline of prayer and the grace of the sacraments. As baptism brings people into Christ's humanity, the Holy Eucharist renewed participation in the body of Christ. Very early on in his ministry ROH instructed Christians in practices that would review their faith and their receptivity to God's love: to read the Bible and pray daily, and take part in the Holy Eucharist at least weekly. Prayer, he considered, could give people direct, personal communion with God:[81]

> Christians are those whose conversation with God is in Christ's name. We pray in Christ's name. Prayer is only one part of our on-going conversation with God and his on-going conversation with us.

This daily prayer he recommended was dialogic and open-ended, not bracketed by prescriptive ritual. Although he agreed that the methodical prayer recommended in prayer manuals was good, he also urged a more spontaneous, less formal style of prayer. People were urged to pray whenever a chance presented itself, and not to feel ashamed about pouring out their hearts to God before falling asleep, as that was the best, if not the only, way for a child of God to end the day. From his own daily prayer and meditation he derived strength, inspiration, and a sense of closeness to God that he wanted others to experience. Throughout his life ROH would pray unselfconsciously with people from all walks of life, always kneeling down in prayer as a sign of obedience and surrender to God.[82]

ROH recommended that Christians read the Bible every day, but in a mature way, not a literal way. ROH did not accept a literal interpretation of stories of creation in Genesis and was most unhappy with the stance of churches that held the Bible, rather than the risen and living Christ, as the standard of faith. He did not see the preservation of the Church of God as depending upon the unquestioning acceptance that the Bible was verbally inspired by the spirit of God.[83]

For ROH, with his Tractarian background, the bread-breaking ceremony of Holy Eucharist was a reenactment of Jesus' living and dying and of His rising again to give Himself to men. He thought that taking the cup in the sacrament of Holy Eucharist "should do more than express our obedience to Jesus' command at the last supper." It should also remind us of Jesus' obedience to God during his sufferings in Gethsemane:[84]

> The cup in the Communion Service will always remind you of the obedience behind the words about "Love and charity with all men" which draw us to the Lord's Table. Every time you kneel and take the cup into your hands, picture to yourself Jesus Our Lord kneeling in the gardens and crying out, "Father if it be possible take this cup from me. Nevertheless not my will but thine be done." The cup is the symbol of all that lies behind the

sentence in the Epistle to the Hebrews: "Though he were son yet learned he obedience through the things that he suffered."

ROH recommended that all Christians should participate in the Holy Eucharist at least once a week. Later, during World War II, he would break with the Church's centuries-old tradition and ordain the first female priest in the Anglican Church, in order to enable Christians in Macao to receive Holy Communion when no male priest could reach them.

When ROH set out to his episcopate in the Diocese of Victoria—whose people he had great affection for—he had by then fully developed his beliefs in God's universal, undiscriminating love. He submitted, with a joyful heart, to the mission that called him to serve the Chinese people for the next 34 years. His love would be realized through action.

Notes

1. Family tree of Cecil Galopine Hall. Hall Family Archive.
2. R. O. Hall, "The Late Rev C. G. Hall," *Outpost* (January–March 1940): 5–6.
3. Information provided by Sir Noel Hall, ROH's brother, to D. M. Paton. 1975. Hall Family Archive.
4. Paton, R. O.: *The Life and Times of Bishop Ronald Hall of Hong Kong*, 6–7.
5. School report of ROH Royal Grammar School, Newcastle, 1909. Chung Chi Divinity School Archive.
6. Paton, R. O.: *The Life and Times of Bishop Ronald Hall of Hong Kong*, 4–5 (ROH as a student in Brasenose College).
7. The Military Cross is the third-level military decoration awarded to officers and (since 1993) other ranks of the British Armed Forces and in other Commonwealth countries. It was granted in recognition of "an act or acts of exemplary gallantry during active operations against the enemy on land to all members, of any rank in Our Armed Forces." The Bar means that it had been awarded twice.
8. "Short Biography of Bishop R. O. Hall." Bishop Hall Jubilee File. Bishop House's Archive.
9. R. O. Hall, "Enthronement Speech." Delivered at St. John's Cathedral, Hong Kong. December 30, 1932. Hall Family Archive.
10. Hall Humphrey on R. O. Hall. Likely written at the request of Percy Smith in 1975. Chung Chi Divinity School Archive.
11. Professor Charles Manning to Sir Noel Hall. Likely in 1975 for the memorial service of ROH. Chung Chi Divinity School Archive.
12. R. O. Hall to N. Baron. May 6, 1919. Written at Brasenose College, Oxford University. Hall Family Archive.
13. R. O. Hall to N. Baron. April 25, 1919. Written at Brasenose College, Oxford University. Hall Family Archive.
14. Sir Herbert Thompson on R. O. Hall. Likely written in 1975 for the memorial service of ROH. Chung Chi Divinity School Archive.
15. R. O. Hall to N. Baron. May 19, 1919. Written at Brasenose College, Oxford University. Hall Family Archive.

16. R. O. Hall to N. Baron. June 19, 1919. Hall Family Archive.
17. Paton, R. O.: *The Life and Times of Bishop Ronald Hall of Hong Kong*, 12.
18. Interview of Canon Alan J. C. Chan in his home by the author. Hong Kong. April 28, 2010.
19. R. O. Hall to A. C. Hall. October 3, 1956. Chung Chi Divinity School Archive.
20. R. Boyd, *The Witness of the Student Christian Movement: Church ahead of the Church* (London: SPCK, 2007), 23, 38.
21. Bishop Herbert St Barbe Holland, *Outpost* (February 1957): 17.
22. Paton, R. O.: *The Life and Times of Bishop Ronald Hall of Hong Kong*, 25 (Glasgow Quadrilennial Conference).
23. Boyd, *The Witness of the Student Christian Movement*, 22–24.
24. Noncollegiate institutions that admitted men and women without reference to religion or social background.
25. Paton, R. O.: *The Life and Times of Bishop Ronald Hall of Hong Kong*, 29 (R. O. Hall, SCM Conference: Science and Industry. Student Movement 1920–21).
26. G. Allen, "Memories of Bishop R. O. Hall." Not dated. Chung Chi Divinity School Archive.
27. Gilbert Baker became the eighth bishop of Hong Kong succeeding ROH (1966–80); Geoffrey Allen, bishop of Egypt (1947–52) and bishop of Derby (1959–69); Gerald Goodban, headmaster of Diocesan Boys' School (1938–54); Harry Baines, bishop of Singapore (1949–60) and bishop of Wellington (1960–72); Leonard Wilson, bishop of Singapore (1941–49) and bishop of Birmingham (1953–69).
28. Paton, R. O.: *The Life and Times of Bishop Ronald Hall of Hong Kong*, 42 (Tatlow's assessment).
29. Personal Communication from Canon Christopher Hall.
30. R. O. Hall to Nora Hall. April 23, 1945. Hall Family Archive.
31. Leslie Hunter to Archbishop C. G. Lang. Lang Papers 115, 216–18. Lambeth Library Archive.
32. R. O. Hall to N. Hall. July 6, 1923. Hall Family Archive (itching to return to China).
33. Paton, R. O.: *The Life and Times of Bishop Ronald Hall of Hong Kong*, 41 (ROH wanted to leave SCM).
34. Ibid., 53 (*Annus mirabilis*).
35. Ibid., 57 (Vicar of Tyneside).
36. H. Mess, "Industrial Tyneside: A Social Survey." 1926. Chung Chi Divinity School Archive.
37. *Newcastle Diocesan Gazette* (July 1931): 117.
38. Octavia Hill, an English social reformer who was concerned with the urban economically disadvantaged people, had shown that it was possible to build housing for low-paid workers and put it on a sound financial footing. She stressed that all managers had to collect rent personally, ensure regular contact with tenants, keep an eye on the property, and make immediate repairs when necessary. She only trained educated women to become housing managers.
39. *St. John's Review* (December 1932): 487.
40. R. O. Hall, "The Church and Social Problems," 1931. Hall Family Archive.
41. R. Lloyd, "The Church of England in the 20th Century," in Paton, R. O.: *The Life and Times of Bishop Ronald Hall of Hong Kong*, 64.

42. M. Challoner to D. M. Paton. October 23, 1982. Chung Chi Divinity School Archive.
43. Paton, R. O.: *The Life and Times of Bishop Ronald Hall of Hong Kong*, 58–59 (Innovations at St. Luke's Church).
44. Ibid., 60 (ROH's curates).
45. T. Rutherford to D. M. Paton. October 20, 1982. Chung Chi Divinity School Archive.
46. R. E. Doggett, *Ridley Duppuy: Friend and Bishop* (London: CMS Press, 1946), 38.
47. Telegram of Bishop Duppuy to the Prime Minister, Accepting the Appointment of Canonry of Worcester. January 19, 1932. CO 129/538/5. National Archive, London, England.
48. G. B. Endacott, "The Dis-establishment of the Bishopric," in G. B. Endacott and D. She, *The Diocese of Victoria, Hong Kong: A Hundred Year of Church History*, 48–49 (Hong Kong: Messrs Kelly and Walsh Ltd., 1949).
49. Chung Hua Sheng Kung Hui, *History of Chung Hua Sheng Kung Hui* (Shanghai: CHSKH, 1949).
50. Paton, R. O.: *The Life and Times of Bishop Ronald Hall of Hong Kong*, 74 (Bishop Duppuy retiring).
51. W. Featherstone to Mr. Ellis. CO 129/539/5. National Archive, London, England.
52. Report of Bishop Duppuy to Archbishop Cosmo Lang on the results of the meeting of the Standing Committee of the Diocesan Synod representing the Chinese and the Executive Council of the Victoria Diocesan Conference representing the British. Lang Papers 115, 196–97. Lambeth Palace Library, London, England.
53. T. Tatlow to Archbishop C. G. Lang on R. O. Hall. Lang Papers 115, 213–14. Lambeth Palace Library, London, England.
54. Bishop H. Bilbrough of Newcastle to Archbishop C. G. Lang on R. O. Hall. Lang Papers 115, 212. Lambeth Palace Library, London, England.
55. L. Hunter to Archbishop C. G. Lang on R. O. Hall. Lang Papers 115, 216–18. Lambeth Palace Library, London, England.
56. Paton, R. O.: *The Life and Times of Bishop Ronald Hall of Hong Kong*, 76 (Archbishop Lang's advice).
57. R. O. Hall to his mother. June 1932. Chung Chi Divinity School Archive.
58. ROH's mother did not approve of CMS because it was a Low Church.
59. Archbishop C. G. Lang to R. O. Hall. Lang Papers 115, 263. Lambeth Palace Library, London, England.
60. S. Hoare, to His Majesty King George V. Appointment of R. O. Hall to be the Bishop of Victoria. CO 129/539/5. Lambeth Palace Library, London, England.
61. *Outpost* (January 1933): 2.
62. D. M. Paton on R. O. Hall. Not dated. Chung Chi Divinity School Archive.
63. R. O. Hall, "Sermon: To Know the Love of Christ Which Passeth Knowledge, Preached on September 22, 1966," *St. John's Review* (October 1966): 191–93.
64. ROH's dictation of part of what was intended to be a book (Appendix 1). Hall Family Archive.
65. R. O. Hall, Letter to Joc Hall, V. Chung Chi Divinity School Archive.
66. R. O. Hall, *Outpost* (January–March 1957): 6.
67. Paton, R. O.: *The Life and Times of Bishop Ronald Hall of Hong Kong*, 75.

68. W. Crockett, *The Anglican Social Tradition from Maurice to Gore* (forthcoming).
69. J. Atherton, *Social Christianity: A Reader* (London: SPCK, 1994), 14.
70. J. Morris, *To Build Christ's Kingdom: F. D. Maurice and His Writings* (Norwich: Canterbury Press, 2007), 16.
71. J. Carpenter, *Gore: A Study in Liberal Catholic Thought* (London: The Faith Press, 1960), 248–49.
72. Atherton, *Social Christianity*, 12.
73. R. O. Hall, "Revised Reviews: V–F. D. Maurice's *The Doctrine of Sacrifice*." Chung Chi Divinity School Archive.
74. *St. John's Review* (May 1935): 181.
75. R. O. Hall, *China and Britain* (London: Edinburgh House Press, 1927), 170–71.
76. M. Ramsey, *An Era in Anglican Theology: From Gore to Temple: The Development of Anglican Theology between Lux Mundi and Second World War 1889–1939*. Hale Lectures, 1959 (Eugene, OR: Wipf and Stock, 1960), 1–15.
77. D. M. Paton on ROH. Not dated. Chung Chi Divinity School Archive.
78. Paton, *R. O.: The Life and Times of Bishop Ronald Hall of Hong Kong*, 221.
79. R. O. Hall, Easter Day Sermon, Easter Monday 1933, in Paton, *R. O.: The Life and Times of Bishop Ronald Hall of Hong Kong*, 244–48.
80. R. O. Hall, Letter to Joc Hall, III-2, "The Obedient Son." Chung Chi Divinity School Archive.
81. R. O. Hall, "Address Given to the First Graduating Class of Chung Chi College, June 23, 1955." Sheng Kung Hui Documents.
82. P. Smith to D. M. Paton. Not dated. Chung Chi Divinity School Archive.
83. R. O. Hall, Letter to Joc Hall, IV, "Why Are There No Records of Jesus' Own—Written in His Own Language?" Chung Chi Divinity School Archive.
84. R. O. Hall, Letter to Joc Hall, VI, "Obedience and God." Chung Chi Divinity School Archive.

Chapter 3
Working under the Threat of the Japanese

The Diocese of South China and Hong Kong (1932–45)

O holy Jesus,
Most merciful Redeemer,
Friend and Elder brother,
May we see thee more clearly,
Love thee more dearly,
Follow thee more nearly,
Day by day.[1]

At the time of ROH's rail journey, political turmoil in China had been churning for decades. In 1928, the Guomindang had set up the Nationalist government in Nanjing and was recognized by the international community as the sole legitimate government of China. The following "Nanjing Decade" (1928–37) was one of consolidation, with a mixed but generally positive record on the economy, social progress, development of democracy, and cultural creativity. The Guomindang government was unable to solve the problem of landownership in the rural areas, however, and many people continued to live in dire poverty.[2] Guangdong province, where Hong Kong is situated, was, between 1931 and 1936, under the rule of the warlord Chen Jitang,[3] who, in an attempt to improve the lives of the farmers, introduced the Cooperative Movement, which unfortunately lasted for only a short time.[4]

The civil war between the Guomindang and the Chinese Communist Party created a window of vulnerability in China, encouraging Japan's aggression. Marching into Manchuria in September 1931, Japan installed the last emperor of China, Puyi, as a puppet ruler of the region. Japan then began to take control of one area after another in northern China.[5] Despite the continuous Japanese offensive in North China, the Guomindang government did not put up strong resistance. Chiang Kai-shek's policy was "internal pacification before external resistance," and it focused on eliminating the Chinese Communist Party. In October 1934, retreating from the advance of Chiang's forces, the Communists gave up their base in Jiangxi and started the famous Long March. Of the 80,000 people who began the more than 6,000-mile march from Jiangxi, less than one tenth reached Yan'an in October 1935. On the way to Yan'an, Mao Zedong became the leader of the Chinese Communist Party.[6]

In 1932, the Diocese of Victoria included Hong Kong, Macao, and South China (Guangdong, part of Guangxi, Yunnan, and Guizhou), a huge domain almost the size of Europe, with a population estimated at 77 million people. Although ROH's bishopric covered Hong Kong and South China, his "seat" was in Hong Kong, consisting, at the time, of the Hong Kong Island, the Kowloon Peninsula, and the New Territories. After the First Opium War in 1842, the island was ceded to the British, and after the Second Opium War in 1860, the British also gained possession of the Kowloon Peninsula. As these opium wars had exposed the weakness of the Chinese empire, different powers began to demand territorial concessions from China. The French acquired Zhanjiang (Canton Bay), southwest of Hong Kong, in 1898. The British immediately sought a 99-year lease to extend its colony to include the New Territories: the rest of the Kowloon Peninsula south of Shenzhen River and 230 surrounding islands, a total area of about 370 square miles.[7]

The population in Hong Kong was just over 900,000 at that time. Most were first-generation Chinese immigrants, temporary workers, or refugees who worked in Hong Kong because they could not find work at home. They had no loyalty to the colonial government, which, in turn, did not try to turn them into citizens.[8] Most of the Chinese resented the privileges the Europeans enjoyed, and their arrogance. At the top of the European pyramid were the colonial officials, who together with European taipans and entrepreneurs, lived mostly in the district of the Peak, which was barred to Chinese. No Chinese were admitted to the Hong Kong Club, the Hong Kong Hotel, Hong Kong Yacht Club, or the Hong Kong Golf Club. They were also denied entry to the Matilda Hospital and the first-class section of the Star Ferry.[9]

In such a politically convoluted and challenging time, how could a man of faith from England accomplish in China and Hong Kong what he felt called to do? The complex politics necessitated that ROH plan meticulously his management of the vast and diverse Diocese of Victoria.

One might imagine ROH falling into a meditative mood on his rail journey to Hong Kong through Siberia, as he contemplated the challenges that he would soon face. No doubt he also sought human support and guidance when he stopped over in Beijing to visit his brother Giles, at the Peking Union Medical College, and Bishop Norris, as well as the leaders of the National Christian Council in Shanghai.[10]

From Shanghai, ROH traveled to Hong Kong on the Japanese N.Y.K. liner *Katoria Mara*, whose captain spoke to him of the loneliness of being in command. When he arrived on December 23, 1932,[11] he was met by the Very Reverend Alfred Swann, dean of St. John's Cathedral, whose description of this occasion captures ROH's prayerful spirit at the time:[12]

> At the rail of the ship there is a figure, still and alone, intently looking across the harbour to the island of Hong Kong. It is the new Bishop, just arrived. He told us later something of what was in his mind. He was,

he said, struggling to let his faith in God overcome all fear of man. That was the spirit in which Bishop Ronald took up his work and it was not long before his people in the diocese were aware of his trust in God.

On his way to Hong Kong, ROH had been meditating on St. Paul's Second Epistle to the Corinthians, particularly the first and second chapters. He told Swann that he longed to be able to bring to Hong Kong and South China the "grace and peace from God our Father." He was praying for God's grace to do His will and to bring the kingdom of Christ to the diocese he would serve. Swann continued:

> There was a great deal in his talk that quite took our breath away! He was new to us, and was quick, in the old sense of that word as well as the new. We often felt left far behind. But we knew that something valuable was going to get done even if we might not always understand or agree . . . We knew that all of us were going to have to get down on our knees more than they had been doing, metaphorically as well as actually . . . He was clearly going to get to know his clergy well indeed, and they him . . . We found immediately that we could talk to the Bishop freely about anything and did so.

Soon after his arrival, a Chinese name, Ho Ming Hua, was bestowed on him by his beloved Chinese friend T. Z. Koo, in accordance with Chinese custom. "Ho," like Hall, is an old family name in China; "Ming," like St. Luke, means light. This linked him to St. Luke's Newcastle and his new work in spreading the light of the gospel in "Hua" (China).[13]

A Promise to Serve: The Enthronement of 1932

ROH's enthronement as Bishop took place on December 30, 1932, in St. John's Cathedral, Hong Kong. While the service was conducted mostly in English, the program was printed in both English and Chinese for the congregation. Archdeacon Mok Sau Tsang of Guangzhou and the Very Reverend Alfred Swann welcomed him warmly to his new position.

In his moving enthronement sermon,[14] ROH revealed his pain in leaving behind his ministry in Newcastle, where he had worked the greater part of his life. However, he felt called by God to serve the Chinese people: "My heart is still sore for my beloved Tyneside, for my fellow townsmen, for the pits and shipyards and heather hills of the north country. In a strange way God has tied my life to China." He also talked for the first time in public about his experience in World War I, how, after losing three of his closest friends, he felt "that something was dead in [him]," and he seemed to have lost the capacity for intimate friendship. During the Beijing Conference in 1922, however, God had restored this capacity to him through his friendship with a Chinese Christian[15] "as strong and deep as those the war had taken." This friendship opened his heart to the Chinese people. He now embraced a twofold ministry whereby he could combine his two great loves: for his "own countrymen and the Chinese people."

His first calling was to share with the Chinese people the knowledge of God, and his second was to help "forge even stronger and stronger links in the fellowship of the Gospel of Jesus Christ between China and Britain, two nations whom God has made to serve one another in brotherhood and peace." As bishop, he asked for their prayers. He also pleaded for a special kind of prayer—a "forgiving prayer"—when he disappointed them, as he inevitably would.

ROH then described ways that we all suffer disappointments: "that life does not fulfil its promise." His examples of creeping disappointments in ministry, in marriage, in business, or in academic work show his deep insight and empathy with all kinds of people. However, he reminded his listeners that it is out of death that true life is born. He drew from the story in St. Luke's gospel of how, after Jesus' death, two men "walk with leaden steps on Emmaus Road." So consumed by their sadness in the loss of the one they thought would redeem Israel and "give life meaning," they did not recognize Jesus when He came to walk quietly beside them (Luke 24: 13–17). ROH emphasized that, just as Jesus allowed Himself to be detained only because the two men invited him to stay, we too must invite Jesus to stay with us.

At the end of the service, the Chinese were pleased when he gave his blessing in Chinese. As he led the contingent out, he bowed to the governor, Sir William Peel, who represented the king. This ritual sign of respect also pleased the British enormously.[16]

Figure 3.1 ROH's Pectoral Cross (Hall Family Archive)

Beginning to Build the Church in South China and Hong Kong (1932–36)

ROH was joined by Nora and the two children in September 1933, when they arrived by the Blue Funnel Steamer *Diomed*. They lived in the Bishop's House on Lower Albert Road for one year; then they purchased a piece of land in Tao Fong Shan, Sha Tin, from the Christian Buddhist Institute.[17] They built a cottage and named it Lin Yin Tai (meaning the flat hilltop beneath the spirit's shade) and lived there while subletting most of the Bishop's House to help with the mortgage payments.[18] The main part of the Bishop's House became the dean's residence.

The Sha Tin property was near enough for ROH to commute to work and remote enough from the city that he could keep goats and pigs and cultivate vegetables and flowers. He believed that every missionary ought to have a hobby so that he could be at home in foreign lands. It would help him to settle down quickly and become part of daily life there.[19] Even the farm animals of the ROH household played key roles in his ministry. The two huge black sows that he kept were inadvertently his best goodwill ambassadors and had brought him closer to the life of his neighbors.

The insight that ROH had developed into the tensions between Chinese and British communities while he was in Shanghai stayed with him. He had no time for the expatriate assumption of British superiority in the Crown colony of Hong Kong, and he said that he would always side with the Chinese when there was a difference of opinion. ROH often looked toward the Island of Victoria and referred to the government as "this comic opera government" for its conservative colonial policies. While Hong Kong had an executive council at that time, the governor, who had supreme power, could ignore its advice if he so wished. There was also a Legislative Council, but only two out of seventeen members were elected.[20] There were also only two elected out of ten members on the Sanitary Board.[21] The British expatriates had little chance of making their voices heard, and the Chinese even less.

From the very beginning of his ministry he discouraged people from addressing him as "My Lord" or "Your Grace," preferring to be called "Bishop":[22]

> the word "Lord" be no more heard on platform or in letter. The word itself was one of respect for the commission which I hold from the Lord Jesus Himself, but I would rather, and I believe he would rather, that respect for Him was shown in his own simple way. So please just plain "Bishop" or "Bishop Hall."

Early on, he also spelled out his thoughts on the relationship between Christianity, Confucianism, and Buddhism to show his sensitivity and respect to the Chinese culture. This was a complete departure from the attitude of most missionaries at that time:[23]

Figure 3.2 Lin Yin Tai, Sha Tin: (upper) exterior and (lower) interior showing its simplicity. Watercolor painted by Molly Challoner in 1934 (Hall Family Archive).

> Either God loves every single soul in China, or there is no God. We are not denying the great things God has done for China. We are not denying that the religion of Confucius or Buddhism came from God. What we are saying is God has given them so much, but it is not yet enough. Confucius gave them a religion of conduct and Buddha a religion of escape but the Christian religion offers them infinitely more.

He compared Confucius with Moses, and Buddha with Elijah:[24]

> The Chinese Moses and the Chinese Elijah have been the companions of the Lord. Confucius like Moses is the Law-giver. He deals in the "Thou shalts" and the "Thou shalt nots" of this life.

In the first four years, as ROH worked to lay the foundation of the Church in Hong Kong and South China, he understood that spreading the gospel of Christ and His love was essential. But his Newcastle experiences had taught him that action was superior to words. ROH's episcopacy was marked by spreading the gospel through love-in-action to improve the lives of people, so that they would come to know the love of Christ. His mission strategy was twofold: to care for the spiritual needs *and* the social needs of his diocese.

Ministry in South China

During the first half of his ministry, from 1932 to 1949, ROH focused his energy on South China. After assessing the needs for this huge diocese, ROH crystallized his plans for how to proceed with its management. When he presented them during the annual meeting of the Diocesan Synod in Hong Kong in April 1933, he divided the responsibilities among three senior people. ROH would be responsible for Hong Kong, Macao, and the Pearl River Delta southwest of Guangzhou; Kunming, a city with a quarter of a million people and the work of the Church centered on the hospital; and Guiyang, which became significant during the second Sino-Japanese War when the Burma Road passed through it from Kunming to Chongqing. Archdeacon Mok Sau Tsang was to be in charge of Guangzhou, a large metropolitan city where he had built up the Church of Our Saviour, the parish, and Holy Trinity School. He would also be responsible for Zengcheng, which had a number of Christian villages as a result of pioneer evangelism. Lee Kau Yan was assigned Beihai, where the diocese had a leper colony, a hospital, and a church. When Lee declined the offer because of family reasons, ROH was further obliged to cover this area himself.[25]

In 1932, except for a handful of assistant bishops, no diocesan bishop in Chung Hua Sheng Kung Hui was Chinese. The various dioceses were financially supported by different missionary societies in England, as well as the American Episcopal Church and the Anglican Church in Canada. ROH recognized that the survival of the Anglican Church in China depended upon the speedy installation of Chinese bishops. He appointed Archdeacon Mok Sau Tsang to be the suffragan bishop of Guangzhou, an appointment which his predecessor had proposed but had not carried out. At the age of three, Archdeacon Mok had gone to a Methodist mission school in Guangzhou, and after having devoted his entire adult life to spreading Christianity to his compatriots, he was nearly 70 years old at the time of his consecration on January 25, 1935.[26]

When his younger son, Christopher, was born in December 1935, ROH asked Bishop Mok to baptize him. The following morning, the headline of the *South China Morning Post* read: "Unique Ceremony—English Baby Baptized by Chinese Bishop," reporting further that it was a pleasing ceremony of historic interest. Christopher was baptized with a Chinese name and given two Chinese godparents and two English godparents.[27] Although a contemporary reader may see this decision as unremarkable, at the time ROH was making a political and theological declaration of his total conviction in the equal status of Chinese and British in the sight of God. He utilized this opportunity to deliver a strong message to his diocese, the kind of policy he would pursue as he had advocated in his book *China and Britain*.[28]

ROH, who regarded the Chinese as essential coworkers in his ministry, wanted to emphasize the training of the Chinese clergy. At that time Holy Trinity College, a boys' school in Guangzhou, was the Anglican component of Canton Union Theological College. Lee Kau Yan was one of its prominent graduates. The students lived in St. Andrew's Hostel with the Reverend Percy Jenkins, a Church Missionary Society missionary who taught at Canton Union Theological College. The college continued to train many Anglican priests during the first part of ROH's episcopate, including some of the senior clergy in the diocese: Edward Y. P. Lee, Kong Chi Wing, John Chou Meng Chou, Cheung Wing Ngok, and Chung Yan Laap. Li Tim Oi, the female priest who would be ordained by ROH during World War II, was also trained there. ROH considered Canton Union Theological College a success story of ecumenical cooperation. ROH continued to send his ordinands there until the separation of the Diocese of Hong Kong from Chung Hua Sheng Kung Hui in 1951.[29]

Recruiting and training the right people to work in arduous conditions is never easy, yet ROH was able to fire up the hearts of a number of expatriates, friends of his from the Student Christian Movement, who came to work with him in China. Gilbert Baker, who would succeed ROH as the eighth bishop of Hong Kong, arrived in 1934 to open a hostel for Anglican students in Lingnan University, with the hope of enlisting some into the ministry. Geoffrey Allen, who became the bishop of Egypt in 1947, worked in St. Andrew's Hostel in Pak Hok Tung in Guangzhou from 1935 to 1940.[30] In 1936, for the rural work in Zengcheng, ROH found an ideal candidate, Arthur Peill, a physician who became a farmer and whose family boasted two generations of missionaries.[31]

While the work of the Church in the cities was critical, ROH knew that China had always been an agrarian country, and the majority of farmers lived in dire poverty. Recognizing that the needs of these country people could not be ignored, ROH appointed the Reverend Harry Wittenbach as director of rural reconstruction in Zengcheng at a time when the Cooperative Movement in Guangdong was also flourishing under Chen Jitang. Using his enthronement collection fund, he sent Wittenbach to attend an agricultural conference in Ding Xian, a county in Hopei, south of Beijing. He was to study with Yan Yangchu, James (James Y. C. Yen),[32] who had published books on agricultural methods and who had developed new strains of rice, chickens, and pigs.[33]

In a village called Pek-taam, Zengcheng, Wittenbach set up a "Christian" fish farm.[34] When the rising water of an adjacent river had damaged a dyke wall and threatened to flood the communal fish farm, he quickly organized an enthusiastic crowd of English laypeople from Hong Kong to help. They arrived with spades and shovels to aide their fellow Chinese Christians in repairing the dyke and preserving the villagers' fish.[35]

ROH established the Rural Development Committee to assess the situation in Zengcheng, which was tied to a landlord economy where the farmers kept getting deeper and deeper into debt. He created The Bishop's Cooperative Trust as a way to buy the rice seeds for the farmers, and allow them to reimburse the trust after harvest. The cooperative would also buy back land that was mortgaged at a high interest rate and lease it back to the farmers at a lower rate. Seeing the great success of this scheme, other villages requested similar assistance.[36]

ROH was never as happy as he was when roaming his vast diocese. He toured different parts of his diocese at least once every two years to visit his clergy, confirm new Christians, assess the status of various projects, and introduce new ones. After a visit to the Agricultural Department of Lingnan University, he returned with creative ideas about goat milk production for Beihai, and papaya plantations for the rural orphanage in Tai Po, Hong Kong.[37] From his farm in Lin Yin Tai he dispatched his goats on "outreach programs": a few traveled with Wittenbach to Zengcheng to start a new herd, while others went with Baker on a French steamer bound for Beihai to improve goat milk production.

Ministry in Hong Kong

In Hong Kong, there were five Chinese-speaking churches (St. Paul's Church, St. Stephen's Church, Holy Trinity Church, All Saints' Church, and St. Mary's Church) and three English-speaking churches (St. John's Cathedral, St. Peter's Church, and St. Andrew's Church). The congregation of St. Peter's Church at West Point[38] had consisted mainly of seamen and of students and teachers from the nearby Diocesan Boys' School. After the Seamen's Institute moved from West Point to Wan Chai, and the school relocated from Bonham Road to Mong Kok, Kowloon, the lack of funding and the decreasing size of the congregation led to the closure of the Church, in August 1933. Since half of the congregation, mostly Eurasians, had come from the school that had moved near Kowloon Tong, it was logical to build a church there. ROH asked Victor Halward to assemble and enlarge the congregation of the new church in Kowloon Tong. He did not need his help as chaplain in the cathedral, commenting that he did not want someone to lick the stamps for him![39] When the work was almost completed, he sent Halward to perform pastoral work in the church in Shamian, Guangzhou.[40]

Mindful of the need to create an indigenous church, and sensitive to preserving Chinese culture, ROH wanted the church in Kowloon Tong to be designed like a Chinese temple. The cost of doing that was twice as much as an English design, however, and not feasible.[41] When the building was completed in 1937 he named it Christ Church, and it was consecrated on October 29, 1938. It was neither traditional nor pretty in design, but the architecture, like its name, had simple, clean lines, in harmony with the residences of Kowloon Tong. In the meantime, two newly built Chinese churches—Holy Trinity Church in Kowloon City and St. Mary's Church in Causeway Bay—had been built in accordance with Chinese architectural design.

When he arrived in 1932, ROH relied mainly on four Chinese clergy in Hong Kong for the Chinese churches: Tsang Kei Ngor, Lee Kau Yan, Edward Y. P. Lee, and Paul S. F. Tso. They were important pillars of the Church and helped lay the foundation for the Church's growth in Hong Kong. But ROH needed still more clergy to fulfil his vision for his Hong Kong ministry. During the first year of ROH's episcopate there were only four young Chinese in training for the ministry, but by the following year the number had more than doubled to nine.

He recruited the Reverend Jack Bennitt and the Reverend Harry Baines from England to work in the English churches in Hong Kong.[42] He also ordained Christopher Sargent,[43] the headmaster of Diocesan Boys' School, as a deacon in St. John's Cathedral and in the following year as a priest in the school chapel, making it possible for him to do pastoral work among his students.[44]

Hong Kong had always had a government with a *laissez-faire* policy in economy and social services, its thriving entrepôt trade built on a policy of no taxation. Before World War II, the proportion of government spending on social services—health care, education, housing, and social welfare—was 15 percent or less of the government's total expenditure.[45] The family and extended family had always taken responsibility for the welfare of the Chinese people, through lineages and clans. In the past, when refugees poured into Hong Kong as a result of political upheavals in China, such as the Taiping Rebellion and Boxer Uprising, this form of safety net failed. A handful of local voluntary agencies had evolved to provide for the needs of economically underprivileged people. The Tung Wah Hospital, which was established in 1872, cared for the sick, the dying, women, and orphans, and carried out relief work among the refugees.[46] Other voluntary agencies eventually developed, including Po Leung Kuk, the YMCA, the Scouts Association, and the Girl Guides.[47]

In the 1930s, Japanese aggression again drove refugees from China into Hong Kong. In 1933, an estimated 17,000 refugees were sleeping on the streets. To help address the needs of homeless people, Victor Halward and George She, a Eurasian barrister who had also studied theology and was ordained by ROH after World War II, formed the Street Sleepers Society. They reopened St. Peter's Church as one of the first shelters for street sleepers,[48] and this was followed by the opening of other shelters.

Concerned about the lack of education for many refugee children, ROH set up a number of clubs in rented or borrowed premises for children between the ages of 9 and 14. In 1936, ROH formed the Boys' and Girls' Clubs Association to administer these clubs, which provided the children with one hour of primary education and another hour of organized games.[49]

Orphanages were crammed with the influx of refugees. The Victoria Home in Kowloon City, run by the Church Missionary Society, had barely enough room for its 100 girls to breathe, let alone exercise. To increase the space, ROH decided to move this home, along with Tin Kwok School for Orphans in Kowloon City, which cared for 20 boys, to the countryside.[50] He purchased a beautiful piece of property situated on a hill in Tai Po to set up a rural orphanage.[51]

In 1935, ROH enlisted S. Y. Lee, a recent graduate from the agricultural studies at Lingnan University, and John Prettejohn, an old boy of Diocesan Boys' School, to set up a camp, with the intention of building the orphanage. They accompanied 10 boys from Tin Kwok School for Orphans in Kowloon City to this magnificent site. The group built a hut, but that same year a typhoon destroyed it. They then put up three Nissen huts. To their exasperation, the following year another typhoon swept the huts away. But they did not give up, and in 1937 a solid granite orphanage was finally constructed, and about half of the girls of Victoria Home moved in. In 1939, the orphanage added another dormitory, which could accommodate about 30 boys, and a primary school consisting of four classrooms.[52] S. Y. Lee was later ordained, and he went on to establish the Bishop Ho Ming Hua Chinese Centre in London after ROH's death.

The orphanage was divided into family units, each responsible for its own cooking, marketing, housework, and, for the girls, the mothering of orphaned babies. Each unit had its own plot of land to grow vegetables for its own consumption, any excess to be sold in the Tai Po market.[53] Children were trained by hand learning, not book learning: tending to animals, horticulture, forestry, gardening, and all the practical matters connected with farming life.[54]

ROH's decision to move the orphanage to Tai Po showed practical foresight and was in line with the Rural Reconstruction Movement in China then. He wanted to prepare the children to participate in rural reconstruction when they grew up and returned to the countryside. While some children did manage to go to Zengcheng to work in the villages before World War II, events in China did not allow that to happen afterward. After World War II, ROH renamed Tai Po Rural Orphanage St. Christopher's Home.

The education of children and young people was not a priority of the Hong Kong government before the mid-1930s. Although there were a few government schools such as Queen's College, King's College, Belilios Public School, and Clementi Secondary School, most schools were private or missionary schools. Since parents who sent their children to private schools had to pay high tuition fees, education was a privilege generally reserved for wealthy people.

The Anglican Church had a long history of taking education seriously. A number of Anglo-Chinese schools, most of which had been in existence since 1915, used English as the medium for instruction: St. Paul's College, Diocesan Girls' School and Diocesan Boys' School, St. Stephen's Boys' College and St. Stephen's Girls' College, and St. Paul's Girls' School.[55] At that time, the Church Missionary Society managed two schools for girls—Fairlea, and St. Stephen Girls' College—on the same site on Lyttleton Road. Although it seemed logical to merge the two schools, the differences in culture and social class worked against amalgamation: the former was for girls from relatively disadvantaged families and the latter for girls from wealthy families. In 1935, ROH and Beatrice Pope, the Church Missionary Society missionary in charge of both schools, concluded that it would be a good idea to move Fairlea to Victoria Home, an orphanage for girls. When Tai Po Rural Orphanage was built, half of the girls from Victoria Home moved there. The remainder merged with the girls from the Fairlea School to become Heep Yunn School.[56]

Scattered in different parts of Hong Kong and Kowloon were about 10 to 12 Church Missionary Society primary day schools, some established as early as 1875. They were mostly small, occupying rented flats of tenement houses. Because of the substandard quality of most of these schools, ROH set up a committee to establish guidelines for teachers and teaching.

Successes and Regrets

ROH was grateful for the work he had accomplished in his diocese in the preceding four years. While on his first home leave, in addition to raising funds for work in his diocese, he met with the executives of Victoria Diocesan Association, the association that supported many of his projects. He reported that he had appointed the first Chinese assistant bishop and begun a search for able Chinese men for further training and had recruited young clergy, teachers, and a doctor from England. He had created an innovative rural program to improve the livelihood of the farmers and established new institutions, including a school and a rural orphanage. The foundation had been laid for a completely different kind of diocese, with a greater emphasis on Chinese culture as well being a champion for the poor.

Despite all these achievements, ROH deeply regretted his inability to speak Chinese. His excuse was that, since he first came to Hong Kong at the age of 37, he was too old to learn Chinese (believing that one would have to start learning it before the age of 30). Anticipating the immersion methods of language learning that are now popular, he had said early on that he would not study Chinese formally but would learn it as a child does, by listening and repeating what he heard. He had even said that he would resign if he could not learn Chinese in this way within two years.[57] He had drastically underestimated the difficulties of learning Cantonese, a dialect with so many different intonations that the same word, spoken in different tones, means bafflingly different things. His detractors criticized his inability to speak Cantonese. At the time of his retirement, ROH would still use the wrong tones even while reciting something he must have spoken hundreds of times: the Lord's Prayer and the blessing in Cantonese.[58]

From 1932 to 1936, ROH enjoyed a relatively peaceful life in the colony. The family was complete and together, and he managed to keep alive his hobby of gardening. Strains within his marriage, however, did emerge during this period.

Although there was a long line of clerics on both sides of the family, Nora and ROH were brought up differently.[59] Being the first boy from a large, loving, but disciplined family, ROH was destined to carry on the family line. He received university education from Oxford, where his lifelong interest in classics, poetry, philosophy, and religion no doubt originated. Despite a very busy ministry, his quest for knowledge persisted throughout his life. Nora was the product of a Victorian education, and instead of going on to college, she nursed severely wounded and traumatized casualties from the World War I trenches.[60] She did not share or understand ROH's affection for the Chinese nor his work as a priest,[61] seeming to have had no interest in philosophy or theology.

Mollie Higgs, a close friend of the family, implied that Nora might have caused much social embarrassment for ROH as a priest and bishop even though he had always remained loving and loyal to her. She blamed Nora for taxing ROH's already overburdened life with her self-centered neediness:[62]

> Loyal and loving as RO[63] always was, the domestic background of his life was—well, comic, stupid, frustrating, muddling and disrupting—and at all times a cruel burden on those already overloaded gallant shoulders. Nora always developed a bad leg or a sore throat just when RO was in the midst of important church affairs. I remember once when a group was with them on a platform and someone was giving an address—Nora developed a terrible tickling cough which refused to be suppressed—she spluttered and choked till our attention was entirely on her instead of on the speaker. That was typical . . .
>
> One evening when he was alone with us, RO did really let his hair down and confided to us the strains of his domestic life and the overpowering influence still of Nora's mother . . . But he finished by saying: "In spite of all, I'd rather go home to her now than anyone else."

Despite his understandable frustrations at times, ROH seems to have worshipped Nora. He thought that God had given him Nora in order to help him be a better, less self-centered person. Nora kept him, he believed, from losing himself in too much activity. She and her love were the center and source of his spiritual life.[64]

In May 1936, ROH went on leave with his family to England. They bought Home Farm at Lewknor, Oxfordshire, which became a home for the family during World War II.[65] He was also able to be by his mother's bedside when she passed away in September that year, no doubt a great source of solace for him.[66]

The First Half of the Sino-Japanese War (1937–41)

Even as the Japanese Imperial Army was shadowing the fringes of Hong Kong, life continued more or less as usual for ROH, Nora, and the two younger children. Nora had taken Joc to England in 1938 to continue his schooling. ROH traveled frequently to various parts of his diocese in South China to do necessary relief work. His most important accomplishment during this period came from his work with the Chinese Industrial Cooperatives.

In his personal life, ROH grieved the loss of his father, the Reverend C. G. Hall, a scholar and a gifted musician who had chosen to serve in a downtown parish in Newcastle but always felt that he had failed in life. ROH's moving obituary in honor of his father recognized the value of his father's "ministry of love":[67]

> But I can never regard his life as a failure because it was spent in tireless parish work, and there is no greater success than such a ministry of love. For nearly half the period of the last war he had three sons on active service and, though they all survived, nearly all the men who helped him in his church were killed . . .
>
> He found in the successes which came to his sons a real compensation for his own sense of failure, and you can imagine now that you have read all this, how grateful I was to the Archbishop for inviting him to preach at the consecration of me, his eldest son in St. Paul's Cathedral. I wonder if that may not be perhaps a record in the history of the Church.

Meanwhile, the Sino-Japanese War was moving from background to foreground. In October 1938, Guangzhou fell to the Japanese. Since Japan was not officially at war with Britain yet, the Japanese Imperial Army stopped at the border of Hong Kong.

South China after the Japanese Invasion

While the Japanese advanced southward, the congregation of the Church of Our Savior in Guangzhou scattered, but Bishop Mok stayed to look after the remaining flock. So did Archdeacon Mo-Yung In, who later became the bishop of Guangzhou, in Beihai. Despite the danger, most of the missionaries remained and persevered in their work in different parts of Free China (areas not occupied by the Japanese).[68] Once travel resumed on the Pearl River, after the fall of Guangzhou in October 1938, ROH organized a ship, transporting as much rice, dried fish, bedding, clothing, cotton, and smallpox vaccine as possible.[69]

The following spring, as ROH toured his diocese, he found that none of the churches in Guangdong province were functioning normally. Many churches were partially or completely destroyed, and the remaining churches were overflowing with people. ROH established refugee camps in three locations in Guangdong province: Shiqi, Cuiheng, and Yinkeng. In addition to providing food and shelter, he set up a hospital in the camp in Shiqi, and a school in each of the other camps. He raised funds to support these activities, but at the same time encouraged the refugees to find ways of supporting themselves.[70]

In Free China, the situation was much brighter. As a result of students arriving from all parts of the country, Kunming, the capital of Yunnan province, hummed with activity. Here, the outstanding institution of higher education was Lian Da (National Southwest Associated University),[71] where Gilbert Baker started his missionary work among students and established Wen Lin Tang (Church in the Forest of Learning) for worship. ROH invited Dr. T. C. Chao, a professor of Yenching University and China's foremost Christian scholar and theologian, who was spending his sabbatical year in Kunming, to help Baker with student work. Chao was a speaker during the Victoria Diocesan Association meeting in London after ROH's consecration in 1932, and an outstanding figure at the Madras Conference organized by the World Council of Churches in 1938. Since that time Chao had been drawn increasingly into the study of the Episcopal Church, its order, and its liturgical heritage, and he had approached ROH for his ordination. In July 1941, during his visit to Hong Kong, ROH confirmed and ordained Chao as a deacon and to the priesthood, in his private chapel in the Bishop's House. ROH also made him an honorary fellow of St. Paul's College.[72]

During the Sino-Japanese War, ROH focused his work in Yun-Gui (Yunnan and Guizhou provinces) district. When Burma Road was opened in 1938, much traffic that came from Rangoon to Chongqing passed through Kunming, bringing in war materials from Britain. ROH, together with the Reverend Y. Y. Zhu, a Yale PhD and the brother-in-law of T. Z. Koo, set up the Transport Workers' Welfare Association. They built two experimental stations: one at Baoshan between Lashio and Kunming, and the other one at Qujiang between Kunming and Chongqing, to provide baths, tea rooms, reading rooms, lectures, games, and, where feasible, a dormitory for the workers.[73] The Reverend Quentin Huang, one of the Student Christian Movement students who survived the protest in front of the Louza police station during the May 30 incident, had set up a very successful ministry among students in Guiyang City.[74]

In 1940, at the recommendation of ROH, the House of Bishops of Chung Hua Sheng Kung Hui elected Y. Y. Zhu as a bishop, responsible for the ministry in Yunnan-Guizhou area.[75] This meant that ROH had two Chinese assistant bishops (S. T. Mok and Y. Y. Zhu) working with him in the Diocese of South China. After the war, Quentin Huang succeeded Zhu as bishop of Yunnan-Guizhou.

Refugees in Hong Kong

As the Sino-Japanese War started in earnest, refugees poured into Hong Kong by the thousands. By the end of 1938, approximately 250,000 refugees had arrived in Hong Kong. The conditions at Shenzhen at the border were

Figure 3.3 ROH and his two Chinese assistant bishops, Mok Sau Tsang (left) and Y. Y. Zhu (right) (*St. John's Review* [November 1957]: 360)

desperate beyond description. There was no electricity and no regular water supply. Food was scarce.

ROH, who sent out an urgent appeal to the whole of Hong Kong to contribute to their utmost capacity for the relief of refugees, received an enthusiastic response. The churches organized a system of food supply and food kitchens for the destitute. With Father T. F. Ryan, SJ of the Roman Catholic Church, and other like-minded individuals, ROH set up the Hong Kong Emergency Refugee Council, which became the Hong Kong Social Welfare Council.[76] Of the five refugee camps he helped open in Hong Kong, three were urban and two rural. Yet with such such a severe need, these camps, which housed about 10,000, accommodated only a small proportion of the total number of refugees.[77]

Among all this gloom, ROH was much cheered in 1938 by having one of his best friends, Leonard Wilson, join him as dean of St. John's Cathedral.[78] Wilson, who was ROH's contemporary at Oxford, had worked as a curate in Tyneside and took over the refugee relief work soon after his arrival.

Chinese Industrial Cooperatives

By January 1938, almost all Chinese industries had been wiped out by the Japanese. A meeting was held between several Westerners—Edgar Snow, author of *The Red Star Over China*, and his wife; John Alexander, secretary to the British ambassador to China; and Rewi Alley, a New Zealander—and a few Chinese nationals. They decided that the best way to revive the Chinese industries was to build small, mobile, or guerrilla units. The Chinese Industrial Cooperatives was formally established in August 1938, supported by Madame Chiang Kai-shek and Finance Minister Dr. Kong Xiangxi. Kong allotted to it ¥2 million and promised ¥3 million more. It was Rewi Alley who carried out most of the organization in the field, leading to its success. At its peak, the number of cooperatives reached 3,000, with a membership of nearly 30,000. They supplied military needs—gloves, caps, greatcoats, padded clothes, gauze, tents, and field cots—very efficiently,[79] and they provided jobs for the refugees as well as the unemployed farmers.[80] Madame Sun Yat-sen arrived in Hong Kong toward the end of 1939 to help with fund-raising, and she received enthusiastic support from the Chinese in Hong Kong and overseas.

Both Chiang Kai-shek and Mao Zedong supported the Chinese Industrial Cooperatives and tried to control it. In January 1939, the International Committee for the Promotion of Chinese Industrial Cooperatives (popularly known as Gong He) was established in Hong Kong, to take over the management of the funds from foreign sources. ROH became the chairperson of Gong He because of his reputation in relief work. He promoted the Chinese Industrial Cooperatives internationally to acquire funds, technology, and raw materials. More importantly, he received the backing of China Bank and Central Bank of China to manage these funds.[81] ROH was able to distribute the funds and supplies to cooperatives in all areas of Free China, ensuring that those in the Chinese Communist Party–controlled areas received appropriate amounts, even from sympathetic overseas Chinese and foreign cooperatives.

Both political parties, the Chinese Communist Party and the Guomindang, appreciated ROH's wartime work. In 1939, Mao sent ROH a personal letter of thanks and acknowledgment for his work in Gong He.[82] In 1941, the Guomindang government awarded him the Red Precious Stone Star for his relief work in China.[83] The respect he showed and received from both Mao and Chiang attests to his political foresight and his lack of political partisanship.

One might wonder why ROH, a busy bishop, would be interested in Gong He and choose to take on such a challenging role as chairing the Gong He International Committee. ROH was a close follower of F. D. Maurice, who in the nineteenth century had spent all his energy and his means in starting cooperative industries. He believed that a cooperative run by Christians, with the aim to make a better common life, was a church embodied in every activity of life and worship, and a perfect picture of God in social life. He thought that cooperatives were particularly important for China, because the family, which had traditionally provided security, was disintegrating as a result of industrialization. The cooperatives, especially those run by the Church, might provide the necessary security for young people.[84]

Despite officially being in a united front, the Guomindang government was unlikely to have the funds and resources distributed to outlying areas controlled by the Chinese Communist Party. As the chairperson of the Gong He International Committee, ROH was able to distribute funds equitably to areas controlled by either political party. ROH wrote a remarkable letter to the Church Assembly Missionary Council on October 15, 1938, just before the fall of Guangzhou, in which he predicted that Communists would take over China after the defeat of the Japanese in the Sino-Japanese War. ROH's letter stated that the popular heroes of China at that time were not General Chiang and his Christian supporters and followers[85] but the gallant Eighth Route Army who, like the legendary Robin Hood and his Merry Men, had exciting adventures and lived lives of hardship and self-denial. When the victory over the Japanese came, ROH predicted that it would be the Communists rather than Christians who had "saved China":[86]

> As we face the future, then we face the kind of situation to which Christians have been accustomed since the days of the gospels. ("In the world ye shall have tribulation"), and we shall need, in the years ahead, the wisest help both in personnel and in practical support that the Mother Church can give, for there is one great possibility: that China, with the help of the Chinese Christian Church, may be able to make Communism safe for the world, and the world a better place for what Communism brings into the family treasury.

By being impartial in distributing the funds, he was trying to build a bridge between the Chinese Christian Church and the Communists. He may have been hoping that it might make it easier for the Christian Church in China to be accepted by the Communists.

Second Half of the Sino-Japanese War (1941–45)

During the summer of 1940, repatriation of British women and children began in Hong Kong. While shiploads went to Australia, Nora stubbornly refused to go anywhere unless she could go home to Britain. This would mean the risk of air and submarine attacks on the way, and danger for her and the children, as the war was being carried into Britain itself. Nora's argument was that their children belonged to England and whatever happened to England, they had a right to share in it.[87] In December, Nora, Judith, and Christopher left for England on the *Anchises* to join Joc, who was already in school there. ROH sailed with them to Singapore. There he disembarked and went to the Relief Committee Headquarters, to ensure that the China Relief Funds could be sent to Hong Kong and then into China for the Chinese Industrial Cooperatives.[88]

A Mystical Vision

ROH worried constantly about the safety of his family as they sailed home aboard the *Anchises*, which was heading for Durban and Cape Town and then making its way up the African coast toward Liverpool. ROH knew the sea was vulnerable to attacks by German planes from above and submarines and torpedoes from below. When ROH returned to Hong Kong in January, he was consumed with worry and anxiety about his family's treacherous journey.

Then, on a Sunday in late January 1941, he celebrated Holy Communion at St. Andrew's Church. While praying on his knees as usual and tormented with fears for his family's safety, he had a vision which he described later to Joc: "Suddenly like a flash, a light filled my being. I saw Nora and the two children standing on the sea, and behind them Jesus himself. He was looking down on them and sheltering them." In that instant, all of ROH's fears, worries, and anxieties vanished. He was at peace. He had neither inkling nor assurance that they would reach England safely. Yet this was immaterial. What mattered was that Jesus was with them, and whether life or death awaited them, it was life or death with Him.[89]

On February 27, 1941, passengers on the *Anchises* heard the drone of a distant plane. The sound grew louder and louder. Then six bombs were dropped. Although none hit the ship directly, the underwater explosion blew a shaft out in the engine room, rendering the ship powerless. The protocol of "women and children first" was followed, and that meant that Nora and the children left the ship on the first lifeboat. After thirty hours tossing rudderless on the dark ocean swells, a naval corvette finally arrived to pick them up.

Nora was astonished that their lives had been spared, considering that several other people were lost from lifeboats that had capsized. On March 1, they arrived in Glasgow instead of Liverpool. From there they traveled to Lewknor, where they were reunited with Joc and his grandmother, Mrs. Baron.[90] Sometime later, over dinner, ROH heard the news that the *Anchises* had been bombed and though the family was safe, he fled from the room and was physically sick.

The vision of Christ had been so real and profound that it became for ROH the seal of his apostleship, and it increased his missionary zeal, his devotion, and his obedience to God. He wrote to Joc of his reflections that God had used his imagination and mind in order to reveal Himself through this vision:[91]

> In St. Andrew's Church that Wednesday morning last January Jesus was no more present than He is at every Communion Service, or indeed than He is all the time. But on that morning He used my imagination and my mind to show Himself to me in a special way, and with a definite purpose. For God to use a person's imagination-and-mind in that way to show Himself to him, is just as *real* as it is to use flesh-and-blood. It has a further advantage from God's point of view, that He can then show Himself only to those He wants to. When He used flesh-and-blood, then anyone who came along could see Him.

Spreading the Word on Spreading the Gospel

In the fall of 1941, ROH faced a dilemma: whether to stay as shepherd to his flock in Hong Kong (as the Japanese must have seemed like wolves at the border), or to go ahead with a lecture tour in the United States that he had previously planned. Given the gravity of the Hong Kong situation, it was tempting to stay. Leonard Wilson, his good friend and dean of the cathedral, agreed to take the position of bishop of Singapore only on the condition that ROH would take a break from his demanding schedule in the diocese by following through with the US tour. ROH assented, Wilson accepted the position, and the die was cast.

ROH left Hong Kong for Evanston, Illinois, in the fall of 1941, and Hong Kong fell to the Japanese on Christmas Day, 1941. As bishop of Singapore, Wilson was taken by the Japanese, imprisoned, and tortured. ROH would later be haunted by guilt about his decision to go to the United States while his friend was being persecuted[92] and by his later realization of his flock suffering through the Japanese occupation of Hong Kong during his absence.

In a lecture called the 27th Annual Hale Memorial Sermon, "New Church Order: The Future of the World-wide Episcopal Church," he criticized the way that foreign missionaries had held onto financial and executive control of the

Chinese churches: the American Episcopal Church for keeping the dioceses that they supported financially as part of the American Episcopal Church, and the British missionary societies for fostering overdependency in the Chinese dioceses they supported. He called for the establishment of a new international order for the World Episcopal Church, which would be a real world fellowship that would retain the Anglican ways.[93] He believed that the job of the missionaries was to provide scaffolding that, once it had served its purpose, should be taken away.

During the lecture tour ROH wrote a small book to urge the change in missionary attitudes and methods in spreading the gospel, which he published in England as *The Art of the Missionary* in 1942. (It was retitled prosaically in the United States, to ROH's dismay, *The Missionary Artist Looks at His Job*.) In it he discussed the reasons for the poor results of missionaries in China since AD 635, and the attitudes of some of the missionaries.[94] Emphasizing that the spirit of missionary work, like the spirit of marriage, as he idealistically envisioned it, should be infused with a kind of self-forgetting generosity:[95]

> Marriage needs the same spirit and the same approach for its fulfilment in true happiness, as this missionary job of being scaffolding to a building which is never yours but always someone else's . . . Those who come to marriage as to missionary work with the unpossessive mind of scaffold poles find an abiding dwelling place in living human hearts that is part of the joy of the eternity of God.

He advised that future missionaries in China go to school with artists. Artists work in words, stone, or music, and missionaries work in human lives. Missionaries should have the same reverence for life as the artist has for his materials. A sculptor must not carve against the nature of the marble or granite, just reveal the beauty hidden in the material; a missionary must do so too. In doing so, missionaries would appreciate what God had already done in China. Their purpose would be simply to reveal to the people God's love for them. Some disagreed with what he said, but many found it prophetic, revealing knowledge of what God intended missionaries to be.

One of the highlights of his US tour was a visit to Reinhold Niebuhr and his wife, Ursula, an Anglican. Niebuhr, a distinguished theologian, engaged in politics but addressed himself to a range of public concerns. They discussed many issues, and specifically, with Ursula, the ordination of women priests.[96]

Returning Home

There was a certain providence in the timing of ROH's US tour. While he was away, Hong Kong fell, Pearl Harbor was attacked, and the Pacific War began. ROH might well have died, or have been interned like his friend Leonard Wilson, who was incarcerated and "examined by scourging" with many others.

Unable to return to Hong Kong, ROH went to England and reunited with his family.

ROH visited the Colonial Office on January 16, 1942, to discuss with the staff what had been on his mind relating to future British rule in Hong Kong. At the end of the meeting, he left behind a memorandum, handwritten on a few scraps of paper, with his ideas for radical political reforms in Hong Kong after the war. "The recent disaster," he scribbled, "gives a chance for radical changes when the administration of Hong Kong by Britain is resumed." First, he recommended that the upper reaches of the colony's civil service should be thrown open to all Hong Kong Chinese and Eurasians who were British subjects. Second, he proposed that the tiny move that had been made toward representative government in the prewar decades be "advanced a stage." An electorate should be constituted to choose all the unofficial members of the Urban Council as well as the Legislative Council, and all men and women who had obtained school certificate qualifications should be entitled to vote. Finally, he advised that the colony's postwar government should provide subsidies for social services and that public housing should be created with vision and energy, as a matter of justice for economically disadvantaged people.[97] ROH shared the same thoughts as those in Whitehall, which had begun to appreciate that if British rule were to be restored in Hong Kong, it would have to be on an altogether different basis from that of the past.

As he had lost his see, ROH was offered an opportunity to succeed Prebendary Carlile as the head of the Church Army,[98] but he refused. Instead, he spent the next few months traveling around England, speaking and writing about China. He worked at raising funds for aid to China for different agencies, such as China Red Cross, Gong He, International Society for Medical Services in South China, and British United Aid to China. He also came into close association with William Temple, who became archbishop of Canterbury in 1942. Before the war was over, the British United Aid to China Fund had reached more than £2 million.

On his way back from the United States, ROH had heard from his brother Noel that he [ROH] was being considered for a bishop's job in England.[99] But when he was in England, the resignation of Archbishop Cosmo Gordon Lang temporarily stalled ROH's prospects. ROH had no wish to desert China, where he had dedicated his life, but toward the end of 1942 the political situation in China and Hong Kong was unclear. If all of China fell under Japanese control, he would have to return to England. He needed to know all his options. ROH unexpectedly paid a visit to Downing Street, the prime minister's office, which was responsible for the appointment of all bishops in the Church of England. He hoped to learn what the prospects of him becoming a bishop in England would be if he were to carry out his intention of ordaining a woman priest. He was told clearly and unmistakably that the consequences would be severe.[100]

Back to Free China

As bishop of Hong Kong and South China, ROH had no doubt in his mind that he had to return to Free China while the war was on. He felt the strong need to be with his flock in such difficult times. It must have been quite a struggle for him to tear himself away from his family to return to a dangerous war zone. Nevertheless, he left England on November 8, 1942. His travels took him on a long and tortuous route, passing through Sierra Leone, Lagos, Khartoum, and Calcutta, arriving in Kunming on Christmas eve.[101]

For the rest of the war, ROH was separated from his family. He missed Nora terribly. He wrote to her several times during the day in tiny handwriting, narrowly spaced on thin paper, bundling the letters together once a week to save on postage. He often ran out of paper, and he resorted to writing on both sides of the paper, or to writing on the reverse side of used ones, making them quite challenging to read.

Few people could match the diligence of ROH's letter writing to his beloved. Still, he admitted to her that he was not writing entirely for her benefit but also for his own solace: "I think it would be dishonest to say that I write for your sake. It's somehow my own—it's something like the comfort I get from your body at night—it's a release and a joy to me. But I'm afraid you must often find it very boring to put up with me."[102] Besides recounting his daily activities, discussing the children's affairs and family finances, these intimate letters contained flashbacks to their love life in the past, recalling, for example:[103]

> Clapton in 1919: about this time—I remember the thought of being loved by you, of tenderness, thoughts for me. Herein is love—not that we loved God—but that He first loved us: and how much more is that wonder of your caring for me and showing it than my eager hunger and care and fury of possessive loving of my woman.

The letters revealed ROH's physical and spiritual longing for Nora. He continued to worship her. He compared her with the wives of his friends, idealizing her in a way that kept him aspiring to higher standards of conduct and spiritual worth:[104]

> Your honesty, tireless devotion to duty and absolute hatred of any shame is always there and I feel if I fail, I am dirtying your whiteness—for you have joined your life so utterly with mine. Even Ursula Niebuhr, whom everyone lauds, is shoddy by comparison. Josephine Tucker comes nearer to you—though she is not as strong.

The reference to his fear of "dirtying her [Nora's] whiteness" may make a contemporary reader uncomfortable, but ROH, inevitably a product of his time and place, was drawing on a metaphor of female virtue and morality that was essentially Victorian. Not so Victorian was ROH's celebration of what he had experienced as the sacred joys of their physical union. Appreciating what he

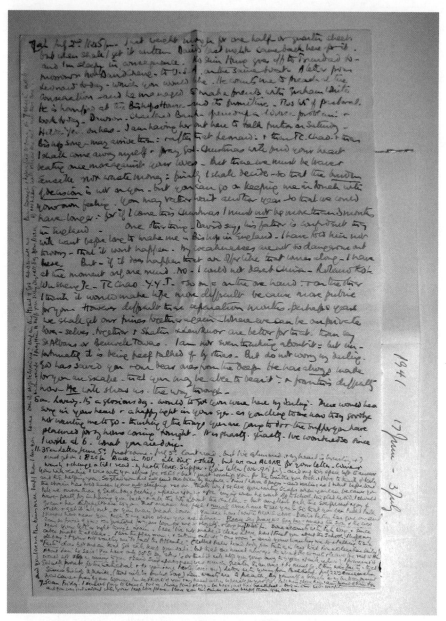

Figure 3.4 Sample of ROH's letter to Nora, July 2, 1941, showing his handwriting, which could be very tiny when paper was scarce. Size of paper 5 × 8 inches (Hall Family Archive).

saw as God-given delight in each other's bodies in the sacrament of hands and eyes and close embrace, ROH believed that God had given humankind something lovely and enjoyable in itself. ROH regarded the enjoyment of things, and particularly of persons, as deeper and more profound than merely understanding them.

From the time he arrived in Free China, ROH became a wanderer. His flock had scattered. He would stay with them in different places for a time, and then move on to do his mission. He spent 1943 and 1944 in almost continuous travel to different parts of Free China: Chongqing, Chengdu, Kunming, Guiyang, Pingshi, Qujiang, Beihai, and Nanning.

Traveling during wartime in China was difficult. Regular train service to places where he wished to go was infrequent, slow, and fatiguing. At times he was lucky enough to have a proper ride, but most of the time he traveled on trucks sitting, with many others, on top of loads of baggage or goods.[105] Even though he suffered badly from varicose veins, he sometimes traveled on foot. He always carried a bedding roll with him and preferred to sleep in a church. He gave away his clothes to those who needed them, or sold the expensive ones given to him by friends, and gave away the money.[106]

He made sure that he did not have more food than the local people did, in order to share with the rest of the Chinese the deprivation of war time (a practice similar to that of Simone Weil during the war).[107] In a time of privation, he did not want to be "greedy," and quickly lost 10 pounds he could ill afford to lose. Between the cold conditions and his self-imposed malnutrition, ROH reduced his resistance to disease to such an extent that he suffered from recurrent episodes of malaria and diarrhea. Yet in his letter to Nora at that time, he confessed that he still felt he was coming up short, not doing enough: "I don't realize enough my own sinfulness—pride and self-will. I'm not disciplined enough in my life. I like comfort and easy ways too much. I don't feel the holiness of God."[108]

Despite wartime travails, he energetically continued to manage the funds of the Gong He to ensure that all the cooperatives received appropriate funding and technical support.[109] While working with the Gong He in Chongqing, ROH had frequent contact with Zhou Enlai, to whom he had been introduced by Rewi Alley over a delightful dinner earlier in 1941.[110] ROH took to Zhou immediately, finding him to be a good and devoted man, simple in his personal living, tireless and hard-working, gentle and quiet in speech.[111] Chou Meng Chou, whom ROH ordained and stayed with at times in Chongqing, recalled that, when Zhou was in Chongqing, he used to visit ROH nearly every week. They would talk for hours, trying to convince each other about what would be good for the future of China.[112]

Privately, ROH wrote to Joc about the similarities and differences of communism and Christianity: "Communism and Mohammedanism are both 'fall-aways' from Christianity. They made it into an easier system. This is what makes it appear to many people a better 'religion' because more practical. And they are willing to accept such an alternative and let the religion of the Risen Jesus go by as too difficult and too hazy."[113] In January of 1943, ROH held a small party in Geoffrey Allen's house in Chongqing, with Zhou Enlai and his wife, and Zhou's secretary (and interpreter), Gong Peng, as his guests.[114]

In 1943, deep sorrow came into his life: the loss of three people he loved and depended upon.[115] Added to the loss of Bishop Mok and William Paton was the heart-stopping loss of Christopher Sargent, who died from pneumonic plague in August 1943, when he was only 32 years old.[116] ROH had consecrated Sargent in 1938 as bishop of Fujian, and Sargent had gone on to set up, despite trying conditions that included poor housing and abject loneliness, a vibrant ministry in Fujian. Sargent had become the beloved Father in God to a large number of Chinese clergy and laypeople, as well as to a devoted team of missionaries. ROH's struggles to come to terms with the death of his good friends may be illuminated by what he said later, in a 1963 sermon, about the way it is friends who provide:[117]

> the only real happiness that ever satisfies our hearts. For the good company of friendship is love at its deepest and sturdiest. No wonder then this Jesus, this God-made-man said to us "Ye are my friends" and again, as He died, to one who responded, "Today thou shalt be with me."

Friendship, then, followed for ROH the pattern of Jesus' love for humanity. No wonder his devastation upon learning the tragic news of Sargent's death. He made a long journey to Fujian and visited the room where Sargent died. It was only after listening to the nurse telling him how Sargent died—as if God had taken a tired child home to peace—that he began to come to terms with the loss.[118] Some people close to ROH felt that he must have blamed himself for sending Sargent to his death.[119] Before he left Fujian, he organized the Diocesan Synod for the election of the next bishop. No one had told him that he had been nominated, and to his embarrassment he received the most votes on the first ballot.

While 1943 was trying, 1944 proved to be even more challenging, as ROH suffered another heartbreaking loss when Archbishop William Temple died.[120] Moreover, ROH must have felt sickened by the realization that all that he and the Church had built before and during World War II had been destroyed: the churches in the cities and the rural districts had been bombed, and the congregations of churches in Free China dissipated, as students from various universities evacuated. His heart ached for his family in England, and he longed to know the whereabouts of his friends in Guangzhou and Hong Kong.

Breaking New Ground: Ordination of the First Female Anglican Priest[121]

After discussing this controversial subject with Ursula Niebuhr during his visit to the United States, an opportunity arose for ROH to ordain the first female Anglican priest, challenging the Anglican Communion for the first time with the issue of women receiving priestly orders.

Li Tim Oi had been a teacher at a school for fishers' children but felt called to study theology. After four years at Canton Union Theological College, where the Anglican Church funded her studies, she began to assist the vicar of All Saints' Church, Kowloon. In 1940, ROH sent her to the church in Macao, and he ordained her a deacon in 1941. The parish in Macao where Li was serving had no priest to administer the Holy Sacraments, and Bishop Mok gave her license to do so.[122] In Macao she quickly built up a congregation of 150, and an additional 72 girls had signed up for baptism.[123]

In a letter dated June 4, 1943, ROH let Archbishop William Temple know of his intention to ordain Li Tim Oi to the priesthood. ROH wrote that he would report to the Chung Hua Sheng Kung Hui General Synod what he had done and hoped that the Lambeth Conference would approve of his experiment in places where there was a shortage of priests.[124] Significantly, he did not ask for permission from Temple in this letter, knowing that Temple, even if sympathetic, could not give it. He also knew that there would be some opposition to women priests.

Figure 3.5 Front: Li Tim Oi, Bishop Mok Sau Tsang, and the Reverend Lee Kau Yan; back: Li's mother and father, after her ordination as a deacon on May 22, 1941 (Hall Family Archive)

It was not until six months later, in a letter dated December 16, that Archbishop Temple replied, indicating that in his view, the ordination of a woman was something quite beyond what the Church had authorized or was probably prepared to authorize. To meet the temporary emergency, ROH was advised to commission her to administer Holy Communion. Nevertheless, this seemed to Temple to be primarily a matter for Chung Hua Sheng Kung Hui.[125]

Temple's reply did not reach ROH in time. In January 1944, ROH asked Li to join him at Zhaoqing, a tortuous seven-day journey for her from Macao. The day before the ordination, he asked not to be disturbed in his room as he had an important decision to make. He did not leave his room until late in the afternoon.[126]

What went on during those hours? As usual ROH meditated, listening for that still, small voice of guidance, and he prayed fervently, wrestling with the knowledge that this controversial act would cost him dearly. He could no longer be a bishop in England should he have to return for any unforeseen reason. Worse still was the prospect of separation from his family. But as bishop, he had to consider the needs of his flock, including the vital need that Christians have for the Holy Eucharist. Moreover, the charisma and dedication of Li were most suited for a priestly career. In the end, his prayer-filled decision was to go ahead. In full consciousness of the cost to him and those he loved, he chose his path.

Still, he did not expect the intense resistance shown by some of his colleagues in the Anglican Church in England. This contentious act was more than a personal sacrifice of his opportunities to return to work as a bishop in England. It almost cost him his job, and it drove a wedge into the Anglican Communion.

The ordination took place on St. Paul's Day, in a small Anglican church in Zhaoqing.[127] Two days later he reported to Temple that he had ordained Li as a priest in the Church of God with a license to work in his diocese, but not as a priest of Chung Hua Sheng Kung Hui, because its canons did not make such a provision. He emphasized to Temple his reasons for ordination were not theoretical views of equality of men and women but the needs of his people for the sacraments, and the gift of Li's charisma.[128] Archbishop Temple wrote back on April 3, 1944, asking him to withhold all comments until Chung Hua Sheng Kung Hui had considered the matter, reached some decision, or referred the matter to him or to the Consultative Body. He continued, "Meanwhile whatever I may think of your action you know that my affection for you remains unchanged."[129]

Six months later the *Church Times* published the news with the headline, "Bishop in Insurrection," strongly denouncing ROH's action and urging the Chinese Church to issue a formal and categorical condemnation.[130] It advocated that, should the Chinese Church fail to do this, the Anglican Church should take unmistakable steps to discharge the obvious duty. The Council for the Defence of Church Principles in Oxford also pounced to censure the bishop of Hong Kong for such an act. When ROH read the editorial that his son Joc forwarded to him, his major worry was that Nora might be hurt by the attack: "I so hope that mother hasn't been hurt by it all. One has to do what is right and not argue about it."

Despite feeling compelled to follow the path he did, ROH also admitted that making a choice unsupported by the larger church community cost him personally: "The trouble is that I probably would have more sympathy myself with the general view of the *Church Times* than with many people who may approve of what I have done. I do believe Church order matters; and so it was not easy to break it."[131]

Temple wrote to the editor of the *Church Times*, Dr. G. L. Prestige, that he was personally against the ordination of women to the priesthood, but he added, "If we could find any shadow of theological ground for the non-ordination of women, I should be immensely comforted."[132]

Another letter to ROH was drafted, but Temple died on October 26, 1944, before signing it. Geoffrey Fisher, who succeeded Temple, forwarded this letter to ROH. It explained why Temple did not respond immediately to ROH's letter of June 1943.[133] While Temple showed certain sympathy with ROH's position, he also could not believe that ROH was serious about ordaining the Chinese deaconess without consulting him or Chung Hua Sheng Kung Hui. His words show a kind of strained and restrained dismay: "The reference was so casual," he wrote, "in the midst of a discussion of the appeal for the Chinese Church, that it never occurred to me that you might act in this way on your own motion without consulting either me or the House of Bishops in China." It cannot be verified whether the letter represented Temple's own views.[134] It opened saying "I have not hitherto sent you any comment upon your action," yet ROH had received a handwritten letter from Temple which arrived after Temple had died.

Unsurprisingly, the letter deferred to the authority of church tradition, which, "on this matter is extremely strong. High authorities have declared that a woman is incapable of receiving Holy Orders. This is a language belonging to a cycle of ideas which my own mind is quite incapable of entertaining. At the same time such a judgment could not have been pronounced unless the whole feeling of the Church was perfectly clear and definite." There was an eagerness to avoid any action which appeared to preempt the archbishop of Canterbury's authority over the bishops of the Chinese Church. The letter concluded with an unmistakable tone of censure, saying that while he understood that ROH's action was "inspired by true pastoral care for souls" he was still obliged to regard it "in principle as quite indefensible."

Geoffrey Fisher, who succeeded Temple, was less sympathetic. Fisher regarded ROH's action as *ultra vires*. In 1945, when ROH was in England, Fisher and ROH had a long talk. ROH indicated that, contrary to Temple's opinion, Canterbury had no jurisdiction over him. Nevertheless, he was ready to abide by the decision of the House of Bishops of Chung Hua Sheng Kung Hui, but rather than suspending Li from priestly duties, he would resign. He did not accept Fisher's judgment, convinced that he had acted in obedience to the Lord's commission, which overrode his ecclesiastical commission from the Church. Fisher was powerless, realizing that he had no legal authority over the Chinese Church. He left it to the Chinese House of Bishops to decide but strongly suggested that the action of ROH was *ultra vires* and that Li should resign her orders.[135]

Under pressure from George She, Li broke the impasse by offering to give up her license to be a priest but not her priestly orders.[136] When the House of Bishops of Chung Hua Sheng Kung Hui met, all bishops except four advised ROH to accept Li's resignation of her license. He reluctantly agreed. The House of Bishops also appointed a committee to investigate the question of women in the ministry.[137]

In 1947, the Diocesan Synod of South China brought a new canon to the General Synod of Chung Hua Sheng Kung Hui in Shanghai, authorizing the experimental ordination of women under certain conditions for a period of 20 years. The General Synod of Chung Hua Sheng Kung Hui did not take any action on this except to ask the Lambeth Conference in 1948 whether the experiment would be in accordance with Anglican tradition and order.[138] The Lambeth Conference replied that such an experiment would be against tradition and order and would gravely affect the internal and external relations of the Anglican Communion.

The ordination of a woman created a huge rift in the Anglican Church and the Anglican Communion. The arguments against the ordination of women to the priesthood were centered on the following: (1) since Christ was a man, the priesthood must be male; (2) since Christ appointed no female apostles, a woman can never be a priest; (3) because St. Paul imposed restrictions upon the liturgical ministry of women, such restrictions must apply today; and (4) the exclusion of females from the priesthood is a long and strong tradition accepted almost universally throughout Christendom.

After stirring up a heated debate in the Anglican Communion and in the 1948 Lambeth Conference, ROH remained quiet on this issue. However, this issue, and the drama around it, would not go away. In 1966, the archbishops of Canterbury and York established a commission on women and Holy Orders. The report of the commission suggested a third view: "Although there may be no absolute impediments to the ordination of women to the priesthood there are strong reasons why it should not in fact be done because to introduce so radical a change in the pattern of the church's ministry would have far-reaching and unpredictable consequences . . . It may be that the Holy Spirit is leading the Church to such changes. But they should not be embarked upon without the most careful consideration, and a greater unanimity between churches and within the Church of England itself than exists at present."[139] Based on this report, the Lambeth Conference of 1968 found the theological arguments either for or against the ordination of women inconclusive.

It was not until 1971 that the Anglican Consultative Council, chaired by Archbishop Ramsey and the most senior advisory body in the Anglican Communion, passed "Resolution 28," which advised bishops that, "with the approval of their province, they might ordain women to the priesthood."[140]

Upon receiving "Resolution 28," Bishop Gilbert Baker, ROH's successor, immediately ordained two women, Jane Huang and Joyce Bennett (who had been ordained as deacons by ROH in 1958 and 1965 respectively),[141] as priests in Hong Kong. The ordination of women began to take place in the American Episcopal Church, the Anglican Church of Canada, and the Anglican Church of New Zealand in the late 1970s, and in Kenya, Uganda, and Australia in the 1980s.[142]

Was ROH a "wild man of the woods," as the *Church Times* referred to him in 1944, or an arrogant extremist who refused to bow to constitutional authority? Michael Ramsey, who succeeded Fisher as archbishop of Canterbury, made a point of getting to know ROH at the 1948 Lambeth Conference. He found not the wild extremist he had expected, but a man of deep godliness.[143]

ROH was strongly criticized for his lack of judgment, lack of prudence, and for placing the Anglican Church at risk of disunion by challenging it with the issue of ordination of women. His decision, however, was not made lightly, since he knew there could be dire personal consequences for himself: the loss of chance to be a bishop in England and the agony of separation from his family. Nor could the decision be considered impetuous when it was made after hours and days of meditation and prayer.

ROH was not ruled by orthodoxy, but it is unlikely that this humble man who did not seek attention wanted to be a trailblazer in the Anglican Communion. His decision was practical and pastoral, based on the needs of the community to receive the Holy Communion at the time. He drew censure from those who pushed for the emancipation of women[144] when he denied that he had ordained a female priest for the philosophical and political reasons of gender equality. He saw that change was called for, and he dared to break with tradition when he was sure that he was acting in obedience to God's will.

He also had the support of his diocese, whose members did not understand the reactionary ideas of the Church in the West. In 1946 the diocese sent a letter to all the diocesan synods in the Chinese Anglican Church, expressing its strong support for ROH's ordination of Li Tim Oi.[145]

> It is our belief that the action taken by Bishop Mok in licensing Li Tim Oi to celebrate the Lord's Supper and Bishop Hall's action later in ordaining her to the priesthood was God inspired. We believe God is using China's age-long respect for women and traditional confidence in women's gifts for administration and counsel to open a new chapter in the history of the Church . . . We believe that the Western Churches expect new things such

as this to happen under God's providence, when Christianity really begins to take root in a civilization as mature as Chinese civilization.

His inner clarity helped him to withstand the disapproval of administrators and the pressure of the archbishop of Canterbury and the Anglican Church of England. The establishment remained intransigent on this issue, even decades after there were already hundreds of ordained women in the Anglican Communion in other parts of the world. In 1992, when the Church of England finally voted to allow the ordination of women, about 470 male clergy left the Church. It was not until 1994 that 32 female priests of the Church of England were ordained in Bristol Cathedral for the first time.

By ordaining a woman of God, ROH took a step that was radical in 1944. He was ahead of his time by 30 years in the United States, and 50 years in his own country. If he were alive today, he might be smiling ruefully, reflecting that what was then seen as revolutionary now seems an unquestioned matter of course. Among his rich legacies, the ordination of women is one of his most lasting contributions to the worldwide Anglican Communion.

Notes

1. One of ROH's favorite prayers by St. Richard of Chichester. ROH requested every church and Christian home throughout the diocese to make special intercession on the day of his consecration. Personal communication from Canon Christopher Hall.
2. Spence, *The Search for Modern China*, 361–70.
3. J. Fitzgerald, "Warlords, Bullies and State Building in Nationalist China: The Guangdong Cooperative Movement 1932–1936," *Modern China* (1997), 23(4): 420–58.
4. Chen Jitang ruled Guangdong province from 1929 to 1936, and contributed much to its development and modernization. He improved the revenue through taxation and monopolizing the sugar industry. He paved roads, established a public school system, and introduced the Cooperative Movement in rural Guangdong which assisted farmers in borrowing money at reasonable rates. By 1935 there were 500 cooperatives. The Cooperative Movement ended in 1936.
5. Spence, *The Search for Modern China*, 390–96 (Japanese invasion of Manchuria in 1931).
6. J. Chen, "The Communist Movement 1927–1937," in *The Cambridge History of China, Volume 13: Republican China 1912–1949, Part 2*, edited by J. Fairbank and A. Feuerwerker (Cambridge: Cambridge University Press, 1986), 226–29.
7. S. Tsang, *A Modern History of Hong Kong* (Hong Kong: Hong Kong University Press, 2004), 38.
8. Ibid., 110.
9. P. Snow, *The Fall of Hong Kong* (New Haven, CT: Yale University Press, 2004), 3.
10. Paton, *R. O.: The Life and Times of Bishop R. O. Hall*, 78.
11. New Bishop Arrives in H.K. HKMS 94-1-9, 1932, 14. Hong Kong Public Records Office.

12. A. Swann, "Those First Days," *Outpost* (February 1957): 7.
13. *Outpost* (April 1933): 5 (Meaning of Ho Ming Hua).
14. R. O. Hall, "Enthronement Speech Delivered on 30–12–1932 at St. John's Cathedral," *Outpost* (1933): 6–10.
15. ROH referred to T. Z. Koo.
16. R. O. Hall to parents. January 2, 1933. Chung Chi Divinity School Archive.
17. The Christian Buddhist Institute was a Christian mission to Buddhists on Tao Fong Shan, Sha Tin, headed by Karl Ludwig Reichelt, who became a very good friend of ROH. See *St. John's Review* (February 1934): 36–37.
18. *Outpost* (April 1934): 5 (Lin Yin Tai, Sha Tin).
19. R. O. Hall, *The Art of the Missionary* (London: International Missionary Council, 1942), 32.
20. G. B. Endacott, *Government and People in Hong Kong 1841–1962: A Constitutional History* (Hong Kong: Hong Kong University Press, 1964), 252–53.
21. Marsh to Secretary of State for the Colonies. August 11, 1886. Unofficial members of the Sanitary Board. CO 129/228 #259, 143.
22. *St. John's Review* (April 1933): 83 (Addressed as "Bishop").
23. R. O. Hall, *Aggressive Church Policy*, March 7, 1933. HKMS 94-1-9. Hong Kong Public Records Office.
24. *St. John's Review* (October 1933): 2–4.
25. *Outpost* (July 1933): 5–8 (Plan to Diocesan Synod).
26. J. Y. L. Chung, "The Biography of Bishop Mok Shau Tsang." Hall Family Archive.
27. A. C. Hall, "Bishop R. O. Hall: A Personal Account." A talk given by Canon Christopher Hall. November 3, 2011. St. Andrew's Church.
28. Hall, *China and Britain*, 1927.
29. P. Wickeri, "Clergy Training and Theological Education: The Sheng Kung Hui Experience in China." Conference paper presented at the International Symposium on the History of Christianity in Modern China, June 10–11, 2011.
30. *Outpost* (July–September 1936): 3 (Friends to work in HK).
31. *Outpost* (January–March 1937): 3 (Arthur Peill).
32. James Yen published the *People's 1,000 Character Literacy Primer* and founded the National Association of Mass Education Movement in 1923. See C. W. Hayford, *To the People: James Yen and Village China* (New York: Columbia University Press, 1990).
33. Hayford, *To the People*, x.
34. *St. John's Review* (August 1934): 255 (Pek-taam).
35. G. Baker, *Outpost* (February 1957): 13 (Repair dyke).
36. *St. John's Review* (May 1934): 132 (Bishop's Rural Cooperative Trust).
37. G. Baker, *Outpost* (February 1957): 12 (ROH roaming in his diocese).
38. West Point is a historical name that is not found on the map now. St. Peter's Church was located in what is Sai Ying Poon today.
39. *Outpost* (October 1934): 21–22 (Christ Church).
40. Paton, *R. O.: The Life and Times of Bishop R.O. Hall*, 84.
41. R. O. Hall to Archbishop C. G. Lang. Lang Papers, 127, 149–53. Lambeth Palace Library, London, England.
42. *Outpost* (July 1935): 6 (Harry Baines).

43. Sargent was appointed headmaster of Diocesan Boys' School, which had a debt of HK$145,000 as a result of its construction during the prolonged boycott-strike in Hong Kong. Sargent succeeded in clearing the debt and raised its reputation. See Y. W. Fung and M. Chan-Yeung, *To Serve and to Lead: A History of the Diocesan Boys' School* (Hong Kong: Hong Kong University Press, 2009), 52.
44. *St. John's Review* (September 1934): 299 (Ordination of Christopher Sargent).
45. *Hong Kong Blue Book*, 1935–1940.
46. L. MacQuarrie, *The Development of Social Services in Hong Kong* (Hong Kong: School of Social Work, Hong Kong Polytechnic, 1984).
47. P. R. Webb, "Voluntary Social Welfare Services, 1951–1976," A Quarter-Century of Hong Kong Chung Chi College. 25th Anniversary Symposium (Chung Chi College, Chinese University of Hong Kong, 1977).
48. R. O. Hall, speech delivered on the First Annual Meeting of the Hong Kong Social Welfare Council, 1940. Hong Kong Council of Social Service (HKCSS) Files. Bishop's House Archive (Street Sleepers Society).
49. Minutes of a Meeting of Boys' and Girls' Clubs Association (BGCA). May 2, 1946. BGCA File. Bishop's House Archive.
50. *Outpost* (October 1935): 5–6 (Tai Po Rural Orphanage).
51. R. O. Hall, *South China* (1937): 6 (Tai Po Rural Orphanage).
52. S. Y. Lee, "Taipo Rural Orphanage to St. Christopher's Home." Hong Kong Sheng Kung Hui (HKSKH) History File. Bishop's House Archive.
53. Annual Report 1936, Taipo Rural Home and Orphanage. DW/060. St. Christopher's Home File. Bishop's House Archive.
54. The 40th Anniversary of St. Christopher's Home. 1975. Summary of Major Events.
55. Fung and Chan-Yeung, *To Serve and to Lead: A History of the Diocesan Boys' School*, 9–10.
56. B. Pope, *Outpost* (February 1957): 51–52 (Church Missionary Society Schools).
57. H. Wittenbach to D. M. Paton, July 5, 1976. Chung Chi Divinity School Archive.
58. M. Fisher, *Autobiography: For the Time Being* (Leominster: Gracewing, 1993), 122 and 134–36.
59. Paton, *R. O.: The Life and Times of Bishop R. O. Hall*, 13 (ROH's brought up).
60. Personal communication from Canon Christopher Hall.
61. R. O. Hall to A. C. Hall. October 13, 1957. Chung Chi Divinity School Archive (Nora unenthusiatic about ROH's vocation).
62. M. C. Higgs to D. M. Paton. December 29, 1976. Chung Chi Divinity School Archive.
63. ROH's friends called him RO.
64. R. O. Hall to N. Hall. October 15, 1946. Hall Family Archive (Nora: Source of his spiritual life).
65. Paton, *R. O.: The Life and Times of Bishop R. O. Hall*, 90 (Purchase of home farm).
66. *Outpost* (October–December 1936): 5 (ROH's mother passing).
67. R. O. Hall, "The Late Rev C. G. Hall," *Outpost* (January–March 1940): 5–6.
68. *Outpost* (January–March 1948): 5–9 (Bishop Mok and missionaries continued their work).

69. *Outpost* (January–March 1939): 2–3 (Fall of Canton).
70. *Outpost* (April–June 1939): 13 (Refugee camps).
71. Lian Da were universities formed when the leading universities and colleges in China chose to move to safer locations during the Sino-Japanese War in the midst of major military upheavals and population dislocation. One was established in Kumming. See J. G. Lutz, *China and Christian Colleges* (Ithaca, NY: Cornell University Press, 1971), 362–95.
72. R. O. Hall, Account of the Confirmation and Ordination of Dr. T. C. Chao, Sunday, July 20, 1941. St. Paul's College Chapel, Hong Kong. *Outpost* (November 1941–March 1942): 2.
73. R. O. Hall, *South China* (1941): 11 (Transport workers' welfare).
74. R. O. Hall, *South China* (1941): 4–5 (Quentin Huang).
75. *Outpost* (January–March 1940): 3 (Y. Y. Zhu).
76. Some people had expressed doubt about whether ROH established the Refugee and Social Welfare Council because of the existence of the British Fund for the Relief of Distress in China, which centralized all charitable donations and distributed to existing bodies such as the Hong Kong Emergency Council for relief in South China and Hong Kong. See 呂大樂：《凝聚力量：香港非政府機構發展軌跡》（香港：三聯書店）, and R. Jarman, *Hong Kong Annual Administrative Report 1841–1949*, Volume 5, 1931–1939, 539–42. ROH provided the strong leadership to get the different social welfare agencies working together to form the council. He had also made a very successful appeal to the public for donations.
77. *Outpost* (January–March 1940): 6–7 (Work among refugees).
78. *Outpost* (January–March 1939): 7 (Leonard Wilson arrived in HK; Sargent consecrated as assistant bishop of Fujian).
79. 朱敏彥：〈抗戰時期「工合」運動的歷史作用〉，《上海師範大學學報》，1995 年第 3 期，9–12 [Gong He during the war and its historical significance]. China Academic Journal Electronic Publishing House, http://www.cnki.net.
80. （日）菊池一隆：〈抗日戰爭時期的華僑和中國工業合作運動 1994–2010〉. China Academic Journal Electronic Publishing House, http://www.cnki.net.
81. 喬玲梅：〈專題研究：試論抗戰時期的工合運動與國際合作〉[Gong He during the war and international cooperation]. Century Link 2003; 5: 38, 1994–2010, China Academic Journal Electronic Publishing House, http://www.cnki.net.
82. Wu Qing, "A Study of Bishop R. O. Hall and His Relationship with China (1922–1966)," PhD thesis (2008), 46–48. The Chinese University of Hong Kong.
83. Brief biography of Bishop R. O. Hall. Bishop Hall Jubilee Celebration. Bishop's House Archive.
84. R. O. Hall, "The Church: A Co-operative," *The Chinese Recorder* (August 1934): 489–91.
85. The Christian community had worked with the Guomindang in the New Life Movement which was set up by General Chiang Kai-shek and his wife, Soong May-ling, in February 1934, at a time when China, already weakened by Western imperialism, faced threats of rising Japanese militarism, domestic factionalism, and communism. The movement, based on Confucianism mixed with Christianity, nationalism, and authoritarianism, attempted to counter such threats through a resurrection of traditional Chinese morality.

86. Bishop's covering letter October 15, 1938 to Church Assembly Missionary Council. Unified Statement 1939–40. Area: Far East; Diocese: Hong Kong. Chung Chi Divinity School Archive.
87. R. O. Hall, sermon "Sheng Kung Hui Day Schools" delivered on March 21, 1954. Hall Family Archive.
88. J. Bennitt to D. M. Paton. March 12, 1980. Chung Chi Divinity School Archive.
89. R. O. Hall. Letter to Joc Hall. Not dated. "The Obedient Son: Jesus in the New Testament. Imagination-and-mind Contacts with Jesus." Chung Chi Divinity School Archive.
90. N. Hall to R. O. Hall. March 4, 1941. The letter was written after Nora and the children returned to England safely after the bombing of the *Anchises* on February 28, 1941. Hall Family Archive.
91. See note 89.
92. *Outpost* (June 1946): 4–8 (Wilson interned).
93. R. O. Hall, "The New Church Order." The 27th Annual Hale Memorial Sermon. Delivered on November 14, 1941. Seabury-Western Theological Seminary. Evanston, Illinois (CHDS), 65.
94. Some Western missionaries had a condescending atitude toward Christians of other cultures, as described by D. M. Paton in his book *Christian Missions and the Judgment of God* (London: SCM Press, 1953).
95. Hall, *The Art of the Missionary*, 52.
96. R. O. Hall to U. Niebuhr, April 12, 1944. R. O. Hall to Dr. and Mrs. R. Niebuhr, March 31, 1971. Chung Chi Divinity School Archive.
97. Snow, *The Fall of Hong Kong*, 197–98.
98. Church Army was founded in England in 1882 by the Reverend Wilson Carlile (later prebendary of St Paul's Cathedral), who formed an orderly army of soldiers, officers, and a few working men and women, whom he trained to act as Church of England evangelists among the outcasts and criminals of the Westminster slums. http://www.churcharmy.org.uk/pub
99. R. O. Hall to N. Hall. November 25, 1941. Hall Family Archive (Possible bishop job at home).
100. A. C. Hall. Bishop R. O. Hall. A Personal Account.
101. *Outpost* (January–June 1943): 2 (footnote).
102. R. O. Hall to N. Hall. October 4, 1945. Hall Family Archive (Letter writing to Nora).
103. R. O. Hall to N. Hall. May 29, 1948. Hall Family Archive (Clapton, 1919).
104. R. O. Hall to N. Hall. November 22, 1941. Hall Family Archive (Comparing Nora with other women).
105. Paton, *R. O.: The Life and Times of Bishop R. O. Hall*, 116–17 (Wartime travel in China).
106. P. Y. C. Pang on Bishop R. O. Hall. July 21, 2010. Hall Family Archive.
107. Simone Weil was a French Jew, a mystic and a philosopher. During the war, she enrolled in the forces for the Resistance. She shared the privation of the French and kept strictly to the rations. See H. Richard, *Simone Weil* (New York: Rowman & Littlefield Publishers, 1998).
108. R. O. Hall to N. Hall. January 1, 1943; January 15, 1943; February 10, 1943 (Travel in China: eating and getting sick). Hall Family Archive.

109. R. O. Hall to N. Hall. February 10–16, 1943; June 10, 1943. Hall Family Archive (ROH working with Chinese Industrial Cooperatives).
110. R. O. Hall to N. Hall. May 12, 1941. Hall Family Archive (Rewi Alley introduced ROH to Zhou).
111. R. O. Hall to N. Hall. September 26, 1949. Hall Family Archive (ROH's description of Zhou Enlai).
112. J. M. C. Chou to A. C. Hall. March 13, 1960. Hall Family Archive.
113. R. O. Hall Letter to Joc Hall. "III – Obedient Son." Probably around 1942–43. Chung Chi Divinity School Archive.
114. G. Allen, Memories of Bishop R. O. Hall. Not dated. Chung Chi Divinity School Archive.
115. R. O. Hall to N. Hall. August 17, 1943. Hall Family Archive (Death of three close friends/colleagues).
116. R. O. Hall to N. Hall. August 2, 1943. Hall Family Archive (Sargent's death).
117. R. O. Hall, "Sermon Preached on Remembrance Day November 10, 1963," *St. John's Review* (January 1964): 4–6.
118. R. O. Hall to N. Hall. February 14, 1944. Hall Family Archive (ROH to Fuzhou).
119. M. C. Higgs to D. M. Paton. December 29, 1976. Chung Chi Divinity School Archive.
120. *Outpost* (January–April 1945): 1–2 (Death of Archbishop Temple).
121. The ordination of Florence Li Tim Oi and its aftermath for ROH has been discussed fully by Paton in his book and by Wu Qing in her thesis, but because it had grave repercussions to ROH, it is dealt with briefly here.
122. T. Harrison, *Much Beloved Daughter: The Story of Florence Li Tim-Oi* (Austin, Texas: Morehouse-Barlow Co. Ltd, 1985).
123. Florence Tim Oi Li, *Raindrops of My Life: The Memoir of Florence Tim Oi Li* (Toronto: The Anglican Book Centre, 1996).
124. R. O. Hall to Archbishop W. Temple. June 4, 1943. Temple Papers 11, 130. Lambeth Palace Library Archive, London, England.
125. Archbishop W. Temple to R. O. Hall. December 16, 1943. Temple Papers 11, 131. Lambeth Palace Library Archive, London, England.
126. Paton, *R. O.: The Life and Times of Bishop R. O. Hall*, 131.
127. R. O. Hall to N. Hall. January 25, 1944. Hall Family Archive (Priesting of Li Tim Oi).
128. R. O. Hall to Archbishop W. Temple. January 27, 1944. Temple Papers 11, 132–33. Lambeth Palace Library Archive, London, England.
129. Archbishop W. Temple to R. O. Hall. April 3, 1944. Temple Papers 11, 134. Lambeth Palace Library Archive, London, England.
130. A Bishop in Insurrection, *The Church Times* (July 28, 1944).
131. R. O. Hall to Joc Hall. December 6, 1944. Hall Family Archive (Regarding Editorial in *Church Times*).
132. Archbishop W. Temple to I. Prestige. July 20, 1944. Temple Papers 11, 136–37. Lambeth Palace Library Archive, London, England.
133. Archbishop W. Temple to R. O. Hall. October 1944. Not signed. Temple Papers 11, 180–81. Lambeth Palace Library Archive, London, England.
134. In 2008, Archbishop George Carey agreed with Canon Christopher Hall's suggestion that Temple's unsigned letter could have been drafted by a civil servant

in Lambeth Palace. The outcome of the 1948 Lambeth Conference could have been different if Temple had been alive and chaired the conference (Archbishop Carey George to A. C. Hall. December 9, 1998. Hall Family Archive).
135. Archbishop G. Fisher to Bishop A. Scott. January 23, 1946. Fisher Papers. Lambeth Palace Library Archive, London, England.
136. Minutes of a Special Meeting of the Diocesan Standing Committee of the Synod on February 23, 1946, held in the Bishop's House. Bishop's House Archive. Li Tim Oi could no longer work in Macao after she had to give up her license. She was sent to a church in Hepu where she worked until the Communists took over the country. In 1981, she received permission to leave China to visit her family in Toronto, Canada, where she lived until her death in 1992. She lived to share the celebration of her priesthood in Westminster Abbey, London, planned by the Movement for the Ordination of Women. In 2003 the American Episcopal Church decided to observe the anniversary of Li's priesting in the Church's Calendar of Lesser Feasts and Fasts, and the Anglican Church of Canada observes the anniversary of her death in the Calendar of Holy Persons. See T. Harrison, *Much Beloved Daughter: The Story of Florence Li Tim-Oi* (Austin, TX: Morehouse-Barlow, 1985).
137. Minutes of a Meeting of the Diocesan Standing Committee of the Synod. March 28, 1946 in the Bishop's House. Bishop's House Archive.
138. *Outpost* (December 1947): 11.
139. Report of a Commission Appointed by the Archbishop of Canterbury and York. Women and Holy Orders. Published by the Church Information Office, London. December 1966. http://www.womenpriests.org/related/arch_cnt.asp.
140. Resolutions of Anglican Consultative Council-ACC1. The Anglican Communion Official Website. http://www.anglicancommunion.org/communion/acc/meetings/acc1/resolutions.cfm.
141. J. Bennett, *This God Business* (Hong Kong: Religious Education Resource Centre, 2003), 218, 265.
142. Ordination of women in the Anglican Communion. http://en.wikipedia.org/wiki/Ordination_of_women_in_the_Anglican_Communion.
143. Paton, R. O.: *The Life and Times of Bishop R. O. Hall*, 87.
144. D. Brown, The Anglican Church in Hong Kong and the Challege of Transition (1949–1993) Seminar. September 22–24, 1993. Centre of Asian Studies, The University of Hong Kong, 1993.
145. Paton, R. O.: *The Life and Times of Bishop R. O. Hall*, 138.

Chapter 4
Managing the Diocese under Political Turmoil
The Diocese of South China and Hong Kong (1946–51)

> The most important moment of this service is the moment you have your hand on the door to go out—to serve him, to whom be ascribed as is most justly due all might, dominion, majesty and power, hence forth and forever.
> —R. O. Hall

Shortly after the conclusion of World War II, civil war began between the Guomindang and the Chinese Communist Party. While the propaganda of the Chinese Communist Party, which dangled the promise to landless and starving Chinese peasants that they would be able to take farmland from their landlords if they won, was no doubt a strong enticement, it was the economic collapse, runaway inflation, and corruption of the Guomindang government that drove the speed and decisiveness of Communist victory in China. The Guomindang government finally lost the support of the disillusioned populace. On October 1, 1949, Mao Zedong declared the founding of the People's Republic of China. The Chinese Communist Party soon took control of all Mainland China except the island of Taiwan, where Chiang and the Nationalist army had fled.[1] On January 6, 1950, Britain accorded diplomatic recognition to the People's Republic of China and Hong Kong was to remain a British colony.

Immediately after World War II, Britain reclaimed Hong Kong and established a military administration with Admiral Harcourt as its head. The old guard who had been interned were shipped home for recuperation, and they were replaced by a group of new young administrators who were no longer so convinced of the white man's mission to rule.[2] The military administration worked efficiently to maintain stability, getting the people fed, and they began the work of rebuilding the economic and public health sectors. By March 1, 1946, Hong Kong had almost returned to normality. The farsighted Sir Mark Young, who arrived in Hong Kong on May 1, 1946 to take over the administration for civilian rule, started to put in place bold political reforms that would allow the Chinese citizens participation in determining their own affairs. However, the Chinese response was lukewarm, and Young's reforms did not outlast his tenure. The next governor, Sir Alexander Grantham, took over the reins in July 1947. In 1951, the Conservative Party in England took power, and the government in Hong Kong became much more conservative.[3]

ROH witnessed the end of the European war when he returned on leave to England from Free China at the end of April 1945. As soon as Japan surrendered in August that year, he rushed to book passage to Hong Kong. On September 14, 1945 he left his family once again and traveled by a combination of airplane and boat, arriving in Hong Kong about one month later. After his arrival in Hong Kong, ROH immediately set about to revive the churches there. Most of the Chinese churches, except St. Stephen's Church, had not been damaged too badly during the war and soon they were kept very busy celebrating Holy Communion several times on Sundays.[4] On Armistice Day, November 11, ROH gave an eloquent sermon that resonated with many expatriates in the congregation. "Under God," he warned, "We dare not stay in Hong Kong unless it is our purpose to build there, as part of the great Pacific civilization of the future, a city in which truth and freedom and justice are not tainted by national pride and racial fear."

Simplicity of Life

ROH was in Hong Kong by himself from 1945 to 1954, except when he was on leave (from December 1946 to June 1947, July 1948 to October 1948 to attend the Lambeth Conference, and from January 1952 to October 1952). Nora remained in England to look after her mother and their children. Joc was in the Royal Air Force while Judith and Christopher were in school. Since ROH was living by himself and accommodation was hard to come by after the war, he subdivided the Bishop's House into several units and let them out at affordable rent to the staff and clergy of the diocese.[5] Although he had intended to use the rent to pay off the loan for the property in Sha Tin, the funds proved insufficient. He eventually rented out parts of his bungalow, Lin Yin Tai, in Sha Tin.[6]

With no means of independent wealth, ROH had to support his family from his salary. This came from an endowment fund (with a capital of £25,000) paying him an annual income of £1,000. He passed on £750 to Nora and kept £250 for himself and to pay his life insurance.[7] At that time the two younger children were in public schools, and their school fees accounted for almost 50 percent of the portion he sent to Nora. He barely managed to get by with the help of the meager rents collected. Interest rates dropped, and in 1948 his annual salary was reduced to £750 and then further to £700 in 1949. This drastic cut of 30 percent meant that ROH was in real financial trouble.

Instead of complaining of salary reduction, he told his family that "actually by the mercy of God, it has come at about the best time: for Marlborough [School] will give C [Christopher] a larger foundation because my income is less and probably Oxford County Council will increase Judith's grant . . . and I pay no income tax."[8] Even so, he reminded them that they should watch how they spend money, adding that he did not want any new summer clothes that year. Unfortunately, he could no longer afford to pay for his life insurance.

He tried to sell part of the Sha Tin property with the house and leave a smaller piece of land on which he would build a smaller house for their own use. When the property failed to sell because of a downturn in the real estate market, he resorted to renting the whole bungalow on a long-term basis and added two small rooms on the roof of the garage as his residence, naming it St. Francis House.[9]

George She, the cathedral chaplain, discovered ROH's financial predicament and informed the Standing Committee of the Diocesan Synod. The members voted unanimously to send him a check for £400 to cover the cost of his children's education that year.[10] Deeply moved, ROH insisted that this would be the only time that he would take it. Dean Rose also suggested that ROH should receive £300 each year from the rent collected by the Church Guest House and that St. John's Cathedral should contribute its share by covering ROH's and Nora's passages once every four years when they went on leave.[11]

ROH lived simply compared with most expatriates in Hong Kong, saving whatever he could to send home. The expatriates could not understand his austerity and his indifference to their way of life and their hospitality. ROH wrote to Nora in 1947 that he had always regarded his cottage, Lin Yin Tai, as his home: "Shatin [Sha Tin]—yes—this is home. But Hong Kong somehow—no: and perhaps this is why I never quite hit it off with the English people."[12] He added, "When you come out next year, I shall not want you to get involved in the English social round—but only with our Chinese friends who love you and understand you."[13]

ROH had always found simple meals most satisfying. His breakfast in Lin Yin Tai regularly included two boiled eggs, tea, goat's milk, bread, butter, and fruit; his supper invariably consisted also of two eggs, usually boiled and occasionally scrambled, or cheese, bread and butter, and vegetables.[14] With the exception of bread and cheese, everything was fresh from his own garden. On most days he had lunch, the most substantial meal of the day, in the Bishop's House. He ordered food from the Church Guest House, which consisted of rice with "sung" (usually fish and vegetables) and soup. Whenever he had some free time, he tended the flowers, vegetables, and goats in Lin Yin Tai. He was able to identify the goats by their names, and their pedigrees from their skin and other features.

It was providential that the property in Sha Tin failed to sell, as this was the place where he could find relief and rejuvenation from the intense demands of his diocese, especially in the postwar years. Lin Yin Tai was also a place for him to meditate, to pray, to be inspired, to be alive, and to be near his Nora. He would drive there late after work, and he told Nora that the place was for him a necessary kind of "Sabbath": "I wonder if I'm crazy to come up here like this, 'apparently' wasting so much time—but I think I would have gone crazy without it, the test will be how much I can get done in the evenings . . . I realize more than ever that this place is my 'Sabbath' God provided."[15]

Lin Yin Tai, built on top of the mountain Tao Fong Shan, commanded the most magnificent view of the valley below, as well as a view of another mountain—Ma On Shan—across the valley. One evening, as he waited to see the goats coming back, ROH described to Nora the splendor of the scene: "I have never seen anything more beautiful, as dapple cloud and sunshine on the sides of Ma On Shan and the low evening light brings out all the green colour. There are also mists of cloud filtering the light and just playing round the top of the high saddle of Ma On Shan: and in the foreground are our eucalyptus which has grown up since it lost its leaves in the typhoon—but the new leaves are just showing, making the most lovely soft dainty pattern against the green misty radiant dappled light of the hill."[16]

Without his family by his side, ROH threw himself into the difficult task of spiritual and social reconstruction of the Diocese of South China and Hong Kong after the ravage of war. Typically he would spend more than 14 hours at work each day, usually past midnight, detailing his activities and concerns in letters to his family and friends and to the Victoria Diocesan Association.

Reconstructing the Diocese in South China

As soon as feasible, he headed north to tour his diocese to assess the postwar situation and to make plans for reconstruction. He found that people needed food for the body, mind, and spirit. He wanted funds to rebuild what had been destroyed during the war and human resources to keep the activities of the diocese going. However, the straitened circumstances of the Church Missionary Society in 1946 resulted in the society granting him only 50 percent of what he had requested, and the number of missionaries the society could support was drastically reduced.[17] ROH had to rely more heavily on local resources. Whenever he went on leave, fundraising dominated his activities. He actively raised funds for British United Aid to China in the United Kingdom and in the United States, for postwar reconstruction work and for promotion of health and welfare of the people in China.[18]

The destruction caused by the war had not ended Chung Hua Sheng Kung Hui's interest in evangelism in China but instead had created a new opportunity for it to reach the Chinese with the Christian message. During the stressful time of rebuilding after World War II, the National Christian Council of China initiated the Forward Movement to spread the Gospel and to provide for the spiritual needs of the community. The Diocese of South China took part in initiating this evangelistic movement on St. Andrew's Day 1946.[19] Bishop Halward, whom ROH consecrated as assistant bishop in 1947[20] to be responsible for the English church in Guangzhou, was in charge of the Forward Movement.

Figure 4.1 Decoration of ROH with the Order of the Brilliant Star by Mr. T. W. Kwok, special commissioner for foreign affairs for Guangdong and Guangxi, Chinese government, in October 1947, in recognition of his relief work in China (Hall Family Archive)

Even though the rural program in Zengcheng that Wittenbach had put in place in 1933 had been revived, there were more people than the land could possibly support. Not for the first time ROH set about solving the problem of local unemployment. ROH proposed using the Bishop Duppuy Fund (see below) to create jobs for unemployed people through the purchase of pedicabs, tricycle-rickshaws that were much less exhausting to operate than traditional rickshaws.[21] In Yunnan-Guizhou district, where farmers paid 50 percent of their harvested crops to the landlord as rent, ROH formed the Rural Service Committee with funds from the Victorian Diocesan Association in Hong Kong. The committee lent $50 for each *mou* (0.165 acre or 666.5 sq. m.) of rented land for the purchase of fertilizer, providing lower interest rates as well as a 25 percent increase in rice crop production.[22]

Reconstructing the Diocese in Hong Kong

The population of Hong Kong was only around 600,000 immediately after the war, as many occupants had fled and others had been forced to leave during the Japanese occupation. By 1946, the population rapidly reached the prewar level of 1.6 million as residents returned. Even before the process of rehabilitation had been completed, refugees started to pour into Hong Kong as civil war raged between the Guomindang and the Chinese Communist Party. When the

Korean War broke out shortly after the establishment of the People's Republic of China, the embargo that the United Nations had imposed on China crippled Hong Kong's reviving entrepôt trade, straining its economy further. This trade had yet to return to prewar levels. Even though Britain had implemented a policy of a modern "welfare state" in Britain and recommended the policy to its colonies, the Hong Kong government had no resources for social services in the postwar years.

In addition to having no means to deal with the massive problems associated with the desperately poor refugees, Sir Alexander Grantham, who had become Hong Kong's new governor in 1947, had chosen to ignore Hong Kong's pressing need for social reforms and social welfare. Having served as a cadet in Hong Kong between 1922 and 1935, Grantham had been troubled by the strike-boycott of 1925–26 that had put Hong Kong into depression. He did not trust the Chinese to be loyal to the British Empire because Hong Kong was far too close to China. His conservative policy could be exemplified by the following argument: "Provided that the government maintains law and order, does not tax the people too much and that they can obtain justice in the courts, they are satisfied and well content to devote their time to making more money in one way or another." This seemingly worked very well as the local Chinese had become increasingly preoccupied with making a living.[23]

Grantham's status quo position and failure to provide relief to the refugees impelled ROH to denounce the government's selfishness from the pulpit of St. John's Cathedral from time to time, especially on Christmas Day and Easter Sunday. This sent Grantham into paroxysms of impotent fury, as he had no right of reply.[24]

With the Hong Kong government preoccupied with the task of getting the city back on its feet again, many local voluntary agencies sprang up to take on the challenge of providing relief for the refugees. The enormity of the refugee problem also drew international attention, and many international voluntary organizations began to set up social welfare offices in Hong Kong. In 1948 the government established the Social Wefare Office within the Secretariat for Chinese Affairs to liaise with various local and international voluntary agencies.

There were a number of social activists and reformers in Hong Kong during the postwar decades. They include Father T. F. Ryan SJ, Elsie Elliott of the YWCA and Reformed Club and later an elected member of the Urban Council in Hong Kong, and Karl Stumpf of the Lutheran World Federation. ROH was one of the most influential individuals providing both the foresight and the continuity that Hong Kong sorely needed in the rapidly changing sociopolitical circumstances of that period. Typically, he gave the credit to others, and often told people that Father Ryan was the leader while he had only assisted.[25]

In Hong Kong, ROH focused on what he told Nora was his "real life work: the central part of [his] life—given to Hong Kong—the Student Christian

Movement and St. Luke's in a way preparation for it."[26] Here, he realized that he would be able to live out his practical theology: to practice his mission theology to improve the spiritual and social situation in Hong Kong.

William Temple, who became the archbishop of Canterbury in 1943, published a book on *Christianity and Social Order* in 1942[27] and had six ideals for a Christian Social Order. The first two were:

- Every child should itself be a member of a family housed with decency and dignity so that it may grow up as a member of that basic community in a happy fellowship unspoiled by underfeeding or overcrowding, by dirt and drab surrounding or by mechanical monotony of employment.
- Every child should have the opportunity of an education till years of maturity, so planned as to allow for his peculiar aptitudes and make possible their full development.

ROH did his best to realize these ideals in Hong Kong after the war, and became an unusual voice quite unlike any other in the colony at that time.

The Forward Movement

When the diocese in Hong Kong took part in the Forward Movement organized by Chung Hua Sheng Kung Hui, ROH appointed the Reverend Edward Y. P. Lee as canon missioner, to establish new parishes in the vicinity of the schools. Each parish was asked to have a daughter church that should become independent at the end of a specified period. At the end of ten years, the organizers were pleased that six new parishes had been created in Hong Kong and Kowloon (Appendix 4, Table A4.1). The momentum of expansion continued to accelerate during the following decade.

Human resources were required for church expansion. After the war, ROH continued to send ordinands to Guangzhou to be trained at Canton Union Theological College, but he also established Ming Hua College on the Bishop's House site. It provided theological training to educated young people so that they could take on the leadership of the Church, teach scripture at schools, and assist the parish priest, and it admitted its first students in 1946/1947.[28] ROH was its first principal and Cheung Siu Kwai its first dean. The teaching staff was initially all English except for George She and Cheung Siu Kwai, but eventually teaching was carried out in Cantonese. It continued to offer courses for studies of the Bible and theology for the following decades although its role broadened to include training of ordinands and parish priests in 1995.[29]

Looking after Economically Disadvantaged People

A familiar sight in Hong Kong at this time was the hundreds of ragged little boys running around in the streets, all carrying little wooden boxes, uttering in English, "Shoe-shine! Very nice shoe-shine!" Some of these children were orphans whose parents died during the war, while others were from families with a single mother. Few of these children went to school. Together with George She and two officers from the Royal Air Force, ROH reestablished, as soon as possible, some clubs for boys and girls to provide these children with some basic reading and writing skills, handicraft training, and recreation.[30] He then brought together representatives from many interested parties such as the Royal Air Force, Police, YWCA, Chinese Youth Society, Toc H,[31] Probation Camp, and Catholic Women's Association, to reestablish the Boys' and Girls' Clubs Association. In the beginning, the clubs offered the children a small meal, some book learning, and a foundation in character building.[32] With increased funding from organized financial campaigns each year, the quality of the clubs improved and their programs expanded.[33] By 1949, there were six boys' clubs and two girls' clubs with 240 members in total.

A few projects arose from the Boys' and Girls' Clubs Association to help the marginalized young people: (1) Stanley Summer Camp, which became a permanent camp for boys on probation and a separate organization on its own, under the supervision of Brook Bernacchi, a liberal lawyer;[34] (2) Hong Kong Sea School, which was set up by the Reverend C. J. W. Faulkner with James C. L. Wong (who later became bishop of Jesselton) as the chairperson of the school committee,[35] and which became a separate organization in 1959;[36] and (3) The Rotary Club "Shoe Black" project, which fitted boys with uniforms, a shoe cleaner's box, and a license, and posted them all over the colony, allowing the boys to make their livings legally.

The Boys' and Girls' Clubs Association, which is still robust, proved very effective in keeping children from roaming the alleys of Hong Kong in the postwar years.[37] It continues to provide a whole range of social services to young people from 5 to 18 years of age.

In early 1946, ROH called a meeting of the officers and committee members of the Hong Kong Emergency Refugee and Social Welfare Council, which had been formed in 1938 to deal with the refugee problem, as a large number of returning residents and orphans found themselves without homes or jobs. He asked the council to resume its work but under a different name: the Hong Kong Council of Social Service. It aimed at not just providing relief to economically disadvantaged people, but also to coordinating social services in the colony to prevent overlapping of tasks, erect permanent centers to assess the needs of economically disadvantaged people, and investigate housing, industrial, and recreational problems in congested areas.[38]

ROH saw that the most pressing need was space where welfare organizations could do their work. Accordingly, the Hong Kong Council of Social Service planned to build permanent welfare centers where a number of organizations could be housed in the same building. The first such center was built at Observatory Path, Kowloon, in 1947–48, and the second on Hospital Road,

Hong Kong, in 1949. They provided rooms for family casework, the Society for Protection of Children, and the Boys' and Girls' Clubs Association.[39]

In 1949, family welfare work, which had been administered by the Hong Kong Council of Social Service, was launched as a separate society—the Family Welfare Society—with its own constitution and funds. To avoid overlapping of relief efforts, the Hong Kong Council of Social Service set up a central records office to track all the services carried out by numerous agencies, including those done on the rooftops.[40] It also liaised with the government's Social Welfare Office, which was established in 1947, voiced the views of its member organizations, and coordinated the social welfare activities in the resettlement estates,[41] in addition to the welfare projects that it had initiated (Appendix 4, Table A4.2). In the beginning, the Hong Kong Council of Social Service had only 20 organizations as members, but when ROH retired in 1966, it included 77 societies under its banner.

Sheltering the Homeless

In 1935, the Hong Kong Housing Commission estimated that there was a housing shortage of between 25,000 and 35,000 flats. Working-class families, unable to rent a whole tenement floor, subdivided the space to rent to separate households, leading to serious overcrowding. The commission recommended that a slum clearance should be financed, and the housing of deprived people subsidized by a special housing tax. However, because of the political instability resulting from the Japanese invasion in the late 1930s, the government did very little to improve housing conditions.[42]

ROH tried to work on improving housing conditions, visiting the slums and the tenement houses on several occasions during the first few years of his ministry. In order to come up with a solution to the housing problem, he corresponded with Ms. E. Hinder, who was responsible for a low-cost housing project in Shanghai,[43] and studied a report on town planning in Singapore.[44] He also discussed the housing situation with local government officials.[45] Unable to find any way out of the difficulty of the high cost of land, and convinced that no private body or government could tackle the problem alone, he came up with a bold proposal of forming a Hong Kong Housing Improvement Trust: a cooperation between the government and the community. Even this scheme had to be shelved because of the political situation in China. His prewar attempts to improve housing bore little fruit.

The extensive damage to houses by shelling and air raids and the lack of resources for repair left one out of four people in Hong Kong homeless after World War II. When unrest and civil war in China caused refugees to flood across the border once again, the effect on housing was devastating. Initially, the government left the task of providing new housing to private enterprise. The demand always outstripped the supply. Hong Kong landlords ingeniously divided tenement houses into cubicles, while others rented out bunk space on which one or more family members slept—sometimes in shifts—daytime for one and nighttime for another member of the family. At night, shanties and shelters, which were bundled up like parcels during the day, filled the streets. Some people slept under staircases and on rooftops and roundabouts, others in wooden cases.[46] By 1948, there were 20,000 squatters on Hong Kong Island and 10,000 in Kowloon, increasing to 300,000 by the end of 1949.[47] These squatters created enormous problems, including fire hazards from cooking in the open amid the debris of the shacks, and widespread proliferation of disease, crime, and despair.

ROH invited Admiral Harcourt, before the admiral's departure, to visit the slum area in the Western District. On April 5, 1946, the two sneaked into the area incognito, in shirts and shorts, to see the horribly overcrowded housing situation. A survey of the tenement houses, which was ordered after the visit, found that the unscrupulous subletting of tenement houses by their tenants was producing absurd profits. One 42 × 13.5 × 15-foot flat, divided into 18 bunks, housed a total of 65 people. The 41 men, 19 women, and 5 children shared one 10 × 13.5-foot kitchen, which would have also included space for a toilet and bathing. The tenant, who paid $30 per month for the whole flat, could, by subletting, collect $45 in rent. After paying the landlord for subletting, and even on a few occasions not being able to collect rent from the subtenants, the tenant still reaped a substantial profit. In addition to marked overcrowding, most of the buildings were in a very poor state of sanitation and repair. The survey gave objective evidence of the degree of congestion and poor sanitation in the tenement houses.[48]

The visit with Harcourt showed the outgoing governor, and therefore the upper echelons of the administration as well as the government in Britain, the gravity of the housing problem in Hong Kong. The British government had discussed the 1938 Housing Report of Hong Kong and had regarded the issue of public housing as urgent and important.

To address the deplorable housing situation in Hong Kong, ROH assembled a group from different professions to form the Hong Kong Housing Society in 1948.[49] In the early stages nothing much was accomplished, because the group was unable to solve the intractable problem of how to get flats built to let at $20 to $25 per month (about one-sixth to one-fifth of the income of a worker with a family of four or five). Due to the high cost of land, site formation in hilly parts, and high mortgage interest rates,[50] it was not possible to meet the minimum standard of 35 square feet of floor area and 350 cubic feet of air space per adult. Meanwhile, the Housing Society, along with the Hong Kong Council of Social Service, petitioned to the government that any premises under the control of the Housing Society be excluded from the application of the Landlord and Tenant Ordinance of 1947.[51] Through the Hong Kong Council of Social Service, the Housing Society received a grant of £14,000 that had been made to the Hong Kong government by the Lord Mayor's Empire Air Raid Victims Fund for the benefit of those who had suffered from Japanese occupation.[52] ROH wanted to use the grant from the Air Raid Victims Fund to start building low-cost housing. Because of high mortgage interest rates and the banks' refusal to give loans for housing for economically disadvantaged people, the project was stalled for the next two to three years.[53]

Restarting the Schools

Most schools, including the Anglican schools, had been closed and taken over by the Japanese for various uses, and enrolment had dwindled to around 5,500. When the war finally ended, the task of rehabilitating the schools to prewar levels was by no means easy, given that most of the school premises were destroyed and there was a lack of resources and funding. With his able assistant, George She, ROH reopened all the Anglican schools as soon as possible, including the Church Missionary Society day schools, reequipped with the government's help.[54]

By March 1947, enrolment in schools in Hong Kong rebounded to the prewar level of around 100,000 due mostly to the private sector working in makeshift premises.[55] The tremendous expansion of primary school education would come in the 1950s and 1960s, to deal with an ever-increasing youth population.

Managing the Diocese

Creative Financing

To get the diocese up and running immediately after the war required funding. At first, ROH found that the diocese had no funds to repair damaged churches and schools. He was adept at what might today be called collaborative problem-solving, however, and he was blessed with the help of George She, who was a barrister but had also studied theology in England and was ordained by ROH as a deacon. George She was in fact a financial wizard. He had previously worked for several years in shipping and other business, before finishing his formal university education. George She was selfless, devoted to the Church, and overflowing with energy. Together, the two not only saved the diocese from bankruptcy but also allowed necessary repairs to be undertaken and vital new projects to be initiated.

Looking around at what resources they could tap, they uncovered several innovative ways to raise and use funds: ways that ranged from the launch of an annual Diocesan Financial Campaign that proved to be highly successful; the conversion of the Church Guest House into a profitable business; the building of rent-generating Stanton House (Central Hospital); creative uses of the

Duppuy Fund; and inauguration of a new scheme whereby all parish churches would share half their income with the diocese. The last three innovative fundraising methods illustrated the duo's ability to create or seize opportunities that other people would have overlooked.

The idea of building Stanton House originated in 1947, when a terrible rainstorm caused a landslide to a small section of the lot (Inland Lot 76) where St. Paul's College, St. Paul's Church, and the Bishop's House were located. Not having sufficient funds to deal with the problem, ROH wanted to sell part of the land. Imagine his astonishment when he learned that the Crown lease had another 900 years remaining![56] As the land had become quite valuable, he decided to develop it despite the legal complexity related to the lot.[57]

Inland Lot 76 was granted to the Reverend Vincent Stanton, the first colonial chaplain of Hong Kong, by Queen Victoria. Stanton used his own funds to build St. Paul's College for the training of native clergy for the ministry. On the arrival of Bishop Smith, he generously donated the land and building to the bishop. The control of the college was vested entirely in the bishop of Victoria as ex-officio warden, and the indenture was signed on October 15, 1849 by Stanton and Bishop Smith.[58] There was, however, another indenture signed on September 5, 1851 by Queen Victoria and the bishop of Victoria. In it, Her Majesty, having given full power to the governor of Hong Kong to grant leases on land, required the bishop of Victoria and his successors not to use that lot or St. Paul's College for any other purpose than the promotion of charitable causes without license from Her Majesty or her heirs, represented by the governor of Hong Kong or other person duly authorized on his behalf.[59]

In 1948, ROH obtained a special license from the governor, Sir Alexander Grantham, to use the lot for the following purposes: as the bishop's and the dean's residence, as premises for the Boys' and Girls' Clubs Association, as a hostel termed the Church Guest House, and as a hospital.[60] With this special license, ROH erected Stanton House, named after Vincent Stanton, in the Bishop's House compound, as well as the building that would house the Juvenile Care Centre.

Since there were already private hospitals for wealthy people and government hospitals for economically disadvantaged people, ROH used Stanton House as a private hospital to serve the middle class.[61] The hospital was known as Central Hospital. ROH envisioned that the income generated from Central Hospital would be used partly to compensate the Church Missionary Society for the construction costs of turning St. Paul's College into a boys' school and partly to train Chinese students for the ministry.

ROH and the committee members needed thick skins to be unfazed by the heated debates on the building of Stanton House that raged in the press. One man who called himself the "Hammer" asked why the bishop of Hong Kong should agree to this moneymaking business.[62] Another remarked on the great need in Hong Kong for more hospitals and nursing homes for economically disadvantaged people, adding that a small hospital that could accommodate only 80 private patients would not contribute much toward solving the problem.[63] Because the list of promoters all had Chinese names, he questioned why the hospital was only for Chinese.[64] The debate persisted even after the new hospital opened in 1950.[65] Although the building of Stanton House on Inland Lot 76 aroused such a heated debate, no one raised a single question when the Juvenile Care Centre was built on the same lot.

The rent collected from Stanton House, the Bishop's House, the Church Guest House, St. Paul's Church, and the schools on Inland Lot 76 were placed in the Victoria Bishopric Fund, for education and charitable purposes.[66] This fund supported the training of many Chinese clergy and many educational and social service projects.

Another source was the Duppuy Fund which originated from the estate of the Reverend J. T. Holman who bequeathed it to the bishop of Victoria, in grateful memory of the episcopate of Bishop Duppuy.[67] In 1939, ROH founded a diocesan mutual investment and loan fund under the title Duppuy Fund, which was to be a discretionary fund or trust for the benefit of the Church. ROH shrewdly noticed that many church schools in his diocese had at the beginning of each academic year large sums of money deposited in local banks, which earned no interest, while churches in need had to pay high interest on their borrowings. The solution was to bring the lenders and borrowers together on a win-win basis.

ROH used the Duppuy Fund to guarantee security to the depositors. He also formed the Duppuy Fund Committee to advise him on the allocation of loans, the fixing of interest rates payable for various kinds of deposits, and the investment of the fund. At no time did ROH surrender to the committee his sole discretion to deal in privacy with individual cases of need. This creative use of the Duppuy Fund, which grew considerably over the years, was a stroke of genius, as the diocese, instead of the banks, reaped the economic benefits. Since its first operation, almost every institution in the diocese (churches, schools, and social welfare institutions) benefited by borrowing at low interest rates from this fund at one time or another.

With advice from George She, ROH began a new financial arrangement for the diocese. Each parish paid the diocese one half of its total income, and out of this contribution the diocese undertook to pay its clergy. The remaining half was retained by the parish to pay salaries for other staff and for the maintenance of the Church. This method proved to be extremely helpful for the missionary work of the Church, as contributions from the financially stronger parishes were more than adequate to meet the stipends for their respective clergy. Further, this system had enabled the diocese to pay the same stipend to every clergy. In this way, an undeveloped field could secure the services of a senior and experienced priest, making growth and progress possible within a short time.[68]

His Lieutenants

ROH had several right-hand aids during his episcopacy who spent years administering and managing vast quantities of work of the diocese under his direction. Immediately after the war, George She not only helped with getting the finances of the diocese in order, but also worked hard on numerous projects for the diocese. At the bidding of ROH, he took up the difficult task of acting as the manager of workers' children's schools, he reestablished the Boys' and Girls' Clubs Association, and he sat on the school committees of a number of established Anglo-Chinese schools. As acting secretary of Church Missionary Society, George She did more than anyone else in getting the Anglican schools—especially the Church Missionary Society day schools—reopened after the war. He oversaw the repair of St. John's Hall and the construction of Stanton House. He also worked as a part-time chaplain in St. John's Cathedral, where his office was constantly crammed with people seeking advice or help. During all this time he supported himself working as a full-time magistrate. His boundless energy, cheerfulness, resourcefulness, and willingness to help was amazing.[69] When George She went on leave, ROH lamented his loss in a letter to Nora "that we shall not see each other again till June 1952. It makes me realize how much I depend on him and how much we do together."[70]

Dr. Charles Harth, who had so courageously defended the Cathedral and its "treasures" and the Bishop's House during the war, stayed on to help ROH in many ways, acting as the diocesan secretary and ROH's chaplain.[71] Harth was ordained in 1947 and became an honorary staff member of St. John's Cathedral and the warden of the Church Guest House, which was originally St. Paul's College Hostel.

By 1950 Harth had left for New York, where he entered a seminary for further studies,[72] and George She left for England in 1954, assuming the headmastership of Diocesan Boys' School a year later. Fortunately, S. K. Loong remained. Ordained in 1941, Loong had been sent to work in Calcutta during the war. After he returned, he helped the architect who designed Central Hospital and supervised the construction work. Soon he became involved with the building of churches in the diocese. Loong was most proud of Kei Oi Church which had a novel design at that time for Hong Kong: the choir deliberately placed around the altar and a space behind the altar for the bishop's chair. This allowed the vicar to celebrate the Eucharist facing the congregation, providing closer participation by the people.[73] The faithful Loong became ROH's secretary, and chaplain and registrar of the diocese in 1949, and remained in these positions until ROH's retirement.

Edward C. C. Johnson, an old boy of Diocesan Boys' School who had been with ROH in Free China during the war, had given up a job with an absurdly high salary at Jardine, Matheson & Co., in order to work in the bishop's office after the war. When Nora was in England, the devoted Edward took it upon himself to look after ROH in small but essential ways: retrieving a lost pen, accompanying him to a restaurant or a movie, and even buying him a new suit. He was one of the very few who would argue with ROH. On rare occasions ROH might get angry with him, but he usually sent him an abjectly contrite note afterward. Johnson also looked after the Duppuy Fund and other funds of the diocese. He and George She were allies and were utterly loyal to ROH. They raised money to purchase a secondhand car to replace ROH's war-surplus jeep, the brakes of which had failed and almost killed ROH and Johnson. Ten years later, they replaced this secondhand car with another one, again with funds raised for the bishop. Without telling ROH they set up an "M. W. Ho Fund" within the Duppuy Fund, which banked donations from friends of the bishop, to provide for his retirement.[74] After ROH's retirement, Johnson also looked after the sale of Lin Yin Tai. He sent detailed statements to ROH at the Home Farm at Lewknor regularly, until all the funds had been transferred to England years later.[75]

It is interesting to note that these right-hand men of ROH were not white Anglo-Saxon: George She and Edward Johnson were Eurasians, Charles Harth an Austrian Jew, and S. K. Loong Chinese.

Committees and Day-to-Day Work

The work of the diocese was governed by several committees, the most important of which was the Diocesan Standing Committee. It made all the major decisions regarding the operation of the diocese. Both clergy and laypeople were represented and it was chaired by ROH. There were a number of other committees: the assistant bishop's Endowment Fund Committee (chaired by Mr. Li Fook Wo), the Youth Training Committee (the Reverend Roland Koh), the Education Board (Canon E. W. L. Martin), the Literature Committee (the Reverend Chung Yan Laap), the Canon and Regulation Committee (Canon Paul Tso), the Prayer Book Committee (the Reverend Chung Yan Laap), the Relationship of Chung Hua Sheng Kung Hui and Church Missionary Society Committee (Archdeacon Lee Kau Yan), the Rural Work Committee (Bishop Victor Halward), and the Medical Board (ROH).[76]

After the war, ROH formed a joint committee with members from the Church Missionary Society and the Chinese churches to oversee the Church Missionary Society primary schools; in 1958, this joint committee would be renamed the Church Missionary Society Day School Council.[77] In 1956, ROH changed the name of the Education Board to Diocesan Education Committee. Its function was to oversee the educational activities of the secondary schools to be chaired by Miss B. M. Kotewall, headmistress of St. Paul's Coeducational College.[78]

ROH appointed the chairpersons of all the committees except the most important ones, which he himself chaired: the Finance Committee, the

Diocesan Synod Standing Committee, and the Church Body of the Chinese Anglican Church in Hong Kong, which was responsible for church properties. He centralized power in his office. In the 1960s when he was traveling either on business or on leave, he appointed individuals to chair these committees and councils during his absence: F. W. Li for the first two committees, Y. W. Penn for the third, and Canon Chung Yan Laap for the fourth.[79] In this way, the whole diocesan enterprise would continue to function efficiently while he was away.

There were very few staff members in the Bishop's House, the "central office" of the diocese, which dealt with day-to-day administration. After the war, ROH was much blessed in having the very patient Kitty Anderson as his secretary, the one person who could be relied upon from long experience to read his handwriting.[80] ROH tended to keep many details in his head. When he was away, it was said that no one knew what went on in the diocese and one could not get any information from his office.[81] This was only partly true, because there was always someone acting as the Bishop's Commissary who had been briefed on what was most urgent. ROH was also in communication by airmail and consistently replied on the same day or the following day.

Support in the Diocese

ROH had the power to inspire numerous individuals and families to find fulfilment in service to the Church. In his silver jubilee sermon in 1957, ROH gave thanks for the "faith and loyalty of the laymen of the Church." Some showed their devotion by donating funds and their time and their talents, serving on various committees for schools and welfare organizations in the diocese. They included Lam Chik Suen and Lam Chik Ho, sons of Lam Woo, whom ROH described as one of the "Grand Old Men."[82] Lam Woo, a prominent builder, who had constructed some of the churches and schools in the diocese, such as Church of Our Saviour in Guangzhou and St. Paul's Church, St. Paul's Girls' College (now St. Paul's Co-educational College) and Diocesan Boys' School in Hong Kong, had served on many committees of the Anglican Church. In addition to serving on committees, Lam Chik Ho met with ROH regularly twice weekly to discuss diocesan matters for many years. Li Fook Wo also served and chaired important committees in the diocese. Other members of the Li family "adopted" St. James' Settlement as their responsibility in fund-raising.

Separation of the Diocese of Hong Kong from Chung Hua Sheng Kung Hui

Establishment of the People's Republic of China in 1949

Toward the close of 1948, the civil war and the corruption in the Guomindang government led to instability of the currency, the value of which dropped daily while unemployment grew. Thousands of people who were disillusioned with the Guomindang government were drawn to communism. The hungry, homeless, and many discharged soldiers now found themselves with no status in the economy, and all became prime recruits for the People's Liberation Army.

Anticipating that a monumental change was imminent, and that it might include more bloodshed, ROH implored the readers of *Outpost*, who had been supporting the Church in South China: "Do not despair of China. God made her, China (like Britain and all people) has been redeemed by the cross of Jesus Christ; and remember, the Kingdom of God has its own momentum."[83]

ROH had been supportive of the Guomindang government with Christians in the leadership in the 1930s. But he lost his trust, as many did, after years of civil war and corruption. ROH could see that the people in China might pass more easily from the old social order to communism than they could to Christianity, because Christianity had always been identified with foreigners and imperialism.[84] He was impressed by some of the Communist leaders through his work with Gong He and felt that communism might be a good option for China and provide a path to self-determination.

Even though ROH had no direct contact with Mao Zedong, he greatly respected aspects of his teaching, which few people in the Church shared then. ROH found a passage in Mao's book entitled *On Practice* that resonated with his sense of Christian faith. Mao's quotations of an old Chinese saying about practice, "If one does not enter the tiger's den, one cannot obtain the tiger cubs"—intimating that knowledge separated from practice was worthless—encapsulated, for ROH, not only the basic principle of empirical science but also the principle of Charles Gore, who valued practice over theory in social theology as well as with Christian faith.[85] For Jesus said, "If any man will do His will, he will know of the doctrine" (John 7:17).

On August 21, 1949, the People's Liberation Army had just liberated Fuzhou and could be expected before too long on the border. At the opening of the Synod celebrating the centenary of the Diocese of Victoria, ROH preached a sermon entitled "The Destiny of the Chinese Church."[86] He was probably influenced by F. D. Maurice's *Kingdom of Christ* and the way it manifest in different nations and civilizations, and how God had prepared the Jews and the Romans for the coming of the Kingdom:

> As God had prepared the Roman Empire for the coming of his Kingdom, so I believe He has prepared the Communist Empire for the coming of that Kingdom. As under the protection of Roman law the mustard seed grew to be a great tree, so under Communist rule I believe the seed will grow into a great tree.

The Roman Empire was orderly, but the cost of spreading the Gospel was the cruel punishment and death of many faithful Christians. God had prepared the Jews and the Romans for the coming of His Kingdom, just as He had been preparing China for the coming of His Kingdom at this hour under the Communist rule. The Christian Church had been able to eventually abolish one of two evils in the Roman Empire: the possession of slaves. The other evil that the Christian Church had not been powerful enough to abolish was the massive accumulation of private property and individual wealth. Is it possible that God had raised communism to destroy this evil? He continued:

> The Christian church has been able to abolish slavery but it has not been strong enough to abolish the evil of great accumulation of private property. So perhaps God has raised up Communism to destroy the evil of accumulated private property just as he raised the Roman Empire to destroy the evil of lawlessness and banditry in Europe. The prophet Isaiah says: "Woe unto you that join house to house and add field to field." You will find the book of Deuteronomy and other prophets also condemn the accumulation of private property. The accumulation of private property has always increased poverty. It was the cause of Taiping rebellion. It has been the cause of the downfall of the Kuomintang [Guomindang].

In thinking about the future of China under communism, ROH went beyond Maurice's Christian socialism, as many English Christian socialists did, in embracing socialism at that era. One can only imagine the reception of such a sermon in the hothouse capitalistic culture of Hong Kong, with its vast number of refugees who had recently escaped from communism! The sermon clearly announced a political stance that few would dare to declare in public, given the anti-communist climate in Hong Kong and in the West at that time.

The year 1949 was marked not only by the establishment of the People's Republic of China and the centenary of the Diocese of Victoria but also by the 150th anniversary of the founding of Church Missionary Society. ROH's busy engagements in 1949 covering several parts of his diocese have been well documented.[87] Even as the People's Liberation Army was approaching the border of Hong Kong, ROH was still giving weekly lectures at Lingnan University in Guangzhou.

During the first months after the establishment of the People's Republic of China, the policy of religious tolerance was apparently observed and the work of the Chinese Church continued without interference. When the People's Liberation Army finally reached Beihai in 1950, the hospital there treated many of its wounded soldiers and gained appreciation and praise from the army. Nanning district also reported a peaceful handover and that the missionaries there had been treated with courtesy.[88] Then sad news came from the Yunnan-Guizhou Diocese: Bishop Quentin Huang had been arrested together with a number of Christians. ROH sent a telegram to Zhou Enlai, whom he knew well from his Chongqing days, but as Zhou was in Moscow at that time, there was no response.[89] The arrest was apparently due to the initial chaos after the takeover, and Huang was subsequently released.

Figures 4.2 (Upper) Clergy and delegates of the Diocese of Kong-Yuet (Hong Kong and Guangdong) to celebrate the 100th anniversary of Chung Hua Sheng Kung Hui, and (lower) names of people in the photograph according to rows starting from front to back (Bishop's House Archive)

In September 1949, once the Chinese Communist Party had gained control of most of Mainland China, Mao convened the People's Political Consultative Conference, inviting delegates from a broad spectrum of political interests and parties to discuss the establishment of a new state. The first conference approved the Common Program, which served as the de facto constitution for the next five years and guaranteed to all, men and women equally, except "political reactionaries," rights of freedom of "thought, speech, publication . . . and the freedom to hold processions and demonstrations." This guarantee of rights allayed much of the fear and suspicion that Chinese church leaders had felt toward the Chinese Communist Party and won their enthusiastic support.

Some Chinese Protestant Church leaders, hoping to clarify the situation as they worried about the fate of the Protestant Christian churches, met with Zhou Enlai, then prime minister and foreign minister. While Zhou was not against religious beliefs, he opposed any foreign influence on Chinese churches. After the meeting, Y. T. Wu and other Protestant Christian leaders began to draft the *Christian Manifesto*, which expressed support for the new government and its efforts to build an independent, democratic, united, and prosperous New China, in which Christians would be required to be independent and free from overseas support and control. They also organized the Chinese Christian Three-Self (self-governing, self-supporting, and self-propagating) Patriotic Movement Preparatory Committee, based in Shanghai. One of the tasks of this committee was to oversee the "Denunciation Movement" introduced in the spring of 1951 during the Korean War, to sever the connection between Christianity and imperialism.[90]

Unfortunately, the People's Republic of China was drawn into the Korean War, which dragged on for more than three years and had huge casualties on both sides, especially the North Koreans and the Chinese.[91] This war reinforced Chinese perceptions of the evils of Western imperialism, and Westerners who had stayed in China for business or as missionaries were forced to leave the country. Together with other missionaries, four American diocesan bishops resigned and left China.[92]

Final Separation in 1951

Shortly after the war, sensing that political changes might take place in China that would affect the Chinese Church, ROH did his best to ensure that the Church would become indigenous. First, he removed the influence of Canterbury, and in 1947 the archbishop of Canterbury took the inevitable step of relinquishing his final authority over the bishopric of Victoria to Chung Hua Sheng Kung Hui.[93] Second, he created the Yun-Gui (Yunnan-Guizhou) Diocese out of the Diocese of Victoria, to be under the jurisdiction of Chung Hua Sheng Kung Hui.[94] Quentin Huang was elected bishop of that district and consecrated by ROH on August 3, 1947 in St. John's Cathedral.

Sadly, no other district at that time was ready to become a new diocese. Requesting Chung Hua Sheng Kung Hui list Nanning as one of its missionary districts, ROH stated that he would help maintain the work there. Only Hong Kong, Macao, and the province of Guangdong were left in the Diocese of Victoria, which was renamed Kong-Yuet Diocese (Diocese of Hong Kong–Guangdong) by Chung Hua Sheng Kung Hui.

Finally, to remove Guangdong from his jurisdiction, ROH proposed Archdeacon Mo-Yung In to fill the vacancy created by the death of Bishop Mok. In 1949, ROH initiated discussion on whether the Diocese of Hong Kong–Guangdong should be further subdivided into the Diocese of Hong Kong and the Diocese of Guangdong, and that Mo-Yung In should become bishop of Guangdong.[95] But time was running out. When Mo-Yung In was consecrated as bishop of Guangzhou on March 25, 1950 by Bishop Tsang of Hankou, with Bishop Halward, who had been working in Guangzhou, and other Chinese bishops, ROH was no longer permitted to enter Mainland China.[96]

ROH's strategic moves to make the Chinese Church indigenous made pragmatic and ethical sense, but they did not stop the final separation. By 1951, the Denunciation Movement was in full swing and all Western missionaries had left China including those in Chung Hua Sheng Kung Hui except ROH, who remained as bishop of the Diocese of Hong Kong–Guangdong.[97] Since Hong Kong was a British colony, it became quite obvious that the Diocese of Hong Kong–Guangdong had to be split into the Diocese of Hong Kong and Macao and the Diocese of Guangdong for political reasons. In May 1951, Bishop Mo-Yung In was officially informed by the new People's Republic of China government that, as a matter of national policy, there should be "no organic relations between religious or cultural bodies within the jurisdiction of the People Republic's government and similar bodies outside the jurisdiction." Funds for preachers and charitable organizations were to be remitted to Guangzhou for the last time through the Chinese People's Bank. Thereafter, Guangzhou would not be allowed to receive any funding. Chung Hua Sheng Kung Hui was to find new sources of income, gear itself for production, and keep expenses at a minimum. The deadline for implementation of all demands was July 1951. Bishop Mo-Yung In wrote to his friend the Reverend Chung Yan Laap, secretary of the Diocesan Standing Committee, "I cannot hold up my tears, when I say I can be separated from Hong Kong and the church work can be re-organized, but my spirit towards Bishop Hall could never be separated. This promise I repeat again and again before God that though the government authority strongly urged me not to see Bishop Hall again, it is possible in the church organization, but it is impossible in personal spirit."[98]

On receiving the letter from Bishop Mo-Yung In, the Diocesan Standing Committee in Hong Kong called an emergency meeting. During the meeting, the committee decided to take the following steps: (1) a petition would be sent to the House of Bishops of Chung Hua Sheng Kung Hui requesting the constitution of a new diocese, the Diocese of Guangdong (excluding Hong Kong and Macao); (2) the bishop of Hong Kong and Macao would resign from the House of Bishops of Chung Hua Sheng Kung Hui;[99] and (3) the Diocese of Victoria would change its name to the Diocese of Hong Kong and Macao (Hong Kong Sheng Kung Hui) and, in his capacity as the head of the international Anglican Communion, the archbishop of Canterbury would act as trustee, supplying the metropolitan functions prescribed in the canons and constitutions of Chung Hua Sheng Kung Hui.[100]

The Diocese of Hong Kong and Macao became separated from Chung Hua Sheng Kung Hui at that time. ROH was completely cut off from his beloved China, something he did not expect even though he had fully accepted that his diocese, with the exception of Hong Kong and Macao, would be taken over by a Chinese bishop.

Notes

1. S. Pepper, "KMT-CCP Conflict 1945–1949," in *The Cambridge History of China, Volume 13, Republic China 1912–1949, Part 2*, edited by J. K. Fairbank and A. Feuerwerker (Cambridge: Cambridge University Press, 1986), 723–88.
2. Snow, *The Fall of Hong Kong*, 289 (Armistice Day).
3. Tsang, *A Modern History of Hong Kong*, 142–44.
4. *Outpost* (January 1946): 1–3 (Status of the churches).
5. R. O. Hall to N. Hall. August 26, 1946. Hall Family Archive (Bishop's House into units).
6. R. O. Hall to N. Hall. November 8, 1947. Hall Family Archive (Letting part of the cottage in Sha Tin).
7. R. O. Hall to N. Hall. February 23–March 6, 1948. Hall Family Archive (ROH's salary).
8. R. O. Hall to N. Hall. December 9, 1948. Hall Family Archive (Further reduction in salary: no income tax).
9. R. O. Hall to N. Hall. November 18, 1947. Hall Family Archive (Garage house).
10. R. O. Hall to N. Hall. June 17/18, 1949. Hall Family Archive (Standing Committee's check).
11. R. O. Hall to N. Hall. April 1, 1949. Hall Family Archive (Dean Rose's suggestions).
12. R. O. Hall to N. Hall. August 5, 1947. Hall Family Archive (Sha Tin, ROH's home).
13. R. O. Hall to N. Hall. November 10, 1947. Hall Family Archive (Chinese friends).
14. R. O. Hall to N. Hall. August 14, 1950. Hall Family Archive (Meals and payment to servants).
15. R. O. Hall to N. Hall. July 13, 1946. Hall Family Archive (Lin Yin Tai: Sabbath God provided).
16. R. O. Hall to N. Hall. September 26, 1949. Hall Family Archive (Ma On Shan).
17. G. Barclay to R. O. Hall. December 14, 1945. Church Missionary Society Archives. Reel 390, Section 1 East Asia, Part 18. *South China, 1935–1951*. Hong Kong University Library Special Collection.

18. R. O. Hall, "The Importance of Assisting China: British United Aid to China," *Monthly Review* (47), April 1947.
19. V. Halward to R. O. Hall. April 7, 1948. Forward Movement. Bishop's House Archive.
20. *Outpost* (August 1946): 1 (Victor Halward became assistant bishop posted in Shamian).
21. R. O. Hall, *Outpost* (December 1947): 5 (Pedicabs).
22. *St. John's Review* (April 1948): 151 (Rural Service Committtee).
23. Tsang, *A Modern History of Hong Kong*, 148.
24. Snow, *The Fall of Hong Kong*, 319 (Grantham's impotent fury). Sir Jack Cater, chief secretary of Hong Kong, told ROH's son Christopher this story in 1979. What he did not confess was that it was he himself who provided ROH with the ammunition. His widow revealed this to Christopher many years later.
25. Interview of Bishop R. O. Hall at Lewknor. November 30, 1972. Bishop's House Archive.
26. R. O. Hall to N. Hall. August 5, 1947. Hall Family Archive (SCM and St. Luke's prepared ROH for the great challenge in Hong Kong).
27. W. Temple, "Christianity and Social Order," *St. John's Review* (September 1958): 260.
28. Ming Hua College, Tutorial Course for Lay Church Leaders. Church Missionary Society Archive. Reel 384, Section 1, Part 18. East Asia Mission, *South China*. G1CHg 01, 1937–50.
29. I. Lam to the Chairman of Diocesan Finance Committee. October 31, 1996. Ming Hua College. Bishop's House Archive.
30. R. O. Hall to Air Commodore W. A. D. Brook. April 24, 1946. Boys' and Girls' Clubs Association File. Bishop's House Archive.
31. Toc H (Talbot House) is an international Christian movement, founded in December 1915 at Poperinghe, Belgium, to provide rest and recreation for soldiers. It was named after Gilbert Talbot, son of the bishop of Winchester, who was killed at Hooge in July 1915. Toc H served others by organizing activities such as hospital visits and entertaining the residents of care homes. http://www.toch-uk.org.uk.
32. Minutes of Meeting of BGCA. May 2, 1946. BGCA File. Bishop's House Archive.
33. A. Cooney, Report on BGCA in Hong Kong. July 15, 1946. BGCA File. Bishop's House Archive.
34. B. Bernacchi to Colonial Secretariat. October 7, 1946. Probation Camp at Stanley. BGCA. February 2, 1948. BGCA File. Bishop's House Archive.
35. Minutes of a Meeting of BGCA. August 9, 1946. BGCA File. Bishop's House Archive (Sea Training School).
36. B. Bernacchi, The Sea School at Stanley. Reasons for Pride. HKMS 94-1-12. Hong Kong Public Records Office.
37. J. Doggett, BGCA. Widening Influence. HKMS 94-1-12. Hong Kong Public Records Office.
38. Constitution, Name, and Objective of the Hong Kong Council of Social Service (HKCSS). November 7, 1950. HKCSS File. Bishop's House Archive.

39. R. O. Hall, Talk to the Rotary Club, "Hong Kong Council of Social Service." November 30, 1954. HKCSS File. Bishop's House Archive.
40. M. I. Palmer to R. O. Hall. Roof-top Welfare List. May 24, 1957. HKCSS File. Bishop's House Archive.
41. Minutes of Executive Committee Meeting of HKCSS. September 2, 1957. HKCSS File. Bishop's House Archive.
42. E. G. Pryor, "Review of Housing Conditions in Hong Kong," *Journal of the Royal Asiatic Society Hong Kong Branch* (1972) 12: 89–130.
43. E. Hinder to R. O. Hall. April 1935. Hong Kong Housing Society File. Bishop's House Archive.
44. Town Planning in Singapore. Not dated, but likely before 1935. Hall Family Archive.
45. W. H. Owen to R. O. Hall. Not dated, but likely before 1935. Hong Kong Housing Society File. Bishop's House Archive.
46. R. Hutcheon, *High Rise Society* (Hong Kong: Hong Kong Housing Society, 1998).
47. A. Smart, *The Shek Kip Mei Myth: Squatters, Fires, and Colonial Rule in Hong Kong 1950–1963* (Hong Kong: Hong Kong University Press, 2006), 48.
48. R. O. Hall. Lecture on Social Service. 1954. HKCSS File. Bishop's House Archive.
49. Formation of the Hong Kong Housing Society. Not dated. Hong Kong Housing Society File. Bishop's House Archive.
50. *South China* (1951): 8–9 (Housing).
51. Petition to the governor from the Social Welfare Council on November 30, 1949 that any premise under the control of the Housing Society to be excluded from the regulations of the Landlord and Tenant Ordinance of 1947. Hong Kong Housing Society File. Bishop's House Archive.
52. Annual Report of Hong Kong Welfare Council. December 1, 1947–November 30, 1948. December 1948 (Lord Mayor's Empire Air Raid Victim Fund). HKCSS File. Bishop's House Archive.
53. R. O. Hall, Notes on "Economic" Nature of Our Housing Society. May 31, 1948. Hong Kong Housing Society File. Bishop's House Archive.
54. B. Pope, "Church Missionary Society Schools," *St. John's Review* (February 1957): 29–31.
55. B. H. K. Luk, *A History of Education in Hong Kong: Report Submitted to Lord Wilson Heritage Trust*, 2000, 66. A. Sweeting, *Education in Hong Kong 1841 to 2001* (Hong Kong: Hong Kong University Press, 2004), 142.
56. All land in Hong Kong belonged to the Crown and leased to landowners with the exception of one: St. John's Cathedral.
57. R. O. Hall, Statement on the Position of the Bishop's House. March 24, 1949. Minutes of Meeting of the Standing Committee. Bishop's House Archive.
58. Copy of Indenture between the Reverend Vincent John Stanton and the Right Reverend George Lord Bishop of Victoria. November 3, 1849. Stanton House File. Bishop's House Archive.
59. Copy of Indenture between Queen Victoria and the Bishop of Victoria signed on September 5, 1851. Stanton House File. Bishop's House Archive.
60. Sir Alexander Grantham to R. O. Hall. December 10, 1948. Permission to use parts of IL-76 for various purposes. Stanton House File. Bishop's House Archive.

61. Stanton House File. Bishop's House Archive.
62. A. S. Abbott to the editor of *South China Morning Post*, June 27, 1948. Stanton House File. Bishop's House Archive.
63. S. W. P. to the editor of *South China Morning Post*, June 29, 1948. Stanton House File. Bishop's House Archive.
64. Correspondence on Stanton House, the New Hospital. HKMS 94-1-11. Hong Kong Public Records Office.
65. The Central Hospital ceased to function on September 2, 2012.
66. S. K. Loong to members of the 39th Synod of the Diocese of Hong Kong and Macao. Hall Family Archive.
67. G. She, The Duppuy Fund. Statement of Purpose and Policy. September 30, 1972. Bishop's House Archive.
68. C. Long, The Diocese of Hong Kong. 1953. Chung Chi Divinity School Archive.
69. A. Rose, *St. John's Review* (April–May 1954): 110–13 (The Reverend George She).
70. R. O. Hall to N. Hall. May 2, 1951. Hall Family Archive (George She on leave).
71. R. O. Hall to N. Hall. January 5, 1946. Hall Family Archive (Charles Harth).
72. Bishop's Secretary to C. J. Harth. HKMS 94-1-11. Hong Kong Public Records Office.
73. S. K. Loong. Kei Oi Church. Not dated. Bishop's House Archive.
74. Minutes of meeting on August 26, 1957 called by George She of friends of Bishop R. O. Hall to create a fund (Ho Ming Hua Fund) to provide for Bishop Hall's retirement. Bishop's House Archive.
75. E. C. C. Johnson to R. O. Hall. April 9, 1973; May 8, 1973; November 14, 1973. Chung Chi Divinity School Archive.
76. Minutes of Meeting of the Standing Commmittee. September 16, 1949. Bishop's House Archive (committees).
77. Minutes of Meeting of the Standing Committee. May 14, 1958. Bishop's House Archive (Joint Committee renamed Church Missionary Society Day School Council).
78. Minutes of Meeting of the Standing Committee. March 19, 1956. Bishop's House Archive (Diocesan Education Committee).
79. Minutes of Meeting of the Standing Committee. March 9, 1964. Bishop's House Archive (Chairperson of various committees).
80. Personal Communication from Canon Christopher Hall.
81. Interview of Dorothy Lee by D. M. Paton. Not dated. Chung Chi Divinity School Archive.
82. *St. John's Review* (February 1934): 34 (Lam Woo).
83. *Outpost* (April 1948): 2–4 (Political turmoil in China).
84. R. O. Hall, "The Development of Social Conscience in Modern China," in *The Christian Movement in China in a Period of National Transition* (Mysore City: Wesley Press and Publishing House, 1938), 40–42.
85. R. O. Hall. Mao Tze-Tung and Practice. Chung Chi Divinity School Archive.
86. R. O. Hall. Sermon, "The Destiny of the Chinese Church Given at the Opening of the Synod Celebrating the Centenary of the Diocese of Hong Kong on August 21, 1949," in Paton, *R. O.: The Life and Times of Bishop R. O. Hall*, 251–55.
87. Paton, *R. O.: The Life and Times of Bishop R. O. Hall*, 171–74 (Activities in 1949).

88. *South China* (1950): 9 (Nanning takeover).
89. *South China Morning Post*, February 9, 1950. Bishop Quentin Huang. "Said still in Yunnan Custody."
90. P. Wickeri, *Reconstructing Christianity in China: K. H. Ting and the Chinese Church* (New York: Orbis Books, 2007), 98.
91. Spence, *The Search for Modern China*, 524–33 (Korean War).
92. Church Missionary Society Statement. Resignation of Bishops in China. *The Times*, London. September 7, 1950. Bishop's House Archive.
93. *St. John's Review* (1947): 114–17 (New status of the bishop of Hong Kong and the diocese).
94. *Outpost* (December 1947): 2 (Creation of a new diocese of Yun-Gui). Petition from the Diocese of Kong-Yuet to the General Synod of the Chung Hua Sheng Kung Hui. July 28, 1947. Translation of the Original Chinese Document. Church Missionary Society Archive. Reel 384, Section 1, Part 18. East Asia Mission, *South China*. G1CHg01, 1937–51.
95. Minutes of Meeting of the Standing Committee. September 16, 1949. Bishop's House Archive (Dividing the Diocese of Kong-Yuet into two).
96. *St. John's Review* (May 1950): 132–35 (Consecration of Bishop Mo-Yung In).
97. In 1947, the Diocese of South China and Victoria came under the metropolitical authority of Chung Hua Sheng Kung Hui except the three English churches in Hong Kong. The name was changed to the Diocese of Kong-Yuet after the Diocese of Yun-Gui was partitioned off.
98. Letter from Bishop Mo-Yung In to the Reverend Chung Yan Laap, Secretary of the standing committee. May 13, 1951. HKMS 94-1-11. Record of Episcopate of Bishop Ronald Owen Hall, Book 2, 1949–53. Hong Kong Public Records Office.
99. R. O. Hall to H. A. Wittenbach. May 21, 1951. HKSKH History, Bishop's House Archive. Minutes of the 22nd (Emergency) Meeting of the Diocesan Standing Committees held at Mr. W. H. Young's Office. May 10, 1951. Bishop House Archive (Bishop Hall resigned from the House of Bishops, Chung Hua Sheng Kung Hui, and the Diocese of South China would be divided into two: the Diocese of Hong Kong and Macao and Diocese of Guangdong).
100. Petition to Archbishop G. Fisher by the Standing Committee of the Synod of the Diocese of Victoria. 1951. Bishop's House Archive.

Chapter 5
Shepherding His Flock in God's Beloved City
The Diocese of Hong Kong (1951–56)

> CHRIST, look upon us in this city
> And keep our sympathy and pity
> Fresh, and our faces heavenward
> LEST WE GROW HARD[1]

Despite the Korean War and the United Nations embargo that devastated its entrepôt trade, Hong Kong's economy began to find its feet again in the 1950s. The capital, skills, and technology brought by wealthy migrants, together with the cheap labor provided by refugees, helped to gradually transform Hong Kong into a city with flourishing textile and printing industries.

However, life was still very hard. The population had risen to 1.86 million by 1949 and 2.1 million by 1951. It escalated thereafter at a rate of 1 million every ten years for the next three decades, due to the influx of refugees and the postwar baby boom. Despite improvements in the economy, the Hong Kong government spent less than 15 percent of its budget on social services until after the riots of 1966 and 1967 when it was forced to question its own legitimacy, and was under pressure from both local and international agencies.[2]

It was during the first two postwar decades that ROH, with his supporters and other social reformers, contributed most in creating a safety net for the refugees, which provided not only immediate relief for young people but also skills to make a living. With his tremendous faith in God, ROH was able to utilize his gifts of ingenuity, administrative skill, and energy to rehabilitate and expand the Church and to help the city with the challenge of social reconstruction at this difficult time. He was deeply rooted in the Anglican Christian Socialist tradition[3] and successfully adapted it to the situation in Hong Kong. While the Roman Catholic Church and many other agencies also participated in the rebuilding of Hong Kong, as bishop of Hong Kong's Anglican Church, ROH was well placed to obtain the government's attention for his projects.

Spiritual Tasks

Cultivating Clergy

ROH strongly believed that the Chinese clergy could spread the gospel much more effectively than any missionary and saw the training of Chinese clergy as an essential part of his ministry. Over the years, he prepared a number of young clergy for the local Chinese churches and even for ministry overseas, but after 1951 he could no longer send ordinands to be trained in Canton Union Theological College, and Ming Hua College at that time was not training clergy.

As the Church expanded, ROH dealt with the shortage of clergy in two ways. First, he sought out talent in other spheres. He ordained not only full-time clergy but also auxiliary priests who were headmasters of schools or fully employed in other professions: for example, James C. L. Wong, a full-time engineer, and George She, a barrister and a magistrate. ROH ordained 13 men as auxiliary priests under a special canon of the Chinese Church through 1959. They were available for service in any parish or school or other institution to perform the duties of a priest, but from time to time they might be appointed to temporary charge of a parish.[4] Until then, the only non-stipendiary clergy in the worldwide Anglican Communion had been teachers. Ordaining clergy who were in other secular employment was a pioneering development.

Second, he established the Hong Kong Union Theological College as a postgraduate institution in September 1955, admitting university graduates as "external students" of the University of Hong Kong. As more people in Hong Kong became better educated and more sophisticated, it was necessary to have some clergy with a broader education, trained to a higher academic level. He invited other churches to join, but only the American Methodist Church, the Church of Christ, and the YMCA agreed to participate. Because there were so few students each year it was not economical to build a seminary to accommodate them. St. John's College, an Anglican residential hall at the university was founded that year, and it provided the ideal arrangement because it could accommodate several theology students and its chapel was perfect for worship. The Council of the Union Theological College was formed with Canon Alaric Rose as the chair of the faculty. Members included representatives from the participating denominations.[5] The Reverend R. Trueman became the first principal of Hong Kong Union Theological College, and Canon Ernest Martin the first chaplain of the college.[6]

ROH had clear rankings for the essentials of a priest's life, which, in his view, began in that quiet inner place of the soul. Prayer came first and preaching was last in the following order: (1) the pastor's knees (prayer); (2) the pastor's feet (visiting); (3) the pastor's heart (love); and (4) the pastor's voice (preaching).[7] He often wrote letters to his clergy when he was on leave. In one of his pastoral letters he underlined what was important for a priest to strive to do: (1) to love passionately the souls that are in your care and never let them go; (2) to commit absolutely and to obey as a soldier; (3) to have endurance and not be discouraged; (4) to strip off pride and envy; (5) to accept things and people as they are; (6) to discipline the tongue; (7) to discipline oneself to meditate and to pray; and (8) to think of the mystery of the universal and the particular.[8]

ROH demanded high moral standards from his clergy and the teachers working in Anglican schools, especially from the Europeans. He believed that the Europeans, even though they were not clergy, should set an example for the local people. He strongly believed in the marital vow: "Those whom God hath joined together let no man put asunder." Once one was married, marriage had the first call,[9] and one should do all one could to work out the difficulties. It was the cross that one had to bear. Wasn't that true in his own case?

There were instances when he asked for the resignation of individuals because of problems with their marriage even though the problems were not of their own making. Donald Brittain, an excellent geography teacher, had not had his contract renewed from the Diocesan Boys' School because his wife had left him and he remarried. Even George She, by then headmaster of the school, was unable to persuade ROH to change his mind.[10] On another occasion he wrote directly, without informing the headmaster, to the director of education asking him to find a post in a government school for a teacher in an Anglican school who had gone through a divorce.[11]

In 1963, he asked for the resignation of Barry Till, dean of St. John's Cathedral, when he heard about the Tills' marital difficulties. ROH's decision was final. Even though Till was not at fault,[12] like others in similar situations, Till was not invited to offer explanations and was no doubt deeply hurt.[13] Naturally some clergy were dismayed by Till's resignation.[14] It is tempting to speculate that ROH's own marital situation might have influenced such decisions. He may have later regretted some of these decisions, especially in the case of Till, whom he did not help to find an alternative appointment. In one case, he annulled the marriage of another priest and allowed him to remarry after his wife had left him twice for someone else.[15]

ROH had a genuine personal interest in each of his clergy. At the same time, all clergy loved and respected him and felt that they could talk to him about their personal problems. The Reverend Charles Long of the American Episcopal Church, who spent two years (1954–56) in Hong Kong, became a close friend. ROH asked Long, who spoke Mandarin, to be one of the clergy in the Mandarin-speaking Church of the Good Shepherd, opened in 1955. Long described the lively tone and inclusive atmosphere of the weekly celebrations that knitted the diocese into a community:[16]

> The heart of life of this Diocese is a weekly corporate celebration of the Holy Communion. Every Thursday morning all of the clergy gather with the Bishop for a celebration of the Eucharist, in Cantonese, at the Cathedral. This is followed by the gay and warm fellowship of breakfast together at the Cathedral Hall. About 9 o'clock the Bishop convenes an informal meeting of all the parochial clergy where every sort of pastoral and Diocesan problem is discussed with complete freedom by all concerned. There is amazing variety of opinion to be expressed. The Chinese clergy here are unusually articulate. The young ones are not afraid to express

themselves before the venerable archdeacons. There are CMS [Church Missionary Society], SPG [Society for the Propagation of the Gospel], and American missionary points of view. No one hesitates even to disagree with the Bishop, who is quite capable of defending his point of view! . . . One cannot exaggerate the value of these Thursday mornings for the sense of unity in the Diocese and for the vitality of ministry found among its clergy. It has meant more than I can say for my own spiritual life since my arrival.

Every Thursday morning ROH welcomed all clergy to the cathedral for morning prayers and Holy Communion, and then opened up a meeting to discuss problems in the diocese. During these sessions, ROH often talked about the collect, epistle, or gospel of the week, and at times the significance of the Holy Sacraments. He wondered whether these talks were helpful and was absolutely thrilled when "Pui Suk," Canon Edward Lee, suddenly said one day, "By the way, I am so glad you come talking to us on Thursday mornings. It makes such a difference." He related gladly to Nora, "I gauged rightly from the way they listened and the kind of togetherness at breakfast afterward that my Thursday morning talks had been God-guided."[17]

During the meetings, clergy would not hesitate to object to ROH's ideas when they thought they had better ones. ROH listened carefully and was happy to accept their point of view when it was clearly valid. Up to the late 1950s, he appeared to have governed the Church in a democratic manner. After Thursday meetings the clergy usually had lunch together and there was a strong *esprit de corps*. Some of the retired clergy still relish the memories of those years.[18] The Thursday morning clergy meetings continue today, another example of ROH's lasting legacy.

ROH followed the Chinese tradition of honoring the old. He gave work to the able and honor to the senior. The archdeacons and the canons he appointed were mostly senior clergy, who had the titles in name, and their work was mostly done for them by younger and able clergy.[19]

Expanding the Church

Six new churches were founded from 1949 to 1956 as a result of the Forward Movement and the hard work of "Pui Suk," the canon missioner, and other clergy: St. Matthew's in Hollywood Road, in an old house; St. James' in Wan Chai, and St. Thomas' in Shum Shui Po, both in Nissen huts initially; St. Luke's in Kennedy Town; St. Joseph's in Kam Tin; and the Church of the Good Shepherd, for the Mandarin-speaking population (Appendix 4, Table A4.1). These churches were in temporary quarters when they were first inaugurated, and proper church buildings were erected as funds became available.

The Mandarin-speaking population made use of Christ Church for their services after the war. Their own church was built and consecrated by ROH as the Church of Good Shepherd, Muk Oi Tong in Chinese, on November 23, 1955. ROH explained that the name "Muk Oi" (Shepherd's Love) was taken from the Chinese characters carved in a stone tablet above an old magistrate's *yamen*[20] in Shensi (now Shaanxi) province. ROH emphasized once again that Christ is not a foreign import to China but a spiritual ancestor, part of the very ground of being in China:

> Before Christ was known to China but not before Our Lord Jesus Christ Himself was in China, for Christ is He by whom all things were made and in whom all people live and move and have their being.[21]

Promoting Social Justice

"Blessed Are the Poor"

ROH's deep concern for ordinary workers was reflected in his tireless work to improve their lives: helping them fight for higher wages, better working conditions, and affordable housing. He also promoted the establishment of workers' children's schools.

ROH was called the "Pink or Red Bishop" less because of sympathy with Communist China than for his involvement in negotiations for workers' wage increases and strikes in the immediate postwar period, when the soaring cost of living and low wages led to many bitter labor disputes.[22] One that was particularly disruptive began in 1949 after a tramway company failed to respond to the workers' demand for a wage increase. The strike that took place was provoked by Guangdong authorities. In attempts to head off the strike, ROH spent a great deal of time meeting with union representatives, company people and lawyers—but without success.

On January 30, 1950, when the police attempted to break up a meeting of over 1,000 strikers and supporters outside the tramway union building, the crisis boiled over. More than 100 were injured, and more than 10 were arrested and deported from Hong Kong. Eventually, the government used emergency regulations to force the workers back to work and the tramway company formally withdrew its recognition of the union. ROH criticized the government for persistently refusing to take action to establish a mechanism for negotiation, saying that it was both unjust and unwise to use emergency regulations to force the workers back to work. If there was an emergency, the government should have acted earlier, before feelings became too bitter and acrimonious.[23]

ROH's special concern for workers led him to help the union leaders form the Workers' Education Advancement Society to provide primary education to their children. With George She's assistance, the trade unions started more than a dozen small schools in different parts of Hong Kong and Kowloon.

ROH and the governor, Sir Alexander Grantham, had a heated dispute in 1949 over the workers' children's schools. The tiny schools, often consisting of only one or two classes, operated in rented space. The premises and even the teachers were often substandard. But because they were run by trade unions, the government suspected that the unions were spreading the seed of communism among the young,[24] and the schools came under very close surveillance by the Special Bureau of the Education Department, an office set up especially to monitor communism-related activity. In the summer of 1949, the schools were ordered to be closed.

The two men had a meeting wherein His Excellency declared that the closure was due to the presence of communist activities in the schools as well as the poor quality of supervision. Grantham insisted that ROH was creating embarrassment for the government, but ROH maintained that the poor condition of the schools was entirely due to the unwillingness of the Education Department to give subsidies to these schools. Arguing that closure of the schools would be unreasonable and repressive, based on prejudice and not on facts, ROH further warned that school closure would be the quickest way of making communists out of the students.[25] In the end they compromised. The smaller schools were closed and the children sent to government schools, but five larger ones reopened after reregistration.[26] These schools later received subsidies and their standards improved.

In 1951, after numerous meetings chaired by ROH involving intense negotiations between the workers and the members of the Education Department, land was finally granted for a new school to be built for workers' children on Nairn Road.[27] In one of his letters to Nora, ROH told of an incident that almost sabotaged any achievement: "Just as we had won the first round to get a new school for them, the school inspector found essays of some of the children saying the new school is to defeat the plans of the imperialists . . . I am afraid it may wreck the whole bag of tricks."[28]

ROH's deep concern for ordinary workers was connected to his Christian beliefs. For ROH, the quality of obedience that manual laborers must show echoed the supreme obedience of Our Lord, who, "though he was son learned obedience" in the manual labor of a carpenter's shop, he lived and died by that obedience, saying "My Father worketh hitherto and I work." In one of his sermons he quoted Simone Weil: "the submission to the daily round of manual labor is an expression of humility with great spiritual worth."[29] More importantly, however, were his Christian beliefs in social justice for workers as well as for economically disadvantaged people, and his embrace of social theology of F. D. Maurice to W. Temple.

Founding Social Welfare Institutions

As part of his ministry of love-in-action, ROH founded several social welfare institutions to look after the young, orphans, and children from economically disadvantaged families, to train them to make a living (Appendix 4, Table A4.2).

The Juvenile Care Centre, St. James' Settlement, and Holy Carpenter Church, Hostel and Youth Centre are discussed below to illustrate how he managed to build up these institutions at a time when funds and resources were scarce.

ROH had deep concerns about the ineffective and inhumane system for managing juveniles, and he worked to establish the Juvenile Care Centre in 1949. After the war, Juvenile Court was inundated by large numbers of juveniles each day. Of the 54,000 cases before the court in 1952, very few were involved in actual crime. These juveniles could be divided into two categories: hawkers without a license, and beggars. Since it was illegal to hawk without a license, the police had to arrest the hawkers, most of whom were recurrent offenders, some having been taken in as many as ten times. Those who were apprehended for begging might face deportation—a very serious penalty. Once deported, however, most of them found their way back to the colony.[30] In 1949, ROH formed the Juvenile Care Center Committee, employing two people to interview the juveniles in the Magistrate's Court to decide whether the boys would be sent to the Boys' Camp in Stanley for training in a trade, or to the Boys' and Girls' Clubs Association for free schooling, or for employment by firms in the colony.[31] A temporary shelter was needed to house these juveniles before placement, but the application to build the shelter was delayed for more than one year because of lack of land, as residents and shops did not wish to have a troublesome group of children in the neighborhood. With special permission from the governor, ROH had the Juvenile Care Centre built next to the Bishop's House.[32] The center had a schoolroom, a club, and accommodations where boys could temporarily be kept pending placement. More importantly

Figure 5.1 St. James' Settlement started in 1949, in Pak Tai Miu, Stone Nullah Lane (Bishop's House Archive)

for ROH, this center gave theology students an apprenticeship in the workings of social justice.

Of the many welfare institutions in Hong Kong, St. James' Settlement stands out in its breadth of activities. The story of its early development and evolution illustrates the spirit in which it serves Wan Chai and is worth recounting here. After the war, there were many families in Wan Chai who lived in very crowded tenements, bed spaces, or cubicles, and whose total income was less than $100 per month.[33] They could not afford to send their children to school. ROH wanted to bridge the wealthy community of St. John's Cathedral with Wan Chai by setting up a settlement.[34] Because of lack of space in crowded Wan Chai, ROH started the settlement first in a Chinese temple, Pak Tai Miu, on Stone Nullah Lane in 1949.

The settlement initially ran clubs similar to those of Boys' and Girls' Clubs Association. ROH called the settlement "St. James' Settlement," for just as James was the brother of John, St. James' Settlement was an outpost of St. John's Cathedral.[35] The chief aim of the project was to help people in Wan Chai face their many problems, regain a feeling of usefulness, develop a healthy community spirit, and help themselves and each other improve their conditions.

ROH asked one of his students from Lingnan University in Guangzhou, the young and enthusiastic Miss Lee Hei Man, to run a club for children who had trouble with the law but had been given another chance by the judge of Juvenile Court to learn reading and writing, and to enjoy games and singing.[36]

Figure 5.2 St. James' Settlement, Nissen hut, 98A Kennedy Road (1950s) (Bishop's House Archive)

When ROH was granted a piece of land at the head of Stone Nullah Lane on the south side of Kennedy Road, he erected a Nissen hut to be used for children's clubs, adult education, Sunday school, and church worship with a generous gift of $10,000 from St. John's Cathedral. It was opened on October 4, 1951. The Nissen hut had a large hall with two tiny rooms for storage and an office at one end. At the other end was a partition separating two rooms: the home of the Reverend James and Mrs. Pun. ROH insisted that the warden should live in the community, to be readily accessible to the people and to demonstrate Christian love.[37]

Gradually, more programs were added and courses were offered in printing, mechanics, carpentry, and car maintenance for young men, and sewing and embroidery for young women. A mothers' club was organized to teach mothers the basics of nutrition, hygiene, home economics, and infant care. The first medical clinic was opened in the settlement in January 1952, run by volunteer nurses from different hospitals, and a clinic that provided inexpensive dental treatment followed in 1956.[38] The Nissen hut soon became too congested to accommodate more programs or staff. Plans were made for a permanent settlement in a complex consisting of a workshop, a four-story building to house clinics, clubrooms, and warden's quarters, a church with a hall, and a five-story primary school. Today, St. James' Settlement, a 14-story multipurpose community center on the same site, opened in 1987, offers a wide variety of services to children, young people, adults, elderly people, families, and people with disabilities, with a staff of 1,000 from across the region.

St. James' Settlement gives us some insight into the policies and principles of ROH. First, he respected other religions in establishing the program in Pak Tai Miu, a Chinese temple. Most Christian leaders would have shrunk from the idea of having anything to do with a Chinese temple, which they would have viewed as a place for worshipping idols. Second, ROH used tested principles that had been shown to work, insisting that the wardens such as the Reverend James Pun and the Reverend Denham Crary must live in the settlement as residents of Wan Chai, to be close to the people they served. Third, when there was no funding, he would start a project on a small scale as a pilot. When it worked well, funds for then-justified expansion would become available through donations. Last, ROH instilled the idea that the giving and helping practiced at St. James' Settlement was not charity but a cooperative enterprise between prosperous citizens and less fortunate ones, with the goal of making a better life for members of both groups.

The Holy Carpenter Church and Hostel, a favorite project of ROH, was initially conceived as a young workers' center primarily to serve young people who were leaving St. Christopher's Home and going into the city to work. When they lost employment in the city, they could go to this hostel instead of returning to St. Christopher's Home.[39]

ROH bought a triangular piece of land, 7,600 square feet in size, situated at Dyer Avenue, Hung Hom, with this project in mind.[40] Located in one of the then main industrial areas of Kowloon, close to the docks, cement works, power station, and numerous factories, this piece of land was encircled by a tangle of narrow twisting streets with small shops, squatter shacks, and a congested resettlement area. In 1954, the cost of $30,400 for the land alone exhausted more than half the funds that ROH had earmarked for this project.[41] With inadequate funds to properly complete construction of a hostel and a church, ROH decided to build them as cheaply as he could, in stages.

Before the hostel could be built, a small hill on the lot would first have to be leveled. ROH came up with a marvelous "dual purpose" idea: to give this work to the unemployed boys from St. Christopher's home. On October 12, 1954, 14 boys from the home, along with the Reverend Denham Crary, began to level the hill.[42] Francis Yip, then an ordinand, drove a truck to remove the soil from the site. Slowly they leveled one section of the hill after another. After years of patient toil, the Holy Carpenter Church and Hostel was finally completed and dedicated on February 16, 1958.[43]

In the beginning, the hostel housed boys from St. Christopher's Home as well as those who had served terms in reformatories or prisons, functioning as a halfway house where these young men were trained in practical skills so that they could become productive members of society. It was occupied entirely by young workers just two years later. When the Reverend Francis Yip became vicar of Holy Carpenter Church and Hostel, different programs emerged to serve the needs not only of the young workers in the hostel, but also of other community members. These programs included a saving scheme for marriage, a day nursery, a children's center, and a medical clinic, and were geared to the changing needs of workers in different life stages. The Holy Carpenter Practical Training Centre was also built to train boys and girls in one of five trades: refrigeration and air-conditioning, automobile repair, metalwork, and wood work for boys, and a combined course of sewing, tailoring, and embroidery for girls.

ROH was very involved with the development of the Holy Carpenter Church and Hostel in its early stages. He chaired the monthly executive committee meetings and attended weekly evening work sessions on Thursdays, sitting and listening to discussions and sharing evening snacks with the staff before going home. The staff was greatly inspired by his presence.[44]

As Hong Kong gradually lost its industries to southern China and turned itself into a financial and service center, some of the services provided by the Holy Carpenter complex became obsolete. At present, the complex no longer has a practical training center, but accommodates a primary school, a secondary school, a guesthouse, and a community center.

Housing Low-Income Families

When refugees streamed into Hong Kong during the late 1940s and early 1950s, tenement housing was already overcrowded. This led to settlements of makeshift squatter huts sprouting on the hillsides. The number of squatters reached about 300,000 in clusters in different parts of Kowloon and Hong Kong Island by the end of 1949.[45]

The government appeared to be doing little about housing during the immediate postwar period for several reasons: its traditional *laissez-faire* political-economic philosophy and policy; the hope that the refugees would return to China after the political situation improved; its unwillingness to spend its limited resources on becoming the landlord of economically disadvantaged people; the immensity of the problem and the inability to find the most economical and efficient way of providing housing for such a huge population of refugees.[46]

The Hong Kong Housing Society, established by ROH in 1948, was incorporated in 1951. Although ROH chaired the executive committee of the Housing Society in the beginning, he passed this role to Mr. J. Finnie (manager of Taikoo Dockyard) soon after its incorporation.[47] Father T. F. Ryan, SJ, and Colonel J. D. Clague acted as the successive chairpersons. ROH continued to serve on the executive committee and helped push the projects ahead after several initial setbacks.

In 1950 the Housing Society had the opportunity to renovate a group of 56 run-down 20-year-old cottages in Ma Tau Chung, Kowloon, and to build an additional 128 cottages. The society was able to fix the rents at $30 per month for each cottage, making them affordable for low income families.[48] Although the project got the Housing Society going, it proved a waste of land resources. From then on the Housing Society built only high-rises, to provide reasonable returns on the high cost of land.

The second project, Sheung Li Uk Estate in Sham Shui Po, took four years to realize. In 1952, after the government offered a 40-year low-interest loan, the Housing Society was able to build units that were relatively small but that satisfied the government minimal standards for housing at 35 square feet per person. Most of the units had one living room and one bedroom, an individual kitchen area, a shower, and an Asian type of toilet. When the 270 units became available, 5,000 applications were received.[49] As no public housing like this had existed in Hong Kong before, the first lucky tenants looked on the estate with awe. Providing cheap housing for the $400-a-month worker and his family,[50] the rent for a four-person flat was $52 and for a six-person flat $69. The flat with rent equivalent to less than one-fifth of total family income seemed heaven-sent.

ROH ensured that the management of the estates followed Octavia Hill's principle. The early managers for the Housing Society, who came from England, trained local managers. They dealt firmly with subletting, late-night mahjong playing, late rent-paying, and dirty families. Tenants came to respect the staff, who were always ready to help and offer advice when asked. Tenants almost never fell behind in their rent payments.[51]

On Christmas Day 1953, a fire broke out in the Shek Kip Mei squatter area, burning it to the ground, making more than 50,000 people homeless overnight. This forced the government to tackle the problem of the squatters on a large scale.[52] Finding that it had to spend about $50,000 each day on emergency relief, the government had no option but to act quickly to rehouse the victims as soon as possible. In 1954, it created the Resettlement Department to resettle the squatters, using a design submitted by the Housing Society but rejected by the government to build the resettlement estate blocks, because the design would only give 24 square feet floor area per adult, below the minimum standard of 35 square feet.[53]

The Housing Society focused on the development of rental estates, providing more than 11,000 units for low-income families by 1970, housing about 124,890 people in different parts of Hong Kong (Appendix 4, Table A4.3). Although it contributed only a small proportion of public housing—5.6 percent of total public housing in 1972, it demonstrated that affordable housing was feasible.[54] In 1972 when the Hong Kong Housing Authority started its own low-cost housing project, it followed Housing Society's well-tried and successful methods.

In the resettlement and low-cost housing estates, ROH made sure that there would be close cooperation with the Social Welfare Office and the Family Welfare Society, to provide help when needed. He worked with the Education Department to have primary schools established within the estate or nearby (see below) and, whenever possible, served undernourished schoolchildren one nutritious meal each school day. The social workers organized activities in the clubs on the rooftops for children and youth, so that they would have a place to go rather than roaming the streets.

The public housing program in Hong Kong has contributed to Hong Kong's economic success by reducing pressure for wage increases, resulting in lower labor costs and competitively priced goods. It had a considerable effect on the redistribution of income. By establishing new towns in more remote sites in the New Territories, the public housing program generated jobs for many workers and at the same time cleared the slums and improved the living environment. For the first time, Hong Kong people developed a sense of dignity and pride and belonging to their city.[55]

Establishing Educational Facilities

The rapid increase in the young population posed an enormous problem in the realm of education. Since most refugees struggled desperately to make a meager living, educating their children was beyond their means. Because the economy was further reduced by the United Nations embargo as a result of the Korean War, the government did not see its way to opening more school placements, but once the economy improved, the government began to spend more on education.[56]

In 1951, D. J. S. Crozier, a member of the congregation of St. John's Cathedral, became the director of education,[57] and he began to implement the highly successful Seven-Year Plan (1954–61) for primary education expansion. At the end of seven years the total increase in the number of primary school places reached 313,000, exceeding the original target by 131,000.[58] Many schools were built during this period, almost at a rate of one every two-and-a-half weeks. In addition to the massive building program, each school operated two (morning and afternoon) or three (morning, afternoon, and evening) consecutive sessions each school day, with 45 children per classroom, per session.

Under ROH's direction, Hong Kong Sheng Kung Hui contributed to the expansion of primary education by providing many primary school places. From 1949 to 1956, five new primary schools were built and two of the old Church Missionary Society schools were rebuilt to accommodate more students (Appendix 4, Table A4.4), all following the rules of operation of the Education Department.

The government did not encourage expansion of secondary education in the 1950s because education beyond primary schools was not necessary for most of the labor-intensive industries in Hong Kong.[59] As a result, while all the established Hong Kong Sheng Kung Hui secondary schools were reopened soon after the war, only one new secondary school, St. Mark's School, was founded, as St. Paul's P.M. English School in Glenealy. In 1953, it became independent of St. Paul's Coeducational College and had its own school committee chaired by ROH.

ROH had always wanted to provide students of higher learning during critical times in their lives in overcrowded Hong Kong with space for reading, for privacy, and for interaction with other students and tutors in a community of minds and personalities. He had also hoped to produce lay Christian leaders for the community.

St. John's Hall, the forerunner of St. John's College, was founded in 1911, by the Church Missionary Society; it was the only hall ready for occupancy when the University of Hong Kong opened, with room for 36 out of the first 71 male undergraduates. The idea of a college arose when George She became warden of St. John's Hall in 1938. He identified the hill promontory above the current University Sports Ground on Pok Fu Lam Road an ideal site to build a larger hall, but then World War II broke out.

After the war neither the Church Missionary Society nor the Church had funds for rebuilding the damaged St. John's Hall or for purchasing a site to

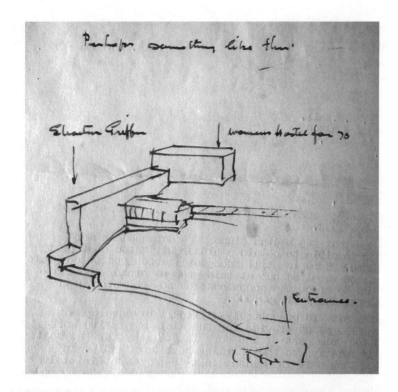

Figures 5.3 (Upper) ROH's sketch of layout of St. John's College (Bishop's House Archive) and (lower) St. John's College in 1955 (*St. John's Review* [October 1966]: 220)

build a new one. Fortunately, the promontory that had captured George She's attention was included in a general university reservation; hence, St. John's College, when it was built, became a subtenant of the University of Hong Kong. ROH and George She worked hard to raise funds from several sources, and when Mr. George Marden agreed to help by guaranteeing any overdraft up to $500,000, the building of the first phase of St. John's College could begin.[60]

ROH would have preferred to build a college quadrangle like the ones in Cambridge and Oxford, but land was at such a premium and site formation on a hill so expensive that it was only sensible to have high-rise buildings. During the design of the building ROH worked very closely with the architect and even determined details such as the number of rooms and washrooms that would be necessary for students and service staff. He frequently visited the site during construction and enjoyed the magnificent view from the college, especially the beautiful sunset. He called it the "promised land."

He invited the Reverend Eric Kvan to be the first master and members of different faculties of the university to be fellows of the College. As bishop, he became the president of the board of governors. The management of the college was to be independent of the board of governors and the court of the university. On October 14, 1955, Sir Kenneth Grubb, the president of Church Missionary Society, with Sir Alexander Grantham presiding, officially opened St. John's College.[61]

St. John's College embraced two novel concepts. It was the first coeducational residence in Hong Kong University, and the only residence where teaching was also carried out (therefore a college rather than a hall). In the late 1950s and throughout 1960, St. John's College was used for training theology students at the postgraduate level.[62] The first phase of St. John's College could accommodate only about 120 students. No sooner had the first phase been completed than ROH began to plan the building of the second phase. St. John's College is now gracefully arranged in a quadrangle through the addition of buildings in different phases on the hill above the University Sports Ground.

Up to 1963, Hong Kong had only one higher education institution, the University of Hong Kong that used English as the language for instruction. It had remained small since its establishment; when it celebrated its 50th anniversary in 1961, it had only 1,800 students. Secondary education in Anglo-Chinese schools in Hong Kong had been preparing students for higher education at the University of Hong Kong or universities in other parts of the Commonwealth or the United States. Before 1948, the Chinese middle schools in Hong Kong had prepared students for universities in China and there was no perceived demand for Hong Kong to provide its own system of university education in the Chinese language.[63] Due to political events in China, many graduates from Chinese middle schools were unable to further their education after high school. Despite its reluctance to expand tertiary education in the 1950s, the government approved the establishment of a number of private postsecondary colleges, including Chung Chi College to offer courses in Chinese.

Although the idea of establishing a Christian Chinese college did not come from ROH,[64] he played a crucial role in the establishment of Chung Chi College; providing leadership, negotiating with the Education Department or the governor, and planning the new buildings for the college. The name of the college, Chung Chi, means "Worship Christ," representing the essentially Christian character of the college.[65] In the beginning, classes were conducted in St. Paul's Coeducational College and St. John's Cathedral. At that time, Chung Chi was supported by donations from the United Board of Christian Colleges in China and some local Chinese. It did not confer degrees, but did issue a diploma upon graduation.

In 1953, the enrolment increased to 350, about one-third that of the University of Hong Kong. To accommodate increasing numbers of students, the college rented a three-story building on Caine Road, Hong Kong, for teaching and for administration. In addition, when the Bishop Hoare Memorial Building in Glenealy was completed, ROH leased it to the college.

From the beginning, the planning committee of Chung Chi College had decided that the new college campus should be located in the New Territories. During the latter part of 1952, a party consisting of ROH and other founding members of the college made several exploratory trips to find a suitable location. They rode on a railway truck provided by the railway administration and were accompanied by an officer from the Land Office to advise the party on questions of landownership, whether the place was privately owned or Crown land.[66]

The group visited many sites, but found only three they considered suitable. One of these was Ma Liu Shui, where green hills enfolded a vast bay, and fishers spread their nets in the blue depths, a spectacle of serenity and gentleness. It was an ideal spot for a college with buildings on the two sides of the valley facing the immense bay beyond. ROH saw the valley "as the cupped hands of Christ, and a meeting place of the sea and rail and road linking the future College by highways of the sea with the Americas, and with all Asia; and bound by the steel bands of the railway to China and on beyond China to Russia and all Europe."[67]

ROH, as chairperson of the planning committee, took great pleasure in sketching designs for the layout of the buildings on this delightful campus. Site formation and construction of five main buildings—administrative, classroom, science, library, and dining hall—began in the spring of 1956. The governor, Sir Alexander Grantham, helped every step of the way, asking various government departments to give the college quick service so that official red tape could be bypassed. The construction of Chung Chi College brought the two old foes together, working toward a common goal.

Only six months from the beginning of construction, in November 1956, the opening of the college took everyone by surprise. When he opened the college, Sir Alexander was unknowingly laying the foundations for the Chinese University of Hong Kong, which would later be spread over 276 acres of the beautiful hills of Ma Liu Shui. Chung Chi College became one of the three founding colleges of the Chinese University of Hong Kong. It fulfilled ROH's dream, at long last, of using the Chinese language as the medium of instruction, affirming the value of their Chinese heritage for coming generations.[68]

Daily Life for ROH

A Typical Hectic Day

ROH's creativity and productivity during this period was achieved through the sacrifice of family life. Typically, ROH was alone, toiling for long hours each day on various projects in new churches, social service, housing, and education. He was always on the lookout for the needs of the community, searching for ways of solving them. He had "many irons in the fire" at any time, as commented by his colleagues in Newcastle.[69]

Although the breathless, rather cryptic style of his writing can be a little hard to decipher, the following letter to Christopher on October 27, 1954 can provide the flavor of ROH's typical hectic work day.[70] In this one day he dealt with pastoral activities, social welfare work at St. James Settlement, the building of St. John's College, entertaining an important official in Hong Kong, teaching at Chung Chi College, and a four- or five-hour meeting with the Hong Kong Tramway Union workers to avoid a strike. These were followed by other activities such as attending a Diocesan Boys' School committee meeting and a business dinner that lasted well into the evening. This daily slogging over all the activities must have required iron discipline. Note how intertwined are the threads of prayer, ordinary relationships and obligations, social justice, politics, and daily administration:

> My dear C,
>
> ... I've just thought back today has been typical and yet perhaps rather more than average in variety. Denham [Denham Crary] soon after breakfast—for £200—to buy an old truck—for his unemployed boys to get on pulling down the earth hill on which the Holy Carpenter Church is to be built (Minneapolis Pan-Anglican money). Along in car to see Godson Philip Hague [son of Eric Hague, CMS missionary], less than 1 year—been nastily ill—just knelt and prayed our Lord to heal his child and ours—(better news tonight).
>
> Met Geoffrey Speak [Headmaster of St. Paul's Boys' College]—had heard this morning his father died on Sunday—(had been expecting and hoping for this—took ill after GS [Geoffrey Speak] left as N's [Nora's] father did after I first left for China).
>
> Onto the promised land first—where at last St John's College is beginning & discuss where Chapel and South Wing is to go—incredibly lovely day and view.

Back to find N's AL [air letter] and get through it before going down to St. James' Settlement where Li Hea Man [Warden of St. James Settlement] and James Pun [Chaplain of St. James' Settlement] are finding cooperation difficult—*both* able independent. Fortunately Li Hei Man—no bigger than this fountain pen though James Pun is like a great bear—had a proposal which I think pleased James and may improve things.

Back to lunch with KC [Yeo] and Florence Yeo [wife] (He is the first Chinese Head of Medical Department—Son—doing Medicine with LEHW [Sir Lionel Whitby—school contemporary, then Master of Downing College Cambridge]. George She had written that Freddie [Temple] had hurt them—so I just had them in—said nothing—but hoped it might heal.

Then an hour in Chung Chi on Plato A:B=C:D=AD:CD on the line of Knowledge and Opinion. I started with the Cave last June and am working back. Forgot before lunch 10 min on phone Frank King US lecturer in Economics + Churchman has got really into the whole strike question and finds himself on the management side—HK Tramways—so I am going to dine with him on Saturday night to hear about it.

I also have a draft addition of the Trades Union Ordinance by [Brook] Bernacchi [a liberal minded lawyer who was responsible for the Stanley Boys' Camp, and a fellow goat keeper]—giving government power to intervene. 4–5 hr a heart breaking session with the workers because I cannot see what I can do because it's all bedevilled with the communist issue: though I have written to Anthony Greenwood—Secretary of Christian Group in Labor MPs to get some questions asked.

Then DBS [Diocesan Boys' School] Council—new primary school (had plan for new St Peter's primary school—almost on stilts just before I left). Mary G. [Goodban's wife] had gallbladder out today—so Gerald [Gerald Goodban—Headmaster of DBS] who hadn't yet seen her was a bit piano. (rang up at 9:30 pm. She is all right.)

Back to sign 35 certificates for St. Mark's Prize Giving and then CMS [Church Missionary Society] missionaries executive supper and business— very little and rather bothersome—for poor Eric Hague acting for Miss Pope [Miss Beatrice Pope, CMS missionary, interned during the war]—is the world's worst meddler in others' affairs—bestest of intentions—of course— but I felt *some* hostility all round tonight—except from one bright bosom friend who is nearly as bad—And so back to Shatin to blow it all away and alas tomorrow has mostly had to go also—

Do you think I am a priest or a Christian company promoter?

My love, R.

As most of the educational, housing, and social activities required funds and raising of said funds, it is no wonder he asked the half-humorous question "Do you think I am a priest or a Christian company promoter?" At times, fundraising became almost a way of life for ROH. Despite his many successful fundraising projects, petitioning for money clearly taxed him, a common challenge facing the supposedly privileged nongovernmental organizations those days. In 1951, he wrote to Nora, "To-day is a begging day . . . to ask these Malayan HKU [Hong Kong University] boys to sign their names for a gift for the new St. John's Hall [St. John's College][71] God bless it!" Adding later, "it's been a hard day begging money and we are still under $20,000." He was hoping for $50,000 for one day of "begging" in 1951![72]

Missing Nora

Despite being constantly busy, ROH missed Nora both physically and spiritually. The frequency, consistency, and tenderness of these letters speak loudly of his intense devotion to her even after three decades of marriage. He claimed to have remained "idiotically" in love with her and wrote poetically of this love: "The one thing that stands out like a deep wild song in my heart—like wild bells ringing madly and deep bells tolling quietly—is my Love loves me, loves me so much that it hurts her. For hurt and pain are an essential part of all time love—for God is Love and that crucifix by the road side which spoke God's picture of Himself of His love for us."[73] It is clear that the love he felt was inseparable from pain.

Wanting to share his life with her while they were apart, he wrote several times during the day. Whenever he had a free moment, his thoughts would turn to her. This letter of August 14, 1946 shows how she was, for him, at times a kind of spiritualized image, with whom he could have an intimate, imaginary dialogue:

> Friday midnight. And a lovely rain coming down. We still need it. Newly planted sweet potatoes will be revelling in it. I'm badly prepared for tomorrow. Come and lie on the bed and while you sleep, I'll prepare and find out how God want me to say it [talk].
>
> Saturday 5:45 a.m. And I didn't get very far. Come and have another 'go' now. It's on the pastor's heart this morning. . . .
>
> 8:00 a.m. I was a bit unhappy that I again missed Church this morning working at the 10 am talk. But now I feel that it was what God wanted for a lot of the old material I had has come back. I've got a main idea and which I think will get across what I wanted to say. It is so important, my dear one—for surely helping Church workers to be better Church workers is the most important thing I can do.
>
> 9:00 a.m. Now we must away love, my darling of the world—come with me . . . I've had a vision that it's your love for me that Christ uses to take away my sin.
>
> 3:45 p.m. They've sent down to come to tea. Beloved of my life and I'd been in the garden to see what had been done: they can wait a bit. I'm just stopping to kiss you and you just wouldn't let go—you wanted to keep me here. I long to have tea on a tray but dare not ask it, lest it hurt them.

> It is nearly 4:30 p.m. now. I have been talking to Fahwong [gardener] about where to plant the Michaelmas daisy . . . Sermon for tomorrow now darling. I'm going to try and write it out.
> Sunday 12:30 a.m. Beloved and I think I've got it clear and down in full notes[74]

He wrote to Nora as though she were at his side. When Nora struggled to write as he did, he was absolutely delighted: "Your letter showed how you wanted me: and the lovely way you did struggle to tell me details of your doings and how all the time you talk and share—as I do—but it takes so long and is so much more for the tired arm to do."[75] Despite longing to receive her letters and his daily checking of the mailbox, he urged her not to write more than once a week so as not to add more stress to her overburdened days.

ROH had tried to keep Nora from staying in England with her mother, if only to protect her. He gave in to her wish because he loved her, a mistake that he later admitted. It meant that Nora was under the influence and control of her mother for another nine years. ROH had warnings about the potential dangers of leaving Nora to look after her mother, which he not had fully understood then. He wrote to Christopher years later, "I just couldn't leave her to that hell."[76] The word "hell" referred to the atmosphere created when Nora was with her mother, a difficult woman who exploited and manipulated Nora's filial duty and love.

Imagining that he could give her rest from the grinding, never-ending work at Home Farm in Lewknor, and longing for the warmth of her physical presence, ROH urged Nora to join him in Hong Kong. After two years of ROH's pleading, Nora finally agreed, only to postpone the visit shortly afterward. His letter to her expressed his deep disappointment. Bitterly admitting the power that his love for her had over him, he wrote in an angry reproach:

> You are NOT coming to me because you *pity* my loneliness. You *are* coming because it is right that you should come and share my life and get a break from *your* loneliness before you are too old or too worn to profit from it . . . You see one thing your humility has kept from you—or perhaps your very strength is how *much* I want you and need you—how utterly and always I love you. Do you think really that any other man in the world after 25 years married—is so utterly a lonely lover still—so that all his thoughts always come round to you or does any woman get letters sharing so much of daily life as you do?[77]

Inevitably the strain of loneliness caused ROH to question the sterling quality of Nora's love at least once. Expressing his doubts relative to a struggle between the forces of light and darkness, he wondered if she was using him to get her needs met, then disregarding his needs. Immediately, however, he trounced this uncharitable thought: "How I long for you to have my love and care at your side *every* day. It was the Devil saying to me 'She doesn't really love you—she has used you to get free from her mother—to get a home and children and now she has all she needs for her life's fullness, she does not understand, cannot understand, your man's need of her' . . . But that has gone."

It was not until 1950 and only at the very last minute that Nora, by then 53, mustered the courage to tell her mother she was leaving for a four-month visit to ROH. ROH's delight in their "grandparents' honeymoon" was followed by the exhaustion of yet another separation. The day after she left, he became sick and had to take two aspirin tablets to sleep it off. He did not even go into his office. He felt not only physical tiredness but also an emotional exhaustion that he attributed to "two lovers being torn apart." As usual, he sought the spiritual meaning of his intense feelings. After admitting in a letter that he did not know that saying goodbye to her would make him physically sick, he said: "I have been praying hard. Overwhelmed with gratitude for your love and the sort of miracles that two people so very different in the way they do things, can yet be so dear to each other—and above all your tenderness to me—must have some meaning and purpose from God to make me a better person."[78]

Reunion and Disunion

Though her mother had died and her children launched, it is not surprising that Nora's plan to finally move back to Hong Kong involved much hesitation and delay. There were practical reasons for delay, as she had to clean and sell her mother's place and organize Home Farm, Lewknor to be rented. More importantly, she was anxious about giving up a life in Lewknor, which had become "natural" to her after so many years, for a life in Hong Kong, which appeared so "unnatural" to her and so public.[79] She asked for one year's time to wind things up.

Although agonized over the prolongation of their separation, ROH's understanding of her helped him to accept yet more delay. His poetic expression of mature desire conveys a sweetness and poignancy: "You wanted time to wind up . . . Like a field that has lain fallow for a year to welcome the new grain I shall sow in your body to grow not as children but in dear tenderness—in flowers of tenderness and joy . . . This year's wait you asked me to give you . . . And if your lover cannot understand your heart, then, my darling, you are lonely indeed even when you are with me. It costs you so much to come to me, so naturally it must cost me long hours of lonely, empty, misery waiting for your coming and I give all gladly to you."[80]

It was not until October 1954 that Nora was finally free to join him in Hong Kong. While both of them had to readjust to marital life after prolonged separation, it was particularly difficult for Nora. She had to adapt not only to the change of role from "mother" back to "wife," but also to the colony's most unwelcoming climate. Without her there, the servants in Sha Tin and the Bishop's House did the housekeeping, leaving Nora feeling displaced and insignificant.

Despite his fervent hopes and prayers, Nora was not happy after she joined ROH. We might even wonder whether she felt burdened by the intensity of ROH's longing for her: it could be difficult for any flesh-and-blood woman to live up to the paragon he had built up, over time, in his mind.

In May 1955, there came a devastating blow that no parents can prepare for. Their son Joc died in a motorcycle accident. When the terrible news of Joc's death came, the brokenhearted Nora felt pulled to return to England to be with her children, but also felt the need to stay with ROH. Realizing her role had changed, she remained.

In the depths of his pain and sorrow, ROH was sustained by his faith in Christ, however sorely tested. Surprisingly, perhaps, he never felt Christ to be so near and so real as during this incredibly difficult period. Somehow he could image his son's broken body, he suggested in a letter to Christopher, as the Broken Body of Christ: "Men are not so badly hit in their deepest insides as women are. Perhaps it's in our minds we feel it most. I am still haunted—perhaps always will be—by that broken body on the roadside. I so wish I could have seen him, helped to pick him up—and could deal with his clothes and so on. But somehow I can see that broken body of our Joc taken up into the Broken Body of Eternity in Time. His photograph is now beside my crucifix."[81]

Nora's grief was no doubt made worse by remorse. In the years before she left England for Hong Kong, her relationship with Joc was strained.[82] In another letter to Christopher, ROH revealed his ability to imagine the magnitude of Nora's grief and sense of helplessness, and the core of her pain: "And it has been specially cruel for her that just when she has given up the mother for the wife, the first really great demand on her as mother comes, she cannot suppress herself with that part of her—cannot even take you into her arms—or keep Judith in bed and take her up breakfast . . . about the terrible shock when the core round which our emotional energy is centred is hurt—and that is what it is with a mother—and it's incredibly hard for her that she can *do* nothing for Joc or for Judith or for you. If she had been home she would have taken charge."[83]

But Nora became desperately unhappy and depressed for so long that a close friend observed, a little unkindly: "I did rather feel that, like Queen Victoria, Nora was determined never to get over it."[84] In addition to developing a range of psychosomatic symptoms that doctors were unable to cure, there were times she treated ROH, and the servants, with cruelty. Her angry outbursts wounded ROH greatly. From time to time, her bitter unhappiness would find expression in tirades of venomous words that he would ponder in sorrow. ROH wrote that she had broken down in a car while coming home, fuming: "I hate religious people and religion! It's all words, words, words. I hate all this adulation of you and I hate you loving it so." When ROH suggested that she be "strong enough to give up coming to Church at all," she replied, "I can't. I'm just trapped."

At such a juncture, ROH must have indeed felt knifed by what he described as the "agony of this to [his] heart."[85]

Nora's insecurity and low self-worth may be seen in several instances that ROH described in his letters: "She was happy when she was 'significant' as in the family party during the Christmas season."[86] She would go out of her way trying to be useful and needed. One not so happy incident was the time she forged on, over objections, to renovate ROH's office. He wrote, "Nora's demonic re-doing of the office—not really her business—doing so much more detail than needed and wearing herself out of it—so that everything else has suffered from worn temper and really exhausted body—she has had more illness and more burden of the heat because of it. I ought to have been strong enough to say—hands off—but the answer: all right I'm not really wanted—you can get on better without me. Everyone's glad when I'm not here."[87]

Nora did not find the role of a bishop's wife in a colonial outpost agreeable. ROH had become very self-reliant after so many years of being alone, and Nora had few interests outside the home. When, after his long days, ROH brought home mountains of work such as preparing for a sermon, or writing letters and reports, he had little time for her. In addition, it must have been painful for them both that Nora did not share ROH's passionate sense of love and dedication to ministry. ROH wrote to his son about his sadness on this account:[88]

> I once wrote to her "I want you to love me not only for myself but because I am going to be a parson": she wrote back "I should love you whatever your profession." Two things jarred there—the use of the word profession which is really due to her particular education—the other, I did and still do—want her *to love my work as a priest*. I'm sure she doesn't and never really "accepted it," and *yet*, lad, she takes such care over the chapel, both here, and at the Bishop's House, hates anyone else to do the flowers and she has taken infinite trouble to get made and give me for the 28th a new cope and miter.

Despite Nora's inability to truly accept the work that her husband had chosen, it would seem that she tried to create a role for herself in the care she took for domestic details at the chapel at home and in the Bishop's House.[89] Out of her element in Hong Kong, Nora yearned for ROH to return to England as a country parish priest. ROH, who had dedicated himself to his calling, had no wish to resign. However, he did his best to placate her, reducing his hours at work, picking roses and putting them on her dresser every morning, and taking time off from work.

At one point ROH wondered whether he should take his unhappy wife back to England and let her stay there for good, visiting her every two years on leave. Fortunately, when the heat of the summer wore off and Christmas finally came, her spirits picked up. There were days when she seemed "almost gay." Whenever she was happy, ROH was happy. He would describe in his letters to his children the dresses she wore, the floor of the hall of their living room, the curtains, and the different variety of flowers in the garden and how glorious they were.

He cared very much about Nora's physical well-being and performed what small services he could to help her be more comfortable. During the following summer, he splurged on an electric fan to combat the terrible heat. Every night he would put down the mosquito nets and turn the fan on over the bed so that Nora would be cool enough to sleep. He would turn it off at around 2 a.m. after she had fallen asleep, and turn it on again when she woke up in the morning.[90]

The 1956 Visit to China: Drawn by Hope

Under Communist rule, China's unity assured for the first time in more than a century, political tides seemed to be shifting. In 1953, the Korean War had ended in a stalemate with the United States. This raised China's confidence as well as its status; the first phase of land reform was completed and the economic base of the bourgeoisie broken. The Chinese Communist Party then began to develop the country's economy along the Soviet model in a sequence of five-year plans. The progressive development of infrastructure, industry, health care, and education raised the standard of living for the average individual. The Denunciation Movement in the churches had also ended, and the general social and political climate seemed to be loosening. By 1956 there was a period of relaxation in the People's Republic of China, and the year ended with the so-called "Hundred Flowers Campaign," when intellectuals were encouraged to criticize the party and the government.[91] Even before the "Hundred Flowers Campaign" ROH received an invitation from Bishop C. T. Chen, chairman of the House of Bishops, to visit the Church in China.

On May 13, 1956, Sir Alexander Grantham sent a telegram about this invitation to the Foreign Office in London. It said that Bishop Hall and his wife had been invited "quite unexpectedly" by the presiding bishop of "Our Church in China" to visit churches. The couple would be leaving early in June, perhaps visiting Guangzhou before going on to Shanghai and then Beijing. The bishop was querying the matter privately for the moment because he thought that visits to China would become an ordinary routine matter in due course.[92]

Although ROH would later be heavily criticized for his sanguine report after this visit to China, he had every reason to be favorably impressed with what he had seen there. After leaving Hong Kong in early June, the couple spent three weeks in China, visiting churches in Guangzhou, Shanghai, Beijing, Hangzhou, Nanjing, and Hankou. They were met at the border between Hong Kong and Mainland China by Bishop Mo-Yung In, the Reverend Shen I-fan, and the Reverend Li Tim Oi. The Reverend Shen accompanied them all during the

Figure 5.4 ROH and Nora outside Nanjing Theological Seminary with leaders of the Chinese Church (*St. John's Review* [August 1956]: 215)

visit and interpreted for them. They noted that churches had regular Sunday worship, prayer meetings, and Bible study, and the bishop of Shanghai had confirmed 600 adults in the previous year. As the couple toured workers' housing, new schools, new kindergartens, and new nurseries, they were gratified to see the health and vigor of children everywhere. In Shanghai, they saw how hospitals and medical colleges had expanded. What they did not see was also notable: there were no beggars in the streets. In Shanghai, they met several old friends such as Bishop Cheng Chien Yah and Bishop Michael Chang. Their Chinese friends, who had been defensive about their government in the past, now spoke with pride and confidence about their Communist government. Gambling, prostitution, cholera, and flies all had disappeared.[93]

Dinner with Zhou Enlai

While in the Great Hall of the People with other visitors, he was surprised to be greeted by his friend from Chongqing days, Prime Minister Zhou Enlai. He was even more astounded when Zhou invited him and Nora to dinner. Deng Yingchao (Mrs. Zhou), whom he met for the first time, welcomed them on their arrival. Other guests included Gong Peng, whom ROH also knew in the 1940s, and her husband, Qiao Guanhua, the foreign minister, and two other heads of the Foreign Ministry Department. Just before dinner, Zhou startled ROH by saying, "Now you like to say your prayers."[94]

ROH's letter to his brother Noel on June 23, 1956 suggests not only the pragmatic nature of their interchange but also the delicacy of ROH's intermediary position:

> He [Zhou] was most alive and vigorous and friendly, but I felt rather more exasperated and impatient, and yes I think him too, about relations with Britain . . . He [Zhou] is very disappointed with O'Neill [Sir Con D. W. O'Neill, British Ambassador to the People's Republic of China 1955–57] "not a patch on Trevelyan" [The Right Hon Lord Trevelyan, predecessor of O'Neill] (I know that on O'Neill's part this is not for lack of trying, but O'Neill seems by temperament pessimistic, so always fears the worst.) I myself doubt if we shall make much more headway with O'Neill there and he has got another year to go. His main point is this. England approaches her trade with China like this. "We have surplus products where can we market them?" At the moment this is tractors. Tractors eat oil and do not drop manure . . . We must depend on man and animal labor for the next ten years. . . .
>
> Then he [Zhou] got on to *kerosene*. This is their most crying need and their whole agricultural program is held up because the ordinary country house lamps is lit normally by imported kerosene. "This is not war making material," he said. O'Neill comment later, Yes, this is fuel for jet planes. . . .
>
> After supper there were three questions[95] about Hong Kong which he wanted to tell me: 1) That there should be a representative of Peking in Hong Kong, as there was of Nanking after 1945 . . . I also know that Grantham has made one serious blunder, allowed one SN Chau [Sir Sik Nin, Ear, Nose Throat doctor turned businessman and politician in Hong Kong] and his gang of Hong Kong *property* owners to dominate the Hong Kong government. Whereas most of the British firms though not all and the great majority of the middle group of Chinese depends on trade with China, but their voices are drowned by the powerful property group . . . 2) Through train to Hong Kong . . . We cannot go on living on China's doorstep without more consultation and the more the better. On the immigration issue, the *last* thing China wants is a large influx to Hong Kong suggesting HK is a better place than Canton to live in. 3) The third point was a small matter, but it has indicated a state of mind to the PM [Prime Minister] which is alas far too common in HK Police and HK Executive Council namely, we must beware of Peoples' Government *Culture*. They have at last let in a Chinese Artistic "Ensemble" but with abnormal restrictions.

When ROH returned to Hong Kong, a swarm of journalists awaited him. He tried to put them off, but when they followed him to Sha Tin, he reluctantly granted them an interview. Having seen firsthand the dramatic improvements in Chinese life since he had last been there, it is not surprising that ROH was impressed with what he saw in 1956. His positive appraisal, influenced perhaps by his passionate affection for Chinese Christians and his close connection with Christian leaders in China, was reported by Reuters on June 25, 1956, and would lay him open to attacks from many quarters.

"There is religious freedom as far as I could see during my three-week stay in China. The Church in China is growing vigorously. There are no impediments to our Church at all." Bishop Hall told reporters that Communist China was now facing a similar question as England did in the sixteenth century. The question then was whether the Church in England was to be English or foreign. The problem in China now was whether the Church in China should be controlled by a Chinese or by a foreign missionary society.[96]

When asked to compare the new and the old China, Bishop Hall said that children in China were much better cared for than at any time he had ever seen and that China gave priority to the children's welfare and considered the younger generation China's future. When asked about the imprisonment of Catholics, he said that there were no religious, only political, prisoners in China.

ROH was not alone in his overly sanguine view of the regime after his visit; many who visited during that short period of openness before and even after the Great Leap Forward, with its disastrous consequences, also heaped praises on the progress in China. The brilliant, cosmopolitan, and long-serving late prime minister of Canada, Pierre Elliot Trudeau, who had fled from Shanghai in 1949 when Mao's army marched into the city, visited it again in 1960 shortly before he took office. After his second visit, Trudeau noted in his book *Two Innocents in China* that the throng of beggars, rickshaw coolies, shoeshine boys, thugs and pests, bars, and brothels that had infested the city in 1949 had disappeared. While ROH and other visitors might have been allowed to see only selected areas, the elusive Trudeau escaped from his imperious guide one night and wandered through the streets of Shanghai until early in the morning.[97] Still, he remarked approvingly that Shanghai had become an industrial city where no one wore rags, and the streets were clean.

The Risks of Optimism: Repercussions from ROH's Visit

ROH's visit, at the height of communist paranoia in the West, stirred controversy not only among those in the local government but also among those back in Britain. His remarks on religious freedom in China and the implication that the Catholics imprisoned in China had been involved in political activities offended Roman Catholics.[98]

A flurry of activities in the Foreign Office followed ROH's visit to China. Noel Hall, ROH's brother, then the principal of the Administrative Staff College at Henley,[99] took ROH's letter to the Foreign Office and met with C. T. Crowe (a diplomat working in the Far Eastern Department of the Foreign Office, London). The letter set off a virulent attack, as an enraged Crowe claimed that this was just communist propaganda and that ROH had allowed himself to become a Chinese tool of propaganda. Crowe also rejected the criticisms of O'Neill and Alexander Grantham as totally groundless. He thought that China had started a campaign against O'Neill because the latter was far too intelligent for China's comfort. Most of all, he was dismayed by ROH's comments on religious freedom in China and by their implication that Catholic priests in prisons had been involved in political issues. He then made enquiries as to how best the Foreign Office might inform the Church of England of their utmost displeasure at the press reports of what the bishop had said and to convey their views to the Church of England at the highest level.[100]

Heated discussions erupted in the Foreign Office, and when Crowe subsequently spoke to the Colonial Office and to Grantham, Grantham indicated that he thought the bishop had been most restrained in public on his return to Hong Kong—but he had not seen the Reuters' report. Lamenting that the bishop had been a thorn in the flesh for many years, he recalled that someone in his office had once tried to get the archbishop of Canterbury to do something about him. The answer was that, unless the bishop was guilty of crime, adultery or larceny, nothing could be done. Grantham finally posited that readers would factor in the bishop's bias, which was so well-known in Hong Kong, and that the report would be not as damaging as one might initially believe.

His remarks on religious freedom were highly offensive to the Catholic Church of Hong Kong, as Bishop Bianchi was in prison in Guangzhou. The Reverend C. H. Vath, director of the Catholic Diocesan Public Relations Office, said that ROH's statements were completely opposite to the views expressed by many hundreds of Catholic priests and nuns who had stated emphatically that they were banished and their superiors imprisoned solely for reasons of religion.[101] Catholics in seventeenth-century England were similarly persecuted for their perceived greater loyalty to the pope than to their country, and thus as a threat to national cohesion.

ROH's comments might have tarnished his image as a progressive liberal leader in the community. One correspondent bluntly charged that ROH was being used by Zhou to spread his ideas in Hong Kong and that he had allowed himself to be "used by the Communists for his own purposes."[102] Did this accusation contain an element of truth? During his enthronement speech, ROH had outlined his twofold ministry: the first was to share with Chinese people the knowledge of God and the second to forge stronger links between China and Britain so that the two nations could serve one another in brotherhood and in peace. The letter to his brother probably represented an attempt on his part to build bridges between China and Britain, as he had strived so hard to do in Shanghai in 1925–26. But looking for a middle way of peace and reconciliation carries its own set of risks.

From our perspective today, it may seem that ROH's appreciation of communism was a little starry-eyed. However, his optimism about communism was a natural outgrowth of his Christian faith, which also emphasized communal sharing and generosity to those who are marginalized and oppressed. It is also critical to remember that he was appraising communism in 1956, before the excesses associated with the Cultural Revolution and the famine arising from the Great Leap Forward that resulted in millions of lives being lost. When an American researcher accused him decades later of a lack of judgment regarding his "quixotic desire to support Communism in China which blinded him to the realities of the Government's overwhelming abuse of power . . . from the beginning of Communist government through the end of Cultural Revolution at a minimum of 29 million lives," she was overlooking that ROH was judging Communist China in 1956.[103] Her accusation that "Hall severely damaged not only the moral integrity of his leadership but also the Anglican Church" suggests that she had forgotten that, at that time, the Communist regime in China was making real progress in improving the lives of people.

ROH felt deeply hurt by these relentless attacks but remained silent, keeping true to his policy of "never defend." Subsequent to ROH's visit, a group of teachers from Diocesan Boys' School and Diocesan Girls' School made the first visit from Hong Kong that had been officially allowed since the Communists took over China.[104] Another consequence was that ROH found himself no longer welcome in Taiwan, where he was scheduled to visit later that year.[105] He had been hoping that the Church in Hong Kong would act as a bridge between Taiwan and the Mainland, so he was left deeply disappointed by this dismissal.

The Tortoise and the Hare: Christianity and Communism in China

ROH was called "the Pink or Red Bishop," but he was not a communist even though he was sympathetic to communism, as were most of the social theologians in England at that time. In 1949, when Western countries were strongly against communism, ROH was one of the very few in Hong Kong who rejoiced at the fall of the corrupt Nationalist regime and the establishment of the People's Republic of China. ROH wrote "China: Anno Domini 1950,"[106] an article in which he quoted from the Epistle to the Hebrews that "God is a consuming fire and He comes to cast fire upon earth to burn up evil in men's hearts." ROH could see obedience to the God of truth in the integrity of the Communist officials and the discipline of the Communist soldiers in China at that time. The self-criticism of the soldiers reminded him of the early Christians. He also thought of Communist China as "a secular arm" of God:

> In a greater period of Christian life and thought, the totalitarian and cruel rulers of mediaeval Europe were christened by theologians as "the secular arm" of an active God, creative and redemptive in history. It may be that world communism should be similarly analyzed as a secular arm of the God of history.

ROH was pleased with what he saw in the New China in 1956, especially the growth of the Church. Upon his return from China, he submitted an article to the *Church of England Newspaper*, "The Church in the New China: Social Evils Have Disappeared in the Revolution," testifying that all the churches in China were in good repair and in use for worship.[107] The people appeared to be contented with their lives and their children happy. Social evils such as gambling and begging had disappeared from the streets. ROH argued that the strong government needed to carry out land reform was crucial to improving the livelihood of the majority of farmers.

In August of the same year, he wrote an article for private circulation, "An Overwhelming Experience and Attempted Interpretation," which attempted to convey his views. This article drew on Maurice's idea that the family and nation—always the foundation of Chinese society—were "creative structures" that helped human personality find its full realization.[108] ROH observed that the Church had been closely involved in both the Chinese family and nation and, carefully weighing all that was happening, concluded that the government was sincere in its integrity of purpose for the welfare of the people. The Church in China had found its true place in the new chapter in the country's national story and justified its existence.

ROH also thought that the Church in China had found another aspect of what F. D. Maurice had called for: continuity with the nation's ancient history and its mysterious meaning. ROH revealed that when Bishop Timothy Lin, bishop of Beijing, took him and Nora to visit the Altar and Temple of Heaven, Bishop Lin prayed for God's mercy on the people of China and upon the Chinese Church. As they prayed, the soft rain began to fall upon them, reminding ROH of the quality of God's mercy evoked so vividly in Shakespeare's play, *The Merchant of Venice*:

> The quality of mercy is not strain'd,
> It droppeth as the gentle rain from heaven
> Upon the place beneath.

The whole tableau—the ancient altar, the living bishop, and the soft rain—were, to ROH, a metaphor for how Christ's love was at work in his church in China. ROH ended the article saying that whatever happened, it would be God's way:

> God who had begun His good work when he began the making of China and set about its fulfilment when he sent the missionaries of Christ will surely perfect in his own way the work he has begun in her using the family, the nation and the Church in the particular way He has planned for each.

He endorsed the Communist regime as both strong and enlightened at that time. Despite knowing about the persecution of Christians during the Denunciation Movement in the early 1950s, he was somewhat reassured by what he saw during his visit. He may have had worries about the possibility of a totalitarian regime when he saw that the government demanded that all Chinese would have to accept socialism, and were compelled to learn about the meaning and way of China's new pattern of life, but he defended this practice by saying "these dictates were fundamentally different from the fascist commands of Hitler's Germany and Mussolini's Italy."

He thought that the Communist regime, like the Roman Empire, had a mixture of good and evil. He compared the suffering and sacrifice of some Christians in the early Communist regime with the punishment and death of the many early faithful Christians, which had brought about the spread of the Gospel throughout the orderly but cruel Roman Empire.[109] He was willing to take the long view, and spoke of Jesus' parable:[110]

> The Kingdom of heaven was like a field of good seed in which an enemy had sown weeds among the rice. But when they asked "Must we not pull up the weeds?" he said "No! let both grow together." Many Christians today are spending too much time deploring the weeds in Communism. They are preparing themselves to go and pull them up. Jesus says to us "Let both grow together, until the harvest."

ROH referred to the competition between communism and Christianity as the race between the tortoise and the hare, but trusted the long-term staying power of Christianity.[111]

> But again, the old family consciousness or social consciousness of China is so strong that it may need the Communist hammer to break it before it can pass into a full Christian social conscience. The situation is like a race between a hare and a tortoise. The Communist is like the hare. He does not carry on his back the hard shell of the past, but in the story, it was the tortoise who had the staying power.[112]

ROH had a strong hope that communism would save China from the chaos and poverty that he had seen firsthand in China in the 1930s and 1940s. He also had great admiration for Zhou Enlai and had expected that Zhou would be able to lead the Communist Chinese government to maturity over time, and allow it to take its place among the nations of the world working for peace and mutual cooperation.

History took an unexpected turn. After a brief period of openness that lasted only a few months, China lowered the bamboo curtain toward the end of 1956 for a long time. Mao retaliated against the intellectuals who had criticized the party and the government during the "Hundred Flowers Campaign." This attack, called the Anti-Rightist Movement, quickly spread to purge the "rightists" within intellectual organizations and academia. This was followed by the disastrous failure of the Second Five-Year Plan and the Great Leap Forward, when an estimated 30 million people died from starvation between 1958 and

1961. To regain his reduced power from the failure, Mao started a revolution again among young people—this time in the form of the Cultural Revolution.[113]

ROH found that he was *persona non grata* both in Communist China and in Nationalist Taiwan, a complete reversal from his experience in the war years. Although he was not officially denounced, he was not allowed to enter China again after the 1956 visit. During the tumult of the Anti-Rightist Movement and the Cultural Revolution, ROH was deeply distressed when his colleagues who left Hong Kong to minister to the people in the diocese of Guangdong were denounced and humiliated repeatedly. Unable to do much for them, ROH could only pray for them as he did for all the people in China.

He turned his energy to where it might best bear fruit, Hong Kong. With the relative political stability provided by the British colonial government, it had become a haven for investment and had reinvented itself as a manufacturing center.

Notes

1. Thomas Ashe, *South China* (October 1951): front cover.
2. Hong Kong Annual Reports, 1945–70.
3. J. R. Orens, "Politics and the Kingdom: The Legacy of the Anglican Left," *Anglican Theological Review* ATR/LXIII.I: 21–41. Accessed on August 30, 2013, through Vancouver School of Theology Library website: www.vst.edu/main.
4. R. O. Hall, "What Happens in Hong Kong," in *Part-time Priests? A Discussion*, edited by Robin Denniston (London: SPCK, 1960), 60–64.
5. P. Wickeri, "Clergy Training and Theological Education: The Sheng Kung Hui Experience in China." Conference paper presented at the International Symposium on the History of Christianity in Modern China, June 10–11, 2011.
6. Minutes of Meeting of the Council of the Union Theological College. February 9, 1956. Bishop's House Archive.
7. *Outpost* (January–April 1945): 3 (Order of a priest's life).
8. The Bishop's Pastoral Letter. *St. John's Review* (July 1958): 199–201.
9. R. O. Hall to A. C. Hall. November 6, 1957. Chung Chi Divinity School Archive.
10. Fung and Chan-Yeung, *To Serve and to Lead*, 179–81 (D. Brittain).
11. G. Goodban to D. M. Paton. Not dated. Chung Chi Divinity School Archive.
12. R. Howard to D. M. Paton. June 24, 1976. Chung Chi Divinity School Archive.
13. R. O. Hall. Resignation of Barry Till. *St. John's Review* (1963): 262.
14. Letter from Barry Till. HKMS 94-1-15. Hong Kong Public Records Office.
15. Bishop Hall Annulled the Marriage of the Reverend John Chou Meng Chow and Hon Yan Oi. Hall Family Archive.
16. C. Long, "The Diocese of Hong Kong 1953." Chung Chi Divinity School Archive.
17. R. O. Hall to N. Hall. January 22, 1954. Hall Family Archive (Thursday Morning Prayers).
18. Interview of Canon Alan Chan by the author. Hong Kong. April 28, 2010.
19. Paton, *R. O.: The Life and Times of Bishop R. O. Hall*, 88 (James Pong on ROH).
20. *Yamen* is a mandarin's office or residence in the Chinese empire.

21. R. O. Hall, "Foreword: The Dedication of the Church of the Good Shepherd." July 14, 1955. Bishop's House Archive.
22. Judge or Bishop as Arbitrator? Labour Disputes. HKMS 94-1-11. Hong Kong Public Records Office.
23. R. O. Hall, "A Record of Certain Conferences, Proposals etc., Held and Made in an Effort to Avert the Tramway Strike." December 1949. Workers' Welfare File. Bishop's House Archive.
24. Appendix VIII. Education Department, Hong Kong. Special Bureau. CO 968/259. The National Archives, London, England.
25. "Notes on Interview with His Excellency the Governor at 9:30 am on Monday July 5, 1949–Re: Workers' Schools Closure Order." Workers' Children's School File. Bishop's House Archive.
26. Education Department to Bishop R. O. Hall. December 15, 1950. Workers' Children's School File. Bishop's House Archive.
27. D. C. Barty for Colonial Secretary to R. O. Hall. November 22, 1950. Workers' Children's Schools File. Bishop's House Archive.
28. R. O. Hall to N. Hall. May 1, 1950 (Students' essays with anti-imperialists remarks). Hall Family Archive.
29. R. O. Hall, "Sermon Preached on 3-10-1965 Harvest Sunday at St. John's Cathedral," *St. John's Review* (November 1965): 227–29.
30. P. Smith, Juvenile Courts. J8. Juvenile Care Centre File. Bishop's House Archive.
31. R. O. Hall to Colonial Secretary. February 10, 1949 and January 6, 1950. J8. Juvenile Care Centre File. Bishop's House Archive.
32. The Governor of Hong Kong to the Bishop of Victoria, Hong Kong. Licence to Use Portion of Inland Lot 76 for a Juvenile Care Centre. Juvenile Care Centre File. Bishop's House Archive.
33. R. O. Hall, "St. James' Settlement," *Outpost* (April 1963): 15–17.
34. H. M. Lee, "The Meaning of 'Settlement.' St. James' Settlement 1949–1987." Special Issue in Commemoration of the Opening of the New Multi-Service Community Centre on May 30, 1987. The idea of a "University Settlement" was first conceived by Edward Denison in 1864, when he lived in miserable lodgings in East London in order to learn firsthand about the people who were economically disadvantaged.
35. Minutes of Meeting held in Ying King Restaurant. October 29, 1949. St. James' Settlement 1949–1954 File. Bishop's House Archive.
36. R. O. Hall, to friends in 1949 on St. James' Settlement. St. James' Settlement File, Bishop's House Archive.
37. Interview of H. M. Lee, founding director of St. James' Settlement, by the author. June 7, 2010.
38. St. James' Settlement. Annual Reports, 1953–55.
39. R. O. Hall to Social Welfare Officer, Hong Kong. December 20, 1952. Holy Carpenter File. Bishop's House Archive.
40. R. O. Hall to Crown Lands. November 17, 1952 and May 15, 1953. Holy Carpenter Church and Hostel File. Bishop's House Archive.
41. Minutes of Preparatory Committee Meeting for Holy Carpenter Church, Hung Hom. March 18, 1955. Holy Carpenter Church File. Bishop's House Archive.

42. R. O. Hall to A. C. Hall. October 27, 1954. Chung Chi Divinity School Archive (A typical day).
43. Holy Carpenter Church and Hostel, *St. John's Review* (October 1959): 277–78.
44. Interview of Mr. Wong Kwok To (黃國度) and Mr. Leung Sze Woon (梁士瑗) by the author. Holy Carpenter Church. May 1, 2010.
45. A. Smart, *The Shek Kip Mei Myth: Squatters, Fires, and Colonial Rule in Hong Kong, 1950–1963* (Hong Kong: Hong Kong University Press, 2006), 54–56.
46. Ibid., 98.
47. Formation of the Hong Kong Housing Society. Not dated. Hong Kong Housing Society File. Bishop's House Archive.
48. Hong Kong Housing Society Annual Report, 1952. Hong Kong Housing Society File. Bishop's House Archive.
49. Hong Kong Housing Society Annual Report, 1954. Hong Kong Housing Society File. Bishop's House Archive.
50. Hong Kong Housing Society Annual Report, 1955. Hong Kong Housing Society File. Bishop's House Archive.
51. R. Hutcheon, *High Rise Society* (Hong Kong: Hong Kong Housing Society, 1998), http://www.hkhs.com/eng/about/milestone.asp6–8.
52. Y. S. Sun, *The Evolution of Public Housing in Hong Kong* (Ann Arbor, MI: UMI, 1993), 89–93.
53. Interview of Bishop Hall at Lewknor. November 30, 1972, 6. Bishop's House Archive.
54. S. Y. Ho, "Public Housing," in *Hong Kong in Transition*, edited by Joseph Y. S. Cheng (Hong Kong: Oxford University Press, 1986), 333.
55. N. M. Yip and K. Y. Lau, "Housing," in *Social Policy in Hong Kong*, edited by P. Wilding, A. Huque, and J. P. Tao Lai (Cheltenham: Edward Elgar, 1997), 39–54; R. Firth, "Houses and People," *St. John's Review* (1963): 95–101.
56. The Hong Kong government invited N. G. Fisher, chief education officer of Manchester to assess local education. Fisher's report of 1951 stressed the need for more primary school places, more subsidized schools, separation of primary and secondary education, and improvement of expatriate teachers' salaries and conditions of service.
57. A. Sweeting, *Education in Hong Kong, 1941–2001: Visions and Revisions* (Hong Kong: Hong Kong University Press, 2004), 58.
58. Fung and Chan-Yeung, *To Lead and to Serve*, 68–69.
59. B. H. K. Luk, *A History of Education in Hong Kong: Report Submitted to Lord Wilson Heritage Trust*, 2000, 64–65.
60. R. O. Hall. St. John's College, 1955. St. John's College File. Bishop's House Archive. The first residence for female undergraduates at the University of Hong-Kong was St. Stephen's Hall in Barbington Path, run by CMS. St. Stephen's Hall was sold, and the proceeds went to the building of St. John's College.
61. Official Opening of St. John's College, October 14, 1955. St. John's College File. Bishop House Archive.
62. New College of St. John the Evangelist. Need of spiritual Things. HKMS94-1-12. Hong Kong Public Records Office.
63. Luk, *A History of Education in Hong Kong*, 75.

64. The idea of establishing a Christian Chinese College came from Mr. David Au (a St. John's University graduate) and Dr. Lee Ying Nam (professor at Lingnan University).
65. The Chung Chi was proposed by Dr. Katie Woo, headmistress of St. Paul's Coeducational College.
66. K. C. Mark, "Historical Sketch of Chung Chi College 1951–1954," *Chung Chi College Bulletin*, 1961. Chung Chi College File. Bishop's House Archive.
67. R. O. Hall, *Chung Chi College Bulletin*, no. 30 (July 1962).
68. R. O. Hall, "Thirst for English Harms Chinese Culture," *South China Morning Post*, December 11, 1965.
69. L. Hunter to Archbishop C. G. Lang. May 2, 1932. Lang Papers 115, 216–18. Lambeth Palace Library Archive.
70. See note 42.
71. In the early days, a proportion of students from Singapore and Malaya studied at the University of Hong Kong and lived in St. John's Hall.
72. R. O. Hall to N. Hall. December 31, 1951. Hall Family Archive (On "begging" in Singapore for St. John's Hall).
73. R. O. Hall to N. Hall. October 14, 1953. Hall Family Archive (My love loves me).
74. R. O. Hall to N. Hall. August 4, 1946. Hall Family Archive (ROH's letter).
75. R. O. Hall to N. Hall. April 10, 1950. Hall Family Archive (Jabbering to Nora).
76. R. O. Hall to A. C. Hall. October 13, 1957. Chung Chi Divinity School Archive.
77. R. O. Hall to N. Hall. August 10, 1950. Hall Family Archive (ROH resented Nora's delay to visit him).
78. R. O. Hall to N. Hall. April 2, 1951. Hall Family Archive (Saying goodbye to Nora).
79. R. O. Hall to N. Hall. December 31, 1953. Hall Family Archive (Nora comparing life in England with life in Hong Kong).
80. R. O. Hall to N. Hall. July 17, 1953. Hall Family Archive (ROH's agony over further delay of Nora's return).
81. R. O. Hall to A. C. Hall. May 15, 1955. Chung Chi Divinity School Archive (Death of Joc).
82. Personal Communication from Canon Christopher Hall.
83. R. O. Hall to A. C. Hall. May 21, 1955. Chung Chi Divinity School Archive (ROH's understanding).
84. M. C. Higg to G. Baker. November 20, 1976. Chung Chi Divinity School Archive.
85. R. O. Hall to A. C. Hall. November 6, 1957. Chung Chi Divinity School Archive (Nora felt trapped).
86. R. O. Hall to A. C. Hall. November 2, 1957. Chung Chi Divinity School Archive (Nora happier).
87. R. O. Hall to A. C. Hall. Sunday, July 1957. Chung Chi Divinity School Archive (Nora's insecurity).
88. See note 76.
89. There were very few options for women when their children grew up and left home: no opportunities to find a job or to return to school. Many European women found living conditions in Hong Kong intolerable. It was not uncommon for couples to leave after a while or for the wife to return to the home country.

It is easy to imagine how trapped Nora must have felt. Her husband was virtuous and faithful, so she had no obvious excuses to leave.
90. R. O. Hall to A. C. Hall. May 4, 1956. Chung Chi Divinity School Archive (ROH's care for Nora).
91. Spence, *The Search for Modern China* (1990), 563–73 (Five-Year Plan; Hundred Flowers Campaign).
92. Telegram from Sir Alexander Grantham to the Foreign Office. FO371/121001-C1182/1. The National Archives, London.
93. R. O. Hall, *Outpost* (August 1956): 5.
94. R. O. Hall to Noel Hall. June 23, 1956. FO 371/12100-C1782/5. The National Archives, London.
95. All three issues were related to Hong Kong government's distrust of the PRC. The Hong Kong government refused to have a consular representative of the PRC in Hong Kong even after Britain had recognized the PRC and there were bilateral diplomatic representations in Beijing. Issue 1: The property owners in Hong Kong did not wish to have such representation while the average entrepreneur would benefit from having a PRC consulate in Hong Kong. Issue 2: Through train to Hong Kong from Guangzhou. The Hong Kong government resisted having a through train from the Mainland for fear of not only an influx of refugees but also Communist infiltration. Issue 3: Hong Kong government had refused entry to groups of performing artists from PRC for fear of Communist propaganda.
96. Reuters. FO 371/12100-C1782/6, The National Archives, London.
97. J. English, *Citizen of the World: The Life of Pierre Elliott Trudeau, Vol. 1: 1919–1968* (Toronto: Vintage Canada, 2006), 348.
98. Political activity did not need to be overt political action. The PRC pursued social control and regulation of religion more strongly than in any other period in Chinese history. Merely by maintaining allegiance to the pope, Catholics were considered unpatriotic and subversive. The PRC sponsored the Catholic Three-Self Movement in 1950–51 to be free of foreign influence. Orthodox Catholics who believed that the pope spoke in the name of Christ were considered by the PRC as unpatriotic and were often attacked and jailed. See E. O. Hanson, *Catholic Politics in China and Korea* (New York: Orbis Books, Maryknoll, 1980), 72–82.
99. The Administrative Staff College was set up in 1945 at Henley-on-Thames as a civilian equivalent of the Military Staff Colleges. In 2008, combining with the Business School of Reading, it changed its name to Henley Business School at the University of Reading.
100. Report to C. T. Crowe. FO 371/121001-C1782/7. The National Archives, London.
101. D. Brown, "The Anglican Church in Hong Kong and the Challege of Transition (1949–1993)." Seminar, September 22–24, 1993. Centre of Asian Studies, The University of Hong Kong, 1993.
102. L. Goodstadt, interview by D. M. Paton, 1976. Chung Chi Divinity School Archive.
103. See note 101.
104. Fung and Chan-Yeung, *To Serve and to Lead*, 86 (Teachers' visit to China).
105. O. K. Yui to R. O. Hall. August 20, 1956. Chung Chi Divinity School Archive.

106. R. O. Hall, "China: Anno Domini 1950. An Attempt at Theological Interpretation." CSCA CHSKH Source Documents. http://www.ttc.edu.sg/csca/skh/index.html.
107. R. O. Hall, "The Church in the New China: Social Evils Have Disappeared in the Revolution," *Church of England Newspaper*. August 1956. Chung Chi Divinity School Archive.
108. R. O. Hall, "An Overwhelming Experience and Attempted Interpretation (for Private Circulation Only)." 1956. HKMS96 D and S 1/31. Hong Kong Public Records Office.
109. R. O. Hall, "Sermon 'The Destiny of Chinese Church' Given at the Opening of the Synod Celebrating the Centenary of the Diocese of Hong Kong on August 21, 1949," in Paton, *R. O.: The Life and Times of Bishop R. O. Hall*, 251–55.
110. R. O. Hall, "Sermon Preached on October 31, 1937 at St John's Cathedral, Hong Kong," *Outpost* (January–March 1938): 11–14.
111. Because Christians met in informal houses churches, accurate estimate of numbers in Christians in China is hard to come by. In 1993, the estimates ranged from 6.5 to 50 million. Zhong and Chan reported a more reasonable estimate of about 20 million, an increase of twenty times since 1949 while the population increased by less than three times. See M. Zhong and K. K. Chan, "The 'Apostolic Church': A Case-Study of a House Church in Rural China," in *Christianity in China: Foundations for Dialogue*, edited by Beatrice Leung and John D. Young (Hong Kong: Centre of Asian Studies, the University of Hong Kong, 1993).
112. R. O. Hall, "The Development of Social Conscience in Modern China," in *The Christian Movement in China in a Period of National Transition* (Mysore City: Wesley Press and Publishing House, 1938), 40–42.
113. Spence, *The Search for Modern China*, 575–617 (Cultural Revolution).

Chapter 6
Consolidating and Expanding His Work
The Diocese of Hong Kong (1957–66)

Almighty God, Father of all peoples,
Bless we pray Thee all who dwell in Hong Kong and Macao
And grant to Thy Church in the Diocese, in China, and throughout the world,
To be ever faithful in obedience to Thy Will, and
Mindful of Thy Love for all men,
Through Him by whom all things were made
Our Lord and our Redeemer, Jesus Christ.
Amen

R. O. Hall's prayer for the diocese

Joy Threaded with Sadness: The Silver Jubilee Year

By 1957 ROH had become a widely respected progressive spiritual leader and social activist in Hong Kong and Southeast Asia. Despite his perceived reputation as a "Pink or Red Bishop," successive governors paid attention to him. In the same year, ROH's 25 years of selfless devotion to the Chinese people was rewarded with the bishop's jubilee celebration in Hong Kong. Members of his diocese rejoiced.

Even though it was painful to be exiled from his adopted country, China, ROH must have felt a sense of satisfaction in what the Church had accomplished under his episcopacy in Hong Kong, and at the same time grateful for God's grace to be the instrument of His love. Although his bishopric had shrunk considerably since he was first appointed bishop of Victoria, the Anglican Church in Hong Kong (Hong Kong Sheng Kung Hui) had grown rapidly since World War II.

Sadly, the happiness of ROH's jubilee celebration was not shared by Nora. Even though she loved him dearly, Nora must not have felt like a full partner with him at this celebration. She had been away from Hong Kong since 1940 and did not take part in the reconstruction of Hong Kong during the crucial postwar years. She had never fully accepted her husband's job as a priest, let alone his work as bishop, and had never really felt at home in Hong Kong. She had still not recovered from the loss of her firstborn son, Joc, two years earlier.

ROH could empathize with Nora's position on the fringe of his life. A priest, especially one with such a hectic schedule, could never belong to his wife as in a more typical marriage. ROH would arrive home late in the evening, utterly exhausted, leaving little time for Nora, and on Sundays his energies went toward preaching. Among her own friends, Nora felt she was the odd one out, married to a bishop.[1]

Although ROH disliked pomposity, he was still the bishop of Hong Kong, looked up to by most people in the diocese. Nora resented the "adulation" people had for him and disliked the jubilee celebration intensely. She longed for ROH to return to England and bury himself in the work of a country parish. Her ambivalence toward his job can be seen in that she went to great trouble to have a new cope and miter made for his jubilee celebration, yet on the day of the Jubilee Dedication Service she did not want him to wear them.[2]

ROH worked very hard to make Nora happy. Gradually he began to spend more time with her whenever he could. In 1957, he took three weeks off and stayed at home in Sha Tin, not even attending church on those three successive Sundays![3]

Fortunately there were some bright spots for Nora. On November 27, 1957, while they were resting in the Bishop's House, they heard the sweep of cars and murmurs on the steps. When they looked out, they saw a delegation led by Canon Paul Tso. Twenty-eight people marched in, representing different parishes, with hymn books, sandwiches and a huge birthday cake. They had come to celebrate Nora's sixtieth birthday (November 20). Mrs. Tso gave a little speech saying that the sixtieth birthday, in accordance with the Chinese customs, was an important milestone. It was a beautiful day with warm sun and a cloudless sky, and they sat on the lawn enjoying the afternoon. ROH's letter to Christopher expressed his hopes—perhaps even his wishful thinking—that the surprise party could lift Nora's spirits: "I so hope it really did help N and that she was cheered by it. She is wonderfully natural and cheerful with folk when she meets them. Says she is play-acting—but I'm not quite sure if that is the whole story." Even though Nora qualified her apparent pleasure as "play-acting" it is possible that the sunlight of attention warmed her heart at least for a short while.[4]

That year, their daughter Judith came to Hong Kong. Although ROH had asked her to visit for the summer, Judith, who had worked with the National Health Service in England for nine years, began to work as a doctor in different medical clinics in the diocese. She also became the warden for female students at St. John's College. Delighted to be in a mother's role again, Nora's depression lifted somewhat.

The year 1957 ended with yet another piece of joyful news for ROH: Christopher wrote that he was considering the path of priesthood. ROH was ecstatic, treasuring what he would refer to as "the most precious letter" and thanking his son "a thousand times for that letter."[5] Still, ROH cautioned his son about the hardships his wife would necessarily endure. His wife, he said, would need to love not only her man, but also his work as a priest.

Calm after Turbulence: The Diocese in 1957

By 1957, after going through one of the most turbulent periods in the history of China, the diocese could view its accomplishments during the previous 25 years with some pride. It had 13 Chinese parishes, of which 8 were new additions after the war, and 3 mission chapels. The membership of the Diocese of Hong Kong in 1955 was 8,097 and would grow to reach 13,690 in 1962.[6] The diocese had one American priest (the Reverend Charles Long),[7] twenty-five Chinese priests, and five Chinese deacons. Of these, only ten were full-time parish priests. The rest were honorary priests, mostly headmasters and teachers of schools, who did not receive their stipend from any parish church.[8]

Even though ROH had dared to ordain a woman, Canterbury appreciated that ROH's diocese, in the far reaches of the empire, had become an "episcopal nursery." Over the previous quarter of a century, ten priests who had served in the Diocese of South China and Hong Kong had been consecrated as bishops, presiding in different parts of the world.[9]

Chinese clergy trained in Hong Kong were working in different parts of the world including London, the United States, the Philippines, Malaya, New Zealand, and Mauritius.[10] Although there were not enough clergy to staff the local parishes or social and educational facilities, whenever there was a request from other dioceses for the loan of a Chinese priest or worker, ROH had gone out of his way to help, often sending one of the best in his diocese.

The clergy and the laity joined to celebrate the joyous occasion of ROH's silver jubilee. They set up a committee, chaired by Archdeacon Lee Kau Yan, to organize a series of events to commemorate it. One of the programs included a dedication service to be held in a sports stadium. ROH was at first concerned about holding such a rally until the Diocesan Synod reassured him that it would encourage the Christian community to realize its own strength and rapid growth.[11]

Celebrating the Spirit of Grateful Obedience

The jubilee celebration started with a million-dollar campaign, launched enthusiastically on the evening of Ascension Day on May 20, 1957, to raise funds for the future development of religious, educational, and social work in the diocese. The celebration commenced with a Holy Communion service at St. John's Cathedral. It was followed by a series of events during the year: Brother Michael's Mission, the Diocesan Dedication Service, and Thanksgiving Dinner, ending with a Holy Communion Service on the anniversary of ROH's enthronement.

Figure 6.1 ROH and his prize goat (*Outpost*, February 1957)

In order to renew the spiritual vitality of the clergy, ROH invited Brother Michael Fisher of the Society of St. Francis[12] to lead a retreat from October 14 to 18, 1957 in Ho Fuk Tong, at Castle Peak. ROH attended the retreat with the rest of his staff. To assess the needs of the community, Brother Michael busily conducted a number of meetings in the parishes and churches, convened with youth and senior groups, and visited all the diocesan secondary schools. After his visit, many students in the secondary schools contemplated seeking baptism and confirmation. At the end of Brother Michael's very successful mission, ROH felt that the spiritual life of the clergy and congregation, including his own, had been appreciably reinvigorated.[13]

The Diocesan Dedication Service, the most outstanding event to mark the silver jubilee of ROH's episcopate, took place at the South China Athletic Stadium at Causeway Bay on October 28 (the Feast of St. Simon and St. Jude), the same day he was consecrated as bishop of Hong Kong and South China 25 years before. About 10,000 people attended. The clergy worked hard to ensure that the service went smoothly. The procession consisted of 1,700 delegates from different parishes, schools, social welfare institutions, choirs, visiting clergy, diocesan clergy, and the cathedral chapter. They all arrived before 7 p.m., dressed in their uniforms, gowns, or unique and colorful robes. They carried hundreds of crosses and brilliant banners that billowed and fluttered under the bright lights in the evening breeze. As they were marshalled in by the Reverends Froud, Kwok, and Pong,[14] a sense of excitement and joy filled the stadium.

Sir Alexander came striding in at 8 p.m., dressed in a simple suit, with an elegantly clad Lady Grantham beside him. ROH, who was wearing the beautiful new golden Chinese brocade cope and miter that Nora had commissioned especially for this occasion, greeted them warmly. The colorful procession circled the stadium. The service started at 8:30 p.m., after members of the procession had taken their seats. Sir Alexander, having completed almost 10 years' service as governor, would be leaving the colony at the end of the year. In his letter of congratulation,[15] he generously acknowledged the contributions of his long-time harsh critic and read the first lesson in the Dedication Service.

In his sermon, ROH thanked God for his clergy, for the leaders in education and social welfare organizations, for the work of Church Missionary Society, and for the "faith and loyalty of the laymen of the Church."[16] He reminded the congregation of Jesus' warnings: "Woe unto you when all men speak well of you." He continued, "The Church, Sheng Kung Hui, today is well spoken of. Perhaps that is because we are not sufficiently on fire for Christ: because we are not fearless enough in warning all who live self-centered lives, that God is the only centre of all life."

He asked the audience to remember three symbols: the tortoise, the pine tree, and the crown of thorns, symbols of his faith and mission in the diocese. Sheng Kung Hui should not be afraid of slow growth, but should keep steadily on its course in discipline like a tortoise. ROH asked the audience to keep their emotions in reserve to help them to keep going steadily on the course, like the tortoise that won in the end. The pine log, split open to dry in the sun— a symbol of how Christ "poured out his soul unto death"—represented self-sacrifice that others may live, and a part of God's self-giving that the Church should follow. The crown of thorns was a reminder that Christ died as a servant but that he rose from the dead; evil could destroy his body but could not break his kingly power. By his death, Christ has redeemed all creation:

> We are here not only because God IS, not only because God RULES, but also because God LOVES us. What are we to do in answer to His love? We can only give ourselves back to him in grateful obedience, not just gratitude, not just obedience but grateful obedience.

Finally he urged his audience to remember the *bent knee*. To kneel in prayer is one of the Sheng Kung Hui rules: a sign of obedience to God. "So much of our praying is false. We try to persuade God to give us what we want. Jesus' great prayer is 'Thy will be done.' So our prayer should always be 'Please God help us to do thy will.' This is the prayer of the bent knee, of the will surrendered to God."

The tribute which the community of Hong Kong paid to ROH was appropriately voiced in an editorial in the *South China Morning Post* on the following day:[17]

Manifold are the festivals and anniversaries of the Christian Church. But the celebrations of its living servants are few. One of these rare occasions was marked by the thousands of people who attended the Service of Dedication in the Caroline Hill Stadium, on the occasion of Bishop Hall's Jubilee. Character always tells in the lives of men and when it is allied to and fortified by a great religious faith and zeal, the personality thus evolved is bound to radiate a great and abiding influence. This is certainly true of Bishop Hall. The works he has performed are greater than the man, yet to most of his friends they are inseparable. It is not given to many ecclesiastics to serve their Church as a bishop for the long span of a quarter-century, and a period, moreover, marked by tumultuous events without parallel in the history of this region.

On December 27, 1957 at the Chung Kwok Restaurant, 750 clergy and representatives from different institutions in the diocese attended a Thanksgiving Dinner. ROH had great misgivings about spending so much on food, but his Chinese clergy would not dream of having such a significant celebration without a proper feast. In his speech, ROH gave credit to his clergy and the laity for all the achievements of the diocese in the past 25 years. In his recollections, he acknowledged both his sadness about the calamities and failures, as well as his happiness in the forward strides that he and the people had made together. He thanked God that he and Nora were privileged to share with his people and rejoice with his coworkers in the diocese that evening.[18]

This extraordinarily busy year ended with a Holy Communion Service held at St. John's Cathedral on December 30, 1957, the anniversary of ROH's enthronement as bishop of Hong Kong. Canon Ernest Martin took the text for his sermon from Psalm 136: "O give thanks unto the Lord, for He is good." Canon Martin recalled extracts from the preaching of ROH at the enthronement service and said that they all thanked God from the bottom of their heart for the fatherly rule and loving friendship that the bishop had administered. "They all should step out in the future with joy and hope and walk with newness of life."[19]

The Work of Building at Home and Beyond (1958–66)

ROH made his marriage a priority during this period. In March, 1958, he and Nora went on leave to England where he attended the Lambeth Conference and fulfilled many speaking engagements. They spent their wedding anniversary in Paris on April 24, 1958,[20] before leaving for Lewknor, where Judith joined them for a family reunion. The leave lasted 10 months. Because of Nora's unhappiness in Hong Kong, ROH was mentally prepared to leave her in England should she ask, planning to return to England every two years to visit her.[21] But to his utter relief, she showed no indication of wishing to stay by herself. Nora finally accepted, no doubt with a great deal of reluctance, that her husband would not leave Hong Kong until his retirement. She eventually settled into the routine of a wife of a bishop, to become a "helpmate" for him, becoming known as "Granny Hong Kong." She often visited families of clergy of English churches, always bringing with her a bunch of flowers, ready to read a bedtime story or to bathe a baby. She baked superb cakes in the English culinary tradition and served them with homemade jam during the Saturday afternoon tea parties.[22]

Despite wanting to spend as much time as possible with Nora, ROH maintained a demanding work schedule. During the latter part of his episcopacy, ROH began to spend more time away from his "prison"[23] to attend conferences and to give lectures in other countries. In 1961, he visited Australia and New Zealand on behalf of the Council of Churches of Southeast Asia,[24] attended the World Council of Churches in New Delhi, and conducted a retreat in Manila.[25] In 1963, he had a prolonged visit to attend the Anglican Congress in Toronto, Canada, and a tour in the US where he raised funds for building churches in Hong Kong.[26] Whenever possible, he organized the business trips outside Hong Kong to take place during summer months, so that he could take Nora with him to escape the oppressive heat of Hong Kong.

He also received many visitors, including the archbishop of Canterbury, Geoffrey Fisher, in 1959,[27] and the primate of Canada, the Most Reverend H. H. Clarke, in 1963.[28] The Anglican Church of Canada had donated generously to the building of the Kei Oi Church and Calvary Church, as well as to the Children's Meals Society. There were also several royal visitors, including the Duke of Edinburgh (1959),[29] Princess Alexandra (1961),[30] and Princess Margaret (1966). Every Thursday morning ROH invited some visitors to join in with the regular clergy meeting.

ROH continued his work to expand the Church during this period. In 1958 he met with clergy to work out an ambitious strategic plan for the diocese aimed at strengthening Hong Kong Sheng Kung Hui by providing more churches, and training more clergy to serve the local and the overseas Chinese communities.[31] In addition to building nine churches, the plan was for the diocese to build two primary schools, six secondary schools, six welfare centers and two college hostels, in partnership with the government.[32] The diocese, with help from the Jubilee Fund, which had grown to $850,000, would be able to expand the existing churches, including St. Thomas', St. Luke's, St. Peter's (North Point), and St. James', and to build a new workshop for St. James' Settlement in Wan Chai.[33]

Strategy for Advance

ROH planned his mission strategy of caring for both the spiritual and the social needs of his diocese more systematically and thoughtfully for the years ahead by placing the parish church, social service center, and school together, so that the three would work as a unit to bring about the salvation of the whole person.[34] This integrated approach, which became the philosophy of Hong Kong Sheng Kung Hui, allowed chaplains and priests to more readily identify and follow through with cases that required pastoral care.

ROH was passionate about education for its own sake, but he also saw how schools and churches could support each other. He had realized that, when he was actively supervising the expansion of schools in the diocese after 1949, the primary schools were fertile mission grounds. These primary schools had Sunday schools for the children, but when they grew up and left school, there were no churches for them. ROH's policy from then on was to have the schools and the churches close to each other so that primary school graduates would continue to be connected with the parish church.[35] He discussed this at the 1958 Diocesan Synod, which passed the resolution "that the relations be strengthened between our schools and their nearby parishes" by having baptisms and confirmations in the parish church nearest the students' homes, sharing facilities between the church and the school(s) in the parish, and considering the church and the school(s) in the parish as one unit.[36] In the new industrial development that sprang up in two clusters along the foothills of Kowloon and the New Territories, ROH built churches and schools close to each other (Table 6.1).[37]

ROH had several beliefs about educational reforms that grew, in part, from his awareness of Hong Kong cultural traditions and social needs. First, unlike most of his fellow missionaries, he acknowledged that education should be more about education than about evangelism. Admittedly, he did realize that primary schools were fertile grounds for evangelism, and he established the linkages between primary schools and the parish churches. He also headed the schools with a priest or a deaconess whenever possible, to expose the students to Christianity. However, he advised teachers that teaching, not evangelism, was their mandate. Even in universities, ROH emphasized that "evangelism" as narrowly understood, was not the concern of the Anglican Church:[38]

> Our Anglican concern is not "evangelism" in this "ism" sense, but the whole activity of the Love of God . . . For the Love of God lays on us the duty to educate his children in science, literature, economics, philosophy and so on. Anglican participation in university life has no evangelistic purpose in the "ism" sense of evangelism. It has everything to do with the proclamation of the news that all creation is good, and means good to men because the God who made it has shown us His heart in Jesus Christ, and has in Christ's dying and rising again broken the power of evil which is the enemy of the good world which God has made.

Second, ROH encouraged the use of Chinese as the medium of instruction in the primary school curriculum.[39] Most parents at that time believed that learning English was the surest way of making a good living in Hong Kong,

Table 6.1 Churches Linked to Schools and/or Social Welfare Centers

Miles	Town or Estate	Church	School	Other Social Service
5	Tsuen Wan	Church (Crown of Thorn Church)	(Chu Yan Primary) Comprehensive Secondary (Lam Woo Secondary)	Workers' Hostel
4½	Tai Wo Hau		Kei Mong Primary (discontinued)	
3	Lai Chi Kok		2 primary schools (Kei Wing)	
1	Li Cheng Uk	(Kei Oi Church)	Kei Oi Primary St. Clement rooftop (St. Clement Primary)	
0	Starting from junction of Castle Peak Road and Tai Po Road			
½	Shek Kip Mei	St. Thomas' Church	St. Thomas' Primary	St. Thomas' Clinic
1	Kowloon Tong	Christ Church	Diocesan Preparatory Bishop Hall Jubilee Secondary	
1 ½	Kowloon City	Holy Trinity Church	Holy Trinity Primary	
1 ¾	San Po Kong		All Saints Middle (Lee Kau Yan Memorial Secondary)	
2	Kai Tak	Kei Tak Church (Calvary Church)	Kai Tak Primary (Kei Tak primary)	Workers' Hostel Children's Meal
2 ½	Wong Tai Sin	(Calvary Church)	Kei Sun Primary	
3	Choi Hung	(Calvary Church)	Kei Po and Kei Lok Primary (Yat Sau and Ching San) Secondary Modern (St. Benedict)	
5	Kwun Tong	St. Barnabas' Church	St. Barnabas' Primary	

Note: The above table, prepared by ROH in 1961, includes churches, schools, and welfare centers that were in use or were being planned to be built (with names in brackets, supplemented by the author).

but ROH persuaded them to teach their children Chinese history, culture, and poetry, and to instill pride about China's past and its great heroes. Although not successful in changing the medium of instruction to Chinese in all primary or secondary schools, ROH was able to implement this vision when he founded Chung Chi College.

Third, while promoting the use of the Chinese language, ROH realized that Hong Kong was a city where East meets West, and knowing that bilingual students from Anglo-Chinese schools had helped create bridges between the two cultures, he urged the Anglo-Chinese schools to retain their bilingual tradition to better serve the population. Proficiency in English of the students in these Anglo-Chinese schools would do much to increase the international status of Hong Kong in the 1970s.

Fourth, ROH emphasized the building of students' moral and spiritual character in the schools. He asked parents to work with a vision of education that prized ethical, moral, and spiritual values above material strivings:[40]

> Will you think about it, and will you not see if we cannot gradually change the spirit of our schools, not to be the slaves of Hong Kong worshippers of money, but to be Chinese who are proud of China's great past and China's great heroes. Our schools exist to teach our children to be good family members and good members of the Chinese race and that must be our first object, rather than to see how many clever students we can get on into middle school. We shall do spiritual harm to all our children if we make that the purpose of our schools.

Finally, ROH urged the schools to "reach out into the neighborhood, into the homes and crowded flats of the resettlement blocks" and to teach the students the spirit of service. He requested that students and teachers learn together the true meaning of community life and respond to each other's needs. ROH asked Miss Cherry, headmistress of St. Stephen's Girls' College, to take over the management of St. Luke's Medical Clinic in order to stimulate the students' interest in social work. He also invited medical students residing at St. John's College to assist the doctor in that clinic.

In 1961, the Church Missionary Society Day School Council was renamed the Hong Kong Sheng Kung Hui Primary School Council to oversee all primary schools,[41] while the Diocesan Education Committee continued to supervise all secondary schools of the diocese. The Diocesan Social Welfare Committee had been created in 1964 in an attempt to oversee the plethora of services provided by the centers within Hong Kong Sheng Kung Hui and to provide a systemic, coordinated approach to social welfare activities for the whole diocese.[42] Subsequently, under the chairmanship of the Very Reverend John Foster, dean of St. John's Cathedral, the Hong Kong Sheng Kung Hui Diocesan Welfare Council was established in 1965, replacing the Social Welfare Committee, to represent all the welfare work of the diocese, communicating information and liaising between various welfare organizations, schools, and parishes, and initiating new projects.[43]

Reaping the Fruits of Labor

During the late 1950s and early 1960s, ROH had the pleasure of ordaining a number of locally trained, enthusiastic young Chinese clergy who were emerging from the Union Theological College in Hong Kong and taking up positions in the new churches. Among them were the future leaders of Hong Kong Sheng Kung Hui (Appendix 3, Table A3.2).

Over the years, there had been requests for Chinese clergy to be sent to Chinese churches in other parts of the world because of the Chinese "diaspora." The diocese even "exported" the Reverend James C. L. Wong to become bishop of Jesselton in 1960[44] and of Taiwan in 1965. James Wong was responsible for the Mandarin congregation at Christ Church after World War II. In 1962, Roland Koh, who was ordained by ROH in 1941 and had set up an active ministry among students in Sun Yat-sen University, became assistant bishop of Singapore and Malaya.[45] The installation of these two individuals helped spread the gospel among the Chinese population in Southeast Asia.

Figure 6.2 ROH and James C. L. Wong, bishop of Borneo (Hall Family Archive)

From 1957 to 1966, 27 students took the three-year course at Hong Kong Union Theological College. Many were ordained and served as vicars in different parts of Hong Kong. After 1966, the students were mostly Anglicans. It became clear that the college, without trainees from other denominations, was no longer viable, and by the late 1960s it had ceased to exist. Most of the Anglican priests after that came through Chung Chi Theological Seminary.

Started in 1963, Chung Chi Theological Seminary associated with Chung Chi College of the Chinese University of Hong Kong, was a union institution set up by seven churches. Affiliated with the Southeast Asia Association of Theological Schools, its council represented by members from different denominations, its vision was that the lives of students could be enriched if they mixed with students in other academic disciplines. The requirements for admission were similar to those for the Chinese University, graduation from high school. Although ROH was one of the founding members of Chung Chi College, he was not enthusiastic about sending theology students to Chung Chi Theological Seminary because it lacked the Anglican tradition of morning and evening prayers and a regular Holy Eucharist. The prayer book and the Anglican tradition were not part of the curriculum.[46]

New Churches and Parishes

Seven more new churches and parishes were established during this period: Holy Carpenter Church (Hung Hom), Calvary Church (Wong Tai Sin), St. Barnabas' Church (Kwun Tong), St. Mark's Church (Hung Hom), St. Peter's Church (North Point), Kei Oi Church (Li Cheng Uk) and Crown of Thorns Church (Tsuen Wan) (see Appendix 4, Table A4.1), each church linked to a school, a social welfare center, or a medical clinic, or a combination thereof. ROH constantly reminded people of God's love. In his sermon on February 9, 1964, consecrating Kei Oi Church, which offered a variety of social services and was close to Kei Oi School, ROH preached again on the demanding nature of God's call to love—something very difficult to hearken to at times:[47]

> Jesus' love was not like a cushion or something comfortable to sleep on. His love was like steel, like fire. Because his love is stern like steel, He commands us, He tells us to obey God. He said that his daily bread was to do the Will of God (St. John 4:34). Finally He said to his disciples, "I have a new commandment for you. It is this: you must love one another as I have loved you."
>
> Kei Oi Church is not a preaching house. We have no loud speakers or radios filling people's ears with words about the Love of God. Kei Oi is a centre for action. Only when our neighbours come to feel the Love that is in our hearts and in our actions, will they be able to believe that what we say is true that behind all the greyness of the world, there is love.

Here we see how ROH called upon his listeners to look deeper, to see through what may appear to be gray dullness to a transcendent purpose.

Unity through Diversity

ROH cooperated extensively with the Roman Catholic Church and other Protestant denominations. Unlike most of his colleagues who supported the ecumenical movement in the Anglican Church and in the Anglican Communion, ROH did not accept ecclesiastical unity as an ideal to strive for, and was notably absent from ecumenical activities. The multinational World Student Christian Federation and the National Christian Council conferences, attended by delegates from over 130 denominations in 1925, showed ROH the difficulties of coming to a consensus, helping him to develop the concept of "unity through diversity."

ROH's experience in China had also convinced him that organizational divisions of the church had led to a wider outreach of the Christian gospel than any single, united church could achieve. He observed that the diversification of the gospel had been on the surface wasteful, yet the resulting conversions were remarkable. He wrote, "No one could dare say that an unbroken visible church would have had a more extensive, more sensitive, more varied contact with the 'world' than these restless sensitive fingers of the divided church including the various Roman orders and the Reformed churches and sects." ROH spoke of the hand needing all its fingers to function fully. ROH believed that Christianity would be able to flourish in Hong Kong and in other parts of the world only if it could embrace the paradox of "unity through diversity," something very different from an imposed unification. He wrote:[48]

> I believe the cause of Christ is well served by having Methodists intensely Methodist, in their enthusiasm and their love of song and their disciplined organization and control; in having Congregationalists intensely Congregationalist in their fellowship with one another in the Spirit; in having Presbyterians augustly Presbyterian in their wisdom, their thoroughness, their efficiency, their impossibility of being wrong and their immensely conscientious theological colleges. And as for Anglicans, I believe there will always be a place for a church so ridiculously amateur, and intensely human, neither one thing nor the another, with a little bit of autocracy, a little bit of fellowship, a little bit of constitutionalism, but, pray God, always with a sense of humor.

He further explained that a "reunited church is a circumferential unity and has psychological limits. The circumference of a circle inevitably excludes, but radii running out from the center are capable of indefinite extension without losing their attachment to Christ in the center like the spokes of a wheel. This, I assume, is the scriptural basis of Maurice's insistence that unity comes from being tied to a common center, not from any definition of circumference."[49]

ROH's ecumenical ideas owed a debt to F. D. Maurice, who expressed much sympathy for the ways that other denominations all contribute to the beauty of a large mosaic dedicated to the honor of God: "No amalgamation of these can create a real harmony, but each may find its highest meaning in that harmony which God has created and of which He is Himself the Centre."[50]

Respect for Other Cultures and Religions

As a practical visionary, ROH advocated that Christians understand and respect other faiths. ROH's reverence for Confucius was displayed when he bowed three times in front of the sage's tomb in 1926, and declared in a letter to his parents, "I felt there somehow that in a natural restrained way, Confucianism really is a religion."[51] In a sermon he talked about the way that Chinese civilization had been created by God, revealed through Christ's incarnation:[52]

> In my Chapel above the altar are the four characters, "Dao Shing Yuk San" (The Word Was Made Flesh). They are printed in triumphant gold on red ground. Why triumphant gladness? It means that the Dao[53] which has always been the creative heart of Chinese life and culture, reveals himself in Jesus Christ . . . Jesus Christ is the Word of God "by whom all things are made." Chinese civilization has been made by the Word of God, whose heart and purpose is revealed to us in the face of Jesus Christ.

ROH ensured that other faiths, including Islam, Buddhism, and Hinduism, were represented and that their followers had a chance to offer their prayers at the unveiling ceremony of the War Memorial at Saiwan Bay. He also paid tribute to Dag Hammarskjöld, secretary-general of the United Nations, who died in a plane crash in 1961, in two interreligious memorial services.[54] He cooperated with other faiths in a number of social welfare activities.

In September 1957, ROH established a Christian Study Center in Chinese Religions at Tao Fong Shan, Sha Tin, to examine and define the activity of God in contemporary Chinese society. The center's goal was "to study the presentation of God to Chinese followers and the way the Chinese Christian perceives God, so that our work will be helpful to those who are responsible to preach gospel to the Chinese."[55] At that time, ROH perceived that the Church was seriously weakened internally by the "civilization vacuum" among new Christians who, in accepting the spirituality of Christ, had lost the traditional Chinese way of life. This vacuum was inevitably being filled by the quest for money-based security. The center published the Chinese journal *Ching Feng*, and it remains active today in its new home in the Theology Building, Chung Chi College.

After his intense encounters in China in 1926 with religions and cultures much older than Christianity and Britain, ROH became convinced that Christianity and other faiths are all different expressions of different cultures and different peoples, but that all were created by God. In his goat yard, ROH noticed a kind of living parable that spoke to him about the incomprehensible vastness of God's truth. In the winter, ROH's goats were fed sweet potatoes, too big for them to chew because their mouths were small, so the potatoes had to be cut up into smaller pieces. Similarly, ROH perceived that the whole of God's truth is far too great to be comprehended by a single mind or a set of beliefs. In his mercy, God cuts up his truth into smaller parts for each believer to take in, digest, and make part of him or herself—but not to assume that his part is the whole truth.[56]

"For I Was Hungry and You Gave Me Food"

As Hong Kong's economy continued to improve from the 1950s into the 1960s, ROH did not create any more new social welfare institutions except for the Children's Meals Society. Although children were not starving in the 1960s, many were undernourished, and this program aimed to serve these children one hot meal every school day.[57]

In 1961, children under 15 years of age made up 40 percent of the population in Hong Kong, where infectious diseases such as measles, diphtheria, and tuberculosis were common. These diseases spread because of marked overcrowding and the poor resistance to infection in undernourished children. While overcrowding was not something that any voluntary agency could solve, improving the nutrition of schoolchildren was something that ROH knew how to do. He had shown earlier that, after being fed one nutritious meal a day for six months, the children of St. James' Settlement improved both physically and mentally, and suffered fewer infections. He had also learned that in England in early 1900s, Margaret McMillan had established the first Children's Meals Services, which made the children more robust, allowing them to read, write, calculate, and sing better in schools.[58]

ROH proposed to the Education Department that the Church would provide one low-cost nutritious meal a day to undernourished schoolchildren during each school day. He estimated that there were 70,000 children (an overestimation) who needed such services in Hong Kong.[59] He started the program in the primary schools in industrial areas: Kei Oi in Li Cheng Uk, Kei Sun in Wong Tai Sin, St. Thomas' in Shum Shui Po, St. Barnabas' in Kwun Tong, Lui Ming Choi in the Western District and Che Nam in Aberdeen. ROH appointed P. Y. Cheung (later bishop of Taiwan) to oversee the running of the program. Children whose family income was less than $35 per person, per month were eligible for the program. A child welfare officer would visit in order to decide whether or not to accept the applicant. If accepted into the program, students would receive a meal of rice with meat or fish, and vegetables.[60]

To fund the program, ROH appealed to the Education Department and various local and international agencies. There were enthusiastic responses from the Church World Service, the Anglican Church of Canada, and the Mennonites, who all became staunch supporters of the program.⁶¹ In the 1964/65 school year, close to 2 million meals were provided to about 13,000 children in 121 schools. Students from Roman Catholic, Anglican, Buddhist, Daoist, Methodist, and secular schools were all treated equally under this program.⁶²

ROH passed on the chairmanship of the Society to Oswald Cheung, a well-known barrister, who later served in the Legislative Council and the Executive Council. Cheung worked hard to raise funds to keep the food program going and in coordinating it with other agencies. In 1974, when Hong Kong had become more affluent, school meals were considered unnecessary and the program was discontinued.⁶³ This program was a massive undertaking and required a great deal of planning and organization, but ROH always had great faith that God would provide.

Helping Meet the Demand for Social Workers

ROH was closely involved in training the social workers that were desperately needed in Hong Kong after World War II. He often gave lectures on social welfare topics to social work students and to general audiences, and offered students from Chung Chi College practical training at St. James' Settlement, as well as with the rooftop work in the resettlement estate schools. As a project to nurture students' interest in social work, he asked St. Stephen's Girls' College to take over the management of the medical clinic in St. Luke's Settlement in Kennedy Town.⁶⁴ He sent Miss Lee Hei Man of St. James' Settlement to England and later to Montreal, to further her studies in social work. In 1964, the highly qualified Lee left to teach social work at Chung Chi College, helping to increase the number of social workers in Hong Kong.⁶⁵ ROH was one of the architects in developing the Hong Kong Social Workers' Association in the late 1940s, and he encouraged the association to publish its own journal, the *Hong Kong Journal of Social Work*.⁶⁶ With characteristic eloquence, ROH uttered a plea that still resonates today in the hearts of civic-minded people in many places:

> We must find ways to enlist many more young men and women into voluntary personal service if this city so beautiful, and so beloved, is to be a real family, a real community, in the truest sense of the word: a City.

Working to Increase Educational Access

In Hong Kong the expansion of primary education occurred between 1950 and 1970, secondary education between 1970 and 1980, and higher education from 1980 onward. By the mid-1980s, Hong Kong not only had universal junior secondary education but was also approaching universal senior secondary education.[67] During the latter part of his episcopate, ROH focused his energy on expanding education, working closely with the government to fulfill their objectives, as by then most of his social welfare projects were maturing and the work of the Housing Society was progressing well.

Of the 187 new primary schools and 109 new secondary schools established in Hong Kong from 1945 to 1969 that were still operating in 2010, 25 (13.4 percent) and 10 (9.2 percent) respectively belonged to Hong Kong Sheng Kung Hui; the equivalent figures for the Roman Catholic Church were 62 (33.3 percent) and 33 (30.3 percent) respectively.[68] In 1955, there were only about 8,000 Anglicans compared to 73,499 Roman Catholics,[69] representing 0.34 percent and 3.14 percent of a Hong Kong population of 2.34 million. Hong Kong Sheng Kung Hui made a proportionately greater contribution to education than did the Roman Catholic Church or the rest of the general population.

From 1958 to 1968, 18 primary schools were founded by Hong Kong Sheng Kung Hui under ROH's supervision; of these, two were church schools, nine were new primary schools, and seven were resettlement schools (Appendix 4, Table A4.4). Two Church Missionary Society schools were rebuilt. Most of the new primary schools that ROH founded were for children in poorer districts. In Hong Kong, he had two primary schools built as part of a social settlement: St. James' Primary School as part of St. James' Settlement in Wan Chai, and Lui Ming Choi Primary School as part of St. Luke's Settlement in Kennedy Town.[70] He did not ignore the rural communities in the New Territories: Ling Oi in Yuen Long was founded in 1932;[71] Kei Shek in Tai Po was built for children in nearby villages, as well as the children in St. Christopher's Home;[72] St. Simon's in Castle Peak accommodated children of the fishing and rural communities;[73] and St. Joseph's in Kam Tin served the local rural community.[74]

Following the superb advice from the Education Department, ROH established a number of primary schools within the resettlement estates, where life was very hard. In most families, both parents had to work to make ends meet, and children as young as 6 to 10 years of age performed the arduous adult tasks of cleaning the apartment, washing clothes, carrying water, cooking, and taking care of their younger siblings. Few lucky ones had the benefit of going to school. Having a school in one of the resettlement buildings in the estate would solve the problem of finding land for a school, while also allowing the children of the estate to attend school with their siblings.

ROH inaugurated the first primary resettlement estate school, Kei Sun Primary School in Wong Tai Sin, Kowloon. Opened in 1960, shortly after the completion of the estate, it occupied the ground floors of Blocks U and V, the upper floors of which were crowded with inhabitants, mostly children. The small school accommodated 810 students in each of the two sessions. The school fees of $50 per year were paid in 10 equal instalments, and approximately 10 percent of students attended free or paid only partial fees.[75]

The school had 20 rooms, and with the exception of a general office and a staff room, the rest were classrooms (three classes for each of the six grades). Each classroom accommodated 45 children, as required by the Education Department. The open space within the H-plan of the blocks served as the school hall for morning and afternoon gatherings. On festivals, neighbors crowded the balcony of the upper floors, looking down to cheer the performances of the children below. On sunny days the open-air courtyard was fine, though on rainy days, teachers needed umbrellas to go from one classroom to another.

In all primary schools in the industrial developments, ROH rented a room on the rooftop as a multipurpose space: it could convert from music room to work room, or room for a Sunday school. ROH also used it as a dining room to serve meals to undernourished children. To provide training opportunities for social work students and use labor efficiently, ROH had students from Chung Chi College assess the families for eligibility for free meals and study the socioeconomic status of the schoolchildren. These clubs not only kept the children off the streets, but also helped to build character.

The noisy and overcrowded resettlement estate schools were far from ideal environments for teaching. ROH empathized with teachers' struggles to show their respect and care for each child, and to encourage the full development of human potential in these overloaded classrooms. At various gatherings, ROH spoke about not letting these schools become factories. He also encouraged teachers to be like the Spendthrift Sower in Jesus' parable, giving themselves freely to their students, not seeking glory for themselves:[76]

> In his parables, Jesus gave examples of how God rules. "You can see," He said, "examples of God's rule in the way leaven works, or in the way a tiny seed becomes a great tree, or as the sower who scattered his seed in spendthrift fashion even on ground that was used as a foot-path, and among thorns and in soil not deep enough for the seed to grow up. But when it fell on good ground it brought forth fruit, some of it a hundred fold."
>
> Let this then be your way as teachers, sowing yourself as recklessly as the spendthrift sower of Our Lord's parable. Let your pupils and your school itself work like leaven, like salt, out into the community. For leaven and salt do not draw the goodness of the flour, or of the food into themselves for their own aggrandizement, but rather lose themselves by going out into the flour and the food. So it is with light, another of Our Lord's picture of how God rules. Light's very nature is to spread out into the darkness around it.

Kay Barker, headmistress of St. Stephen's Girls' College, remarked that ROH's charismatic personality provided much inspiration for the teachers, who simply did not want to let him down.[77]

The resettlement estate schools served their purpose by bringing mass primary education to the disadvantaged sections of Hong Kong in the 1960s and 1970s. In the 1980s when Hong Kong became more prosperous, the resettlement estate schools were rebuilt to provide environments more hospitable to learning.

The expansion of primary school education in the 1950s without an accompanying increase in secondary schools led to the formation of a bottleneck in Form 1 (or Grade 7). In 1961, there were fewer than 100,000 students in secondary schools from a population of 270,000 12- to 16-year-olds. The growth in Hong Kong's economy resulted in rising demand for both skilled workers and secondary school places. The government responded to these pressures, after consultation with external and local experts in education, by publishing the White Paper, *Education Policy, 1965*, which included, among other things, the recommendation to provide universal primary education by 1971.[78] ROH, who had been pushing the government for free primary education since the end of the war, finally had his dream realized after his retirement.

From 1958 to 1968, Hong Kong Sheng Kung Hui under ROH founded five academic secondary schools (Bishop Hall Jubilee School, Tang Siu Kin Secondary School, Lee Kau Yan Memorial School, St. Mary's Church, and St. Stephen's Church College) and one was planned (Sheng Kung Hui Lam Woo Memorial School), but did not materialize until 1970 (Appendix 4, Table A4.5).[79] These schools prepared young people for tertiary education.

A pragmatist as well as an idealist, ROH did not believe that every child would benefit equally from receiving academic instruction, especially in the competitive economic environment of Hong Kong in the first two postwar decades. He was convinced that there should be two types of education, one leading to employment after leaving school, and the other leading to higher education. After receiving a report of the Technical Education Committee of the need for vocational schools,[80] the Education Department requested that ROH cooperate with them to build and run two modern secondary schools on an experimental basis in two industrial districts: St. Basil's Secondary Modern School in Shau Kei Wan, near St. Mark's School, and St. Benedict's Secondary Modern School in Choi Hung Estate, a public housing estate.[81] These modern schools offered courses for three years. Instead of regular classrooms, these schools had rooms for woodwork, metalwork, handicraft, dressmaking, typing, music, and art.[82] Unfortunately, parents did not appreciate the value of these schools because they wanted their children to be in the academic stream toward becoming doctors, lawyers, nurses, teachers or chief executive officers. In the end, these schools were closed and St. Basil's became St. Mark's Primary School.

ROH chaired the school committees of all secondary schools and determined the composition of these committees to ensure a close bond between the schools and the parish churches. For example, the school committee of

Lee Kau Yan Memorial School consisted of the headmaster, vicars from the nearby Anglican churches—All Saints' Church, Holy Trinity Church, and Calvary Church—and one lay representative from each of these three churches, as well as one or two lay representatives from churches from a wider area. The principal of an Anglican secondary school was generally the supervisor of the school.[83] Even though decision-making for the secondary schools, especially the selection of headmasters or headmistresses, was supposed to be a democratic process decided by the members of the school committee, ROH often made these appointments unilaterally. At times his arbitrary decisions caused dissent (see below). For secondary schools, he preferred the headmaster to be a priest, and when a suitable priest was not available, a devout Anglican with appropriate educational background would be chosen.

ROH met regularly with officials of the Education Department to assess the status of schools in Hong Kong and to find out which districts would require new schools. At the end of these meetings, he often came up with a long list of schools planned for future development.[84] ROH worked closely with the Education Department and the Resettlement Department to solve the problems of providing education for thousands of children in the resettlement estates. At times the Education Department asked ROH to build schools in certain areas where a need had been identified, the two primary schools (Yat Sau and Ching Shan) in Choi Hung Estate being an example of such a request.[85] The Education Department had great faith in Hong Kong Sheng Kung Hui's ability to build and manage these schools.

In the 1960s, when it became easier to obtain interest-free loans, capital grants, and free land to build schools, ROH was personally involved in negotiation with the Education Department for the planning of each school. From the mid-1950s to the time of his retirement, ROH might be working with the Education Department on five or six school projects at varying stages of development at any given time. This close partnership with the Education Department resulted in the founding of 22 new primary and 10 new secondary schools, and the rebuilding and expansion of most of the established primary and secondary schools during ROH's episcopacy—an immense achievement.

ROH's *Modus Operandi*

To build up such a diocese with its numerous activities in evangelism, social welfare, and education, and to keep it operating successfully and developing in new directions, required someone with extraordinary foresight, strong will, tremendous energy, the ability to delegate, and great political skill and power. Let us examine ROH's *modus operandi*.

It can be particularly difficult for someone as creative as ROH to know when to relinquish power to others, trusting them to take up ideas and carry them to fruition in their own ways. ROH had a remarkable ability to find, in both the Chinese and English churches, the right men and women to carry his work forward.

When ROH delegated a certain job to a person, he completely trusted that person and seldom intervened. By not hovering over people, ROH showed confidence that even those who might not have any previous training for the job, which was common enough, were still highly capable. ROH's faith in people inspired them to do their best. He would follow up when necessary, to address ongoing concerns, especially with some projects of an experimental nature, such as St. James' Settlement and Holy Carpenter Church and Hostel. In addition to the monthly executive committee meetings, he met with his inexperienced delegates in these institutions weekly, at least in the beginning.[86] They were also encouraged to go to him if there was any problem. ROH did not lavish praise, but they all felt they were loved.[87]

Funding for social work after World War II was not easy to secure, and to establish a settlement required diligent planning and promotion. Starting St. James' Settlement as a small pilot project illustrates the strategic way ROH operated. When people saw the good results, he was able to request more funding from various sources. Holy Carpenter Church and Hostel, St. Luke's Settlement, and St. Thomas' Church and Clinic were all founded using this pilot strategy. Objective evidence is important and, just like action, speaks louder than words.

Impatient by nature, ROH disliked red tape and bureaucracy, and he had a tendency to cut corners. He often did what was expedient in order to move projects ahead. For example, because of a lack of teachers, he allowed less qualified ones to teach in the workers' children's schools. He felt that it was better to get results—giving children some education—rather than getting swallowed up in a morass of details and accomplishing nothing.

ROH's three-in-one principle for buildings was not only an innovative way for maximizing the use of space, but also provided for both the spiritual and social needs of the community, his mission strategy. A single building might function as a school on weekdays, a medical clinic in the evenings, and a church on Sundays. Other combination of flexible use could be found in Holy Carpenter Church and Hostel: a canteen at lunch time, a hostel at night, and a church on Sunday evening.

ROH, who became a brigade major during World War I when he was barely twenty years old, was comfortable in positions of command. Chairing the important committees for his projects really meant that he had ultimate control over the work of the diocese, as few would defy his wishes. Habitually impatient with slow processes, it is not too surprising that he lapsed into the habit of autocracy from time to time, especially as he became older.

Although the Thursday morning clergy meetings were democratic, and young clergy were encouraged to express their views, as the years wore on, around late 1950, there were murmurs that ROH was increasingly authoritarian.

He admitted as much in a letter to Gerald Goodban, headmaster of Diocesan Boys' School, saying that he had become so trusted by people that he often felt he could act on his own.

The appointment of George She to succeed Goodban as the headmaster in 1955 represented what some viewed as an executive overreach of authority. Even though George She was a magistrate, a chaplain of the cathedral, and the supervisor of a number of schools, he was a Eurasian and had no experience as a teacher. Despite objections from almost every European member of the school committee of Diocesan Boys' School to She's appointment, ROH fought hard to obtain an unanimous vote.[88] Believing that ROH had used the prestige of his position to overrule the committee,[89] Goodban pointed out to him that there was no sense in asking men of quality to serve on the committee if they were to be ignored when the most important decisions had to be made. ROH replied that the committee was interested only in anglicizing the Chinese students, and that the members did not come from the same social milieu as the parents of the boys; therefore, as bishop, he was prepared to overrule them.

Goodban thought this response both ungracious and absurd. ROH's objections to the European members of the committee applied equally well to ROH himself, and would have disqualified any missionary. It was ironic that ROH was ignoring the input of the school committee members that he had previously praised as not being "yes-men," as he felt that their Catholic school counterparts were. The appointment of George She as headmaster angered the members of the school committee, the old boys, and the "Westernized" teachers in the school, even though they were Chinese.

ROH did not explain to the school committee or to Goodban his primary reason for appointing George She as headmaster. Diocesan Boys' School at that time was modeled after the British public school tradition, with emphasis on the English language. Chinese language was mostly ignored by students or treated flippantly.[90] ROH wished to change the attitude of the students and the staff, since he was sure that Hong Kong would be returned to China in the near future. He told Nora, "I am so convinced that he [George] will make it [DBS] a better school than it has ever been—more belonging, less England conscious—more Hong Kong conscious and less division between European and Chinese staff." The other reason was purely personal. ROH felt that George She, now married and a father, should direct his full attention to one job—the school—instead of being pulled in several directions.

Although She's appointment was backed by Crozier, Crozier told ROH that the situation might have been managed better. Feeling miserable afterward, ROH confessed to Nora, "If I could be really humbled, should I be a better man. I feel Gerald [Goodban] and Mary [Mrs. Goodban] are so straight and I am so crooked."[91]

As headmaster, George She brought about the changes that ROH had sought. He expanded the school to accommodate a larger number of primary school graduates and called on the government to conduct a review of education in Hong Kong. He elevated the status of the Chinese teaching staff and merged the two staff common rooms so that the Chinese and the European teachers would have closer interaction with each other. Chinese music was taught in the school and an orchestra featuring traditional Chinese musical instruments was formed. He brought a more egalitarian ethos into the school and practiced the principle of ethnic equality.

Working with the Government

Even though the Anglican Church in Hong Kong was not an established church, it counted some of the most important senior British officials in the congregation of St. John's Cathedral, including the governor. ROH made full use of his position as their spiritual leader for the greater good of Hong Kong, meeting with the governor, and his successors, about once every two months.

Although they respected each other, the relationship between Governor Grantham and ROH was strained from the beginning due to differences in political outlook. After the row over the workers' children's schools in July 1949,[92] their relationship chilled to such a degree that the regular meetings halted while each tried in vain to find a replacement to negotiate with. The government asked Canterbury to remove ROH. In turn, when ROH heard that the more liberal members of the government, David MacDougall and Geoffrey Herklots,[93] had been let go in November 1949, he asked Cecil Rogers (a Bank of England representative and advisor to the previous Guomindang government in China) to ask Prime Minister Attlee to replace Grantham.[94]

In the end, the governor sent an olive branch. After he wrote a personal note inviting ROH to dinner in his home in April 1950, the regular meetings resumed.[95] Over the years, gradual improvements in the working relationship between the two culminated in great success in 1956, with the founding the Chung Chi College. The following year, Grantham retired.

Immediately after the war, the government wanted to exert more control over the grant schools. ROH had to negotiate hard with the government for more freedom in hiring teachers and charging *tong fai*, which were fees to be retained and used by the school to cover extra expenses, in addition to the tuition fees collected on behalf of the government. ROH arranged for a meeting over this disagreement with the Education Department with Sir Christopher Cox, who was in charge of the education section of the Colonial Office, and the Director of Education of Hong Kong, who happened to be in London while ROH was on leave in 1948. ROH thought he got what he wanted from Sir Christopher, but on returning to Hong Kong, he found that Education Department interpreted the results of the meeting differently and revoked all the decisions made in London.[96]

When D. J. S. Crozier, a member of the congregation of St. John's Cathedral, became the Director of Education in 1951, ROH formed a close working relationship with him. Negotiation over the workers' children's schools had been very difficult, often soured by unrealistic worker demands and the "repressive" attitude of the Education Department representatives.[97] In 1951, ROH felt he had been sidelined when the governor sent a proposal for establishing a Christian college to someone else for comments.[98] Despite these strains, even after Crozier's retirement in 1961, the Anglican Church and the Education Department maintained the cooperative relationship they had worked hard to achieve.

ROH had a difficult balance to strike, harshly criticizing Grantham's policies, but working to cooperate with various government departments, including the Public Works Department, the Resettlement Department, and the Social Welfare Department. Although successive governors respected ROH, people in the government were wary of him and scrutinized any proposal from him with great diligence. ROH needed land to build schools, churches, and social welfare organizations. He would read the lease conditions of land very carefully, finding possibilities that had not been seen by others. He "out-thought" them in ways that did not always go down well with government officials.[99] When ROH was puzzled by the lukewarm nature of government officials' responses, Dean Rose of St. John's Cathedral explained, "The trouble is, Bishop, you are always right and government departments don't like being proved wrong."[100]

As the 1950s wore on, ROH lost something of his old fire, slipping gradually into a "less aggressive, less prophetic social commentary." Age might have mellowed and softened his edges. Sir Jack Cater, a close friend of ROH after the war, who became the director of Independent Commission Against Corruption, recalled that there was a great deal of opposition within the government to the so-called "Red Bishop" and "do-gooder" after his visit to China and subsequent press interview as well as his support of the labor unions.[101] There were also criticisms of his autocratic ways in dealing with some government officials, which aroused antagonism toward Hong Kong Sheng Kung Hui, something his successor would have to deal with after assuming office.

Preparing for Future Ministry

By the 1960s, the Anglican Church of Hong Kong had become a huge enterprise. ROH had installed strong leadership in both the English and the Chinese churches, and he had inspired many individuals to dedicate their lives to the service of the Church. In the Anglican secondary schools, there was a group of devoted headmasters and headmistresses. In social welfare, he also had strong, faithful persons to head each organization.

To cope with the expansion of the Church and the activities of the diocese, more clergy and devoted laypeople would be needed, and ROH worked hard to recruit young people into the ministry. He saw this role as similar to the roles of St. Peter and St. Paul with the early Christians: "My job is to try and give them that sense of meaningfulness not by saying what I've just said to you—but by shewing them in what sense they are those who hold in their hands the reins of history and the destinies of the nations."[102] ROH visited schools and attended youth fellowships and summer camps whenever possible, to scout for possible candidates. Thanks to fortunate timing, ROH was able to tap into a large pool of talent as more and more young men were graduating from the Hong Kong Union Theological College. Others were completing their training in the United States; among them bright, enthusiastic young priests such as Alan Chan and Peter Kwong. They would become the next generation of pillars of the diocese.

With such robust leadership in place in the diocese, ROH was no longer preoccupied with his domestic ministry. As he was cut off from his beloved mainland Chinese, he wanted to expand his ministry to hundreds of thousands of Chinese scattered around the world, especially those in Southeast Asia. He devoted time to establishing the Council of Churches of Southeast Asia, which would become a regional grouping of Anglican bishopric in that area.

The council was originally planned in 1933 to enable the bishops in Southeast Asia to counsel each other on common regional problems, but the war stopped all efforts. The idea was revived in 1954 at a meeting in Minneapolis of the Central Anglican Council on Missionary Strategy, and there was a proposal to hold a series of regional councils and conferences including the region of Southeast Asia comprising Singapore, Borneo, the Philippines, Korea, and Burma.[103] ROH, the most senior bishop in East Asia, having served for over 20 years, assumed the role of chair of the regional council. Discussions took place in two conferences, one in Manila in 1957 and one in Kuching in 1960, with bishops, priests and lay delegates from Southeast Asia. After Kuching, the four dioceses, Singapore, Borneo, Rangoon, and Hong Kong, took further action to initiate a province that could provide metropolitical authority for their dioceses, and they sent a petition to Archbishop Geoffrey Fisher to this effect.

In 1960, the transfer of Harry Baines from bishop of Singapore and Malaya to Wellington, New Zealand created a vacancy. This led Archbishop Fisher to propose constituting Singapore an archbishopric for the region of Southeast Asia in the pattern of the Jerusalem Archbishopric. Fisher asked ROH whether he was prepared to move to Singapore and be archbishop of the region of Southeast Asia.[104] ROH, who turned 65 that year and remained healthy, was not yet ready to retire. He looked forward to new challenges, but was ambivalent about Fisher's proposal. At that time, while the leadership in both the English and the Chinese churches was strong, Archdeacon Lee Kau Yan and Canon Paul Tso were about to retire, and St. Peter's Church in North Point and St. Andrew's Church in Kowloon each had a new vicar, and St. John's Cathedral had brought on a new dean. There would soon be a number of young people graduating from the Theological College and ready for the ministry, and ROH needed to be around for another year or so to "protect" them. Nevertheless, he felt confident that all these problems would be resolved in another year.

If ROH was tempted to accept Fisher's proposal and leave for Singapore in 1960, he did not like the title of archbishop. The Council of Churches of Southeast Asia worked well with the bishops taking turns to chair. Nora, who was tired of living in East Asia and had wanted ROH to retire, strongly opposed the idea. Though distressed and conflicted, he finally decided not to accept Fisher's offer.[105] Because other dioceses also opposed the idea, Fisher withdrew his proposal.

In 1961, the Diocese of Borneo was divided, providing the opportunity of forming a province composed of four dioceses: two in Borneo, one each in Singapore and Burma. Hong Kong withdrew its offer to join, for political reasons, but requested that the Council of Churches of Southeast Asia assume the trusteeship of the canons and constitutions of Chung Hua Sheng Kung Hui, which had been held by the archbishop of Canterbury since 1951. Michael Ramsey, who succeeded Geoffrey Fisher as archbishop of Canterbury, agreed to the request once the constitution of the council had been fully drawn up.[106]

In 1962 at Quezon, a formal constitution for the council was drawn up. ROH resigned as chairman of the council and the bishop of Rangoon was elected to succeed him. The following year, the council officially accepted the trusteeship of the canons and constitutions of Chung Hua Sheng Kung Hui to provide metropolitical authority over the Diocese of Hong Kong and Macao. Hong Kong Sheng Kung Hui became more aligned with its neighbors and was no longer under the jurisdiction of Canterbury. The Province of Southeast Asia, however, was not formed until 1996.

The establishment of the Council of Churches of Southeast Asia was a move for the dioceses in the region toward obtaining independence from Canterbury, to become part of the Anglican Communion, in the same spirit as decolonization after World War II. For Hong Kong, it meant more than that. As long as the diocese was under the metropolitan authority of the archbishop of Canterbury, the bishop appointed was likely to be English or European. ROH removed the influence from Canterbury to ensure that, when he retired, there would be a democratically elected bishop in Hong Kong, and better still, a Chinese. This was, among many others, one of his legacies to his beloved diocese.

Who Comes Next? The Question of a Successor

As he advanced in years, ROH began to think about his possible successor. Even though bishops should not choose their successor, they can certainly make

Figure 6.3   ROH and Nora in 1966 (Hall Family Archive)

recommendations for nomination. ROH had considered Michael Goulder, a brilliant biblical scholar who had worked in Hong Kong in 1949 and the early 1950s, as a possible candidate.[107] However, Goulder left Hong Kong in 1966 for Birmingham.[108] Another name that had been discussed was David Paton, a missionary, a member of the Student Christian Movement, a devotee of ROH, and later his biographer; yet interestingly, ROH showed little enthusiasm for this choice.[109]

ROH wrote an article that appeared in the *Church Times* on October 25, 1957, indicating that to have an English bishop in Hong Kong in 1957 was an anachronism.[110] This article caused quite a stir and sparked a lively debate among the expatriates who began to question if the continuation of an English governor in Hong Kong was also an anachronism. They judged that the bishop's intense affection toward the Chinese people threw him off balance, alienating him from the rest of them.[111]

On August 10, 1965, he submitted his resignation to Bishop James C. L. Wong, chairman of the House of Bishops of the Council of Churches of Southeast Asia, which had the metropolitan authority over the Diocese of Hong Kong. He gave his reasons as "advancing years" and "bodily infirmity."[112] Although there was no rule on the retirement age for bishops, he followed the rule for priests. Because Hong Kong Sheng Kung Hui was no longer under the jurisdiction of Canterbury, he summoned the Diocesan Synod to meet in early November to elect the new bishop in a democratic manner.

The election took place on January 6, 1966, preceded by a bilingual celebration of Holy Communion. The Diocesan Conference (English-speaking) clergy and laity and the Diocesan Synod (Chinese-speaking equivalent) clergy and laity took part in voting. Before the balloting, ROH said, "I pray God that my successor will put right what I have done wrong and that he will be a better leader than I have been able to be." Then he went into the cathedral chancel to pray, remaining on his knees while his successor was being elected.[113] There were three candidates: Joost de Blank, former archbishop of Capetown; Roland Koh, assistant bishop of Singapore and Malaya; and the Reverend Cheung Wing Ngok, vicar of St. Stephen's Church. The balloting, which began at 8 p.m., ended around 11 p.m. The announcement of the result was signaled by the ringing of the cathedral bells: Dr. Joost de Blank had been elected.[114]

An outspoken opponent of apartheid, de Blank had become involved in a bitter feud with the South African government and the Dutch Reformed Church. He left South Africa on medical advice in 1963, returning to Britain where he became canon of Westminster. He recovered well enough to allow himself to be nominated to be bishop of Hong Kong and he accepted the offer, planning to take up the position in November 1966. A social and political activist, de Blank would have likely proven a brilliant successor to ROH. Sadly, in March 1966, de Blank became so seriously ill that he could not take up the position.[115]

The diocese held another election. On this occasion, two candidates were nominated: the Reverend Gilbert Baker and Canon Paul Burrough. Baker had worked in Hong Kong and in China before, during and after the war. He was fluent in Cantonese and spoke some Mandarin, and was well respected by all clergy in Hong Kong. Burrough came from an ecclesiastical family and had distinguished himself as a rower in Oxford. During World War II he served in Malaya and spent three and a half years in a Japanese prisoner-of-war camp; he was awarded the MBE on his release, for his leadership in the camp. The wartime experience led him to seek ordination and he returned to East Asia, serving in the market town of Chung-ju in Korea, where he worked among refugees, as well as arranging treatment for lepers. He then returned to work in Birmingham under Bishop Leonard Wilson.[116] With such a background, Burrough was the favored candidate of ROH, who asked some of his clergy to vote for Burrough,[117] an inappropriate and unwise move, even though he did what he thought was best for the diocese.

During the second election, ROH, as before, went into the cathedral chancel to pray. If ROH was disappointed with the election of his successor, Gilbert Baker, very few would have noticed.[118] ROH's preference would have been someone who was a leader, a trailblazer rather than a scholar. Baker told Archbishop Ramsey that he had no intention of entering the race, but he was approached by several Chinese clergy to do so.[119]

One may wonder why ROH didn't nurture someone locally, if he had really wanted a Chinese to be his successor, but at the time his choices would have been very limited. Most of the senior Chinese clergy had attended only Canton

Union Theological College and, with rare exceptions, did not have a university degree. In 1964, ROH wrote to Archbishop Ramsey that if something happened to him in the next year or two, Roland Koh, at that time assistant bishop of Singapore and Malaya, ordained in 1941 in China, would be an excellent candidate for his successor. However, he believed that a European would be elected because both the Chinese clergy and the laity would feel that it would be much easier for a European to work with the Hong Kong government.[120] His assessment was absolutely correct in this remnant of the British Empire, because a Chinese bishop would not have been accepted by the local government at that time.

Looking back with Gratitude and Forward with Hope

On his retirement, ROH was awarded the CMG (Companion of the Order of St. Michael and St. George) for his contributions in Hong Kong.[121] The University of Hong Kong conferred an honorary degree of divinity on ROH and an honorary degree of law on Sir Lindsay Ride, vice-chancellor of the University of Hong Kong, on December 18, 1965. ROH was asked to address the congregation on behalf of Sir Lindsay and himself. Toward the end of the address, he said, "In conclusion, I am going to be unfair to Sir Lindsay and claim that there is one great difference between us. He is interested in the past, even in tombstones, or at least in the historic tombstones of Macao. I am more concerned with the future. Only the short spell of thirty-four years separates Hong Kong today from the twenty-first century. By then this beloved city will be one of the pillars in the New World Order now waiting to be born; a world order which, I believe, will be at once disciplined and liberal."[122] He had great faith in China even though he was cognizant of what was going on in the Mainland at that time.

ROH and Nora had planned to leave Hong Kong at Easter, but the second election delayed their departure. In the meantime, they were overwhelmed with invitations to speak to different organizations. In many farewell speeches, presentations, and banquets, the community poured out their gratitude for ROH's lifetime work in Hong Kong and in China: 34 organizations, including several from other faiths, sent their letters of thanks and gratitude, their love, and their best wishes for his retirement.

ROH and Nora had finally completed their packing and were ready to set sail for England. As they stepped onto the gangplank, ROH felt deeply mixed emotions. In one sense he was going home. But in another he was leaving his adopted home, going into what may have felt like a wrenching kind of exile. In contrast, Nora, exhausted from weeks of packing, still exulted at the thought of finally going back to England.

ROH's modest, quiet farewell message to his beloved people in Hong Kong expressed his love and gratitude for his time in service:[123]

Thank you all and God bless you always.

I write to you all in Our Lord's name to say "thank you" for all that you have done and are doing for Him in His beloved city of Hong Kong: sharing His joy "over one sinner that repenteth."

I have written to say "thank you" to all the Officers and Committee members of the Thanksgiving Fund for all that has been done this year.

This message is to every one of you who have prayed and cared and worked and given to our Lord's work this year and in the long years that are past

Our Lord bids us look for no thanks and for no reward.

But then there comes the unexpected reward of His dear words, "Well done thou good and faithful servant."

You do not give, you do not work, you do not pray for Our Lord's work in order that you may hear those words. You do it because you long above all things to do His Will and to share with others the wonder of His Love and of His mercy.

I pray and shall always pray for you and for all whom the Lord will through each one of you, draw into the radiant happiness of being His friend and servant that you hear Him saying in your heart "Well done thou good and faithful servant, enter thou into the joy of thy Lord."

Notes

1. R. O. Hall to A. C. Hall. October 1957. Chung Chi Divinity School Archive (Nora odd one out among her friends, married to a bishop).
2. R. O. Hall to A. C. Hall. November 6, 1957. Chung Chi College Divinity School Archive.
3. R. O. Hall to A. C. Hall. Sunday in July 1957. Chung Chi Divinity School Archive (ROH took three weeks off not even going to church on Sundays).
4. R. O. Hall to A. C. Hall. November 27, 1957. Chung Chi Divinity School Archive (Celebration of Nora's 60th birthday).
5. R. O. Hall to A. C. Hall. October 13, 1957. Chung Chi Divinity School Archive (The most precious letter).
6. 刑福增、劉紹麟：《天國、龍城：香港聖公會聖三一堂史 1890–2009》(香港：基督教中國宗教文化研究社，2010)，126.
7. The Reverend Charles Long, secretary of the National Council of the Episcopal Church in New York, was released by the National Council to help establish the New Asia College in Hong Kong by Yale-in-China. ROH invited him to be a priest in the Church of the Good Shepherd and an observer of the Standing Committee of the Synod of the Diocese of Hong Kong and Macao.
8. C. Long, "The Diocese of Hong Kong, 1953." Chung Chi Divinity School Archive.
9. R. O. Hall, "Hong Kong Episcopal Nursery: Ten Bishops in Twenty-Five Years," *Fragrant Stream* (October 1959): 3. They were: Mok Shau Tsang, bishop of Guangzhou; Christopher Sargent, bishop of Fujian; Leonard Wilson, bishop of Singapore and later Birmingham; Geoffrey Allen, bishop of Egypt and later of Derby; Y. Y. Zhu, bishop of Yunnan and Guizhou, to be succeeded by

Quentin Huang; Mo-Yung In, bishop of Guangzhou to succeed Bishop Mok; Victor Halward, assistant bishop of Guangzhou and later bishop of Vancouver; Harry Baines, bishop of Singapore and later of Wellington, New Zealand; Noel Chamberlain, bishop of Trinidad.
10. R. Koh, "The Chinese Anglicans in the Four Seas," 1957. Bishop's House Archive.
11. The Bishop Hall Silver Jubilee Celebration. Bishop Hall Jubilee. Bishop's House Archive.
12. The Society of St. Francis is an international religious community, within the Anglican Communion, with members in many parts of the world, seeking to follow Christ in the way of St. Francis of Assisi. The movement was revived in England after World War I by the Reverend Douglas Downes, an economics don at Oxford University, and a few friends. http://www.franciscans.org.uk/Page33.htm.
13. Brother Michael Fisher Mission. Bishop Hall Jubilee File. Bishop's House Archive.
14. Diocesan Service of Dedication. Bishop Hall Jubilee File. Bishop's House Archive.
15. A. Grantham, *St. John's Review* (November 1957): 341.
16. R. O. Hall, "Sermon Preached at the Diocesan Dedication Service on October 28th, 1957 Commemorating the First 25 Years of R. O.'s Episcopate," in Paton, *R. O.: The Life and Times of Bishop R. O. Hall*, 271–74.
17. *South China Morning Post*, October 29, 1957.
18. The Bishop Hall Silver Jubilee Thanksgiving Dinner. Bishop Hall Jubilee File. Bishop's House Archive.
19. Bishop Hall Silver Jubilee Thanksgiving Holy Communion Service. Bishop Hall Jubilee File. Bishop's House Archive.
20. R. O. Hall to A. C. Hall. April 21, 1958. Chung Chi Divinity School Archive (Arriving in Paris for their wedding anniversary).
21. R. O. Hall to A. C. Hall. December 23, 1957. Chung Chi Divinity School Archive (Nora did not stay in England).
22. R. Howard, Bishop Hall's Resignation. Extract from *Christ Church Kowloon Tong Newsletter*. September 1965.
23. ROH jokingly referred to Hong Kong as his "prison" because he could no longer go into China.
24. Minutes of Meeting of the Standing Committee of the Diocesan Synod. March 27, 1961. Bishop's House Archive (ROH to visit Australia and New Zealand).
25. Minutes of Meeting of the Standing Committee of the Diocesan Synod. August 28, 1961. Bishop's House Archive (ROH to attend World Council of Churches in New Delhi and a meeting in Manila).
26. Minutes of Meeting of the Standing Committee of the Diocsean Synod. October 30, 1962. Bishop's House Archive (ROH to visit Canada and US).
27. Minutes of Meeting of the Standing Committee. Febuary 2, 1959. Bishop's House Archive (Archbishop Fisher's visit).
28. Minutes of Meeting of the Standing Committee. October 30, 1962. Bishop's House Archive (Visit of Primate of Canada).
29. *St. John's Review* (April 1959): 105 (Duke of Edinburgh's visit).
30. *St. John's Review* (January 1962): 10 (Princess Alexandra's visit).

31. R. O. Hall, "The Jubilee Mission, 1958." Bishop Hall Jubilee File. Bishop's House Archive.
32. Anglican Church Plans Ambitious Program. Sixteen Schools and Nine Churches in Two Years. HKMS 94-1-14. Hong Kong Public Records Office.
33. Hong Kong Diocesan Program of Advance Detail. Appendix to Minutes of Meeting of the Standing Committee. January 23, 1958. Bishop's House Archive.
34. E. Chong, "R. O.'s Mission Strategy Today," *Diocesan Echo* (June 1997): 3–5.
35. Interview of Bishop Hall by W. Smyly, "Topics: Religious Education," *A History and Records of the Diocesan Boys' School*, 2008, 61–62. Diocesan Boys' School Archive.
36. Report on the Meeting of the Subcommittee on the Relationship between Parish and School. May 14, 1958. Minutes of Meetings of the Standing Committee Book. Bishop's House Archive.
37. *Outpost* (March 1961): 8–9 (Churches and schools).
38. R. O. Hall, "The Vocation of Anglicanism in Asia: The Sense of Belongingness," 1962. HKMS 96-1-29. Hong Kong Public Records Office.
39. R. O. Hall, "A Talk on Primary Education to the YMCA of Hong Kong on December 4, 1952." HKMS 96-1-29. Hong Kong Public Records Office.
40. R. O. Hall, "Sermon: Family-Nation-School and Christianity. Preached on March 21, 1954 to Sheng Kung Hui Day School." Hall Family Archive.
41. Minutes of Meeting of the Standing Committee. September 19, 1960 (HKSKH Primary School Council). Bishop's House Archive. Development of Hong Kong Sheng Kung Hui Primary Schools. Bishop's House Archive.
42. Minutes of Meeting of the Standing Committee. March 9, 1964. Bishop's House Archive.
43. Minutes of Meeting of the Standing Committee. March 30, 1965. Bishop's House Archive (Diocesan Welfare Council).
44. *Fragrant Stream* (October 1959): 2.
45. *St. John's Review* (September 1962): 18–19 (Roland Koh's consecration).
46. P. Wickeri, "Clergy Training and Theological Education: The Sheng Kung Hui Experience in China." Conference paper presented at the International Symposium on the History of Christianity in Modern China, June 10–11, 2011.
47. R. O. Hall, "Sermon Preached on the Consecration of Kei Oi Church, February 9, 1964." Kei Oi Church File. Bishop's House Archive.
48. R. O. Hall, "Why I Am Not a Reunionist?" *The Chinese Recorder* (April 1941): 197–202.
49. R. O. Hall to M. Warren. October 24, 1961. Church Missionay Society File. On Reunion. Bishop's House Archive.
50. R. O. Hall to M. Warren. October 24, 1961 (F. D. Maurice, on reunion). Bishop's House Archive.
51. R. O. Hall to parents. August 26, 1926. Chung Chi Divinity School Archive.
52. R. O. Hall, "Sermon 'The Destiny of the Chinese Church' Preached on August 21, 1949 at St. John's Cathedral," in Paton, *R. O.: The Life and Times of Bishop R. O. Hall*, 251–55.
53. The word *Dao* or *Tao* has been used by Protestant theologians seeking to indigenize Christianity, to translate "word" as in John 1, 1. ROH explained in a letter

to Dr. Dewart, "The Chinese word *Tao* (*Dao*) is in my judgment a better form of expression than Logos for the self-giving of God."
54. Mr. Dag Hammarskjoeld, "Memorial Service in St. John's Cathedral and the Inter-religious Tribute," *St. John's Review* (November 1961): 233–36.
55. R. O. Hall, "A Suggested Defintion of the Purpose and Basis: The Hong Kong Study Centre in Relation to the Contemporary Situation," 1957. Chung Chi Divinity School Archive.
56. Personal Communication from Canon Christopher Hall.
57. Children's Meal Society File. File C28. Bishop's House Archive.
58. R. O. Hall, "My Interest in Children's Meals: Talk Given to Notary, Hong Kong." October 24, 1960. Children's Meal Society File. Bishop's House Archive.
59. R. O. Hall to Director of Education. October 15, 1959. General, Children's Meals Society File C21.3. Bishop's House Archive.
60. J. Cheng, "Report of Visits to Schools." May 7, 1962. Children's Meals Society File C26. Bishop's House Archive.
61. E. E. Gates to R. O. Hall, July 23, 1960; K. R. Marshall to R. O. Hall, July 15, 1960; L. E. Hatfiled to R. O. Hall, August 18, 1960. Children's Meals Society File. Bishop's House Archive.
62. O. Cheung to R. O. Hall, March 9, 1966; O. Cheung to T. J. Skiller, October 5, 1966. Children's Meals Society File C21.3. Bishop's House Archive.
63. P. Y. Cheung to G. Baker. December 10, 1974. Children's Meals Society File C21.3. Bishop's House Archive.
64. R. O. Hall to K. H. Cherry, Headmistress of St. Stephen's College. June 5, 1959. St. Luke's Settlement File. Bishop's House Archive.
65. *Outpost* (October 1964): 5.
66. R. O. Hall, "Social Work and Social Responsibility," *Hong Kong Journal of Social Work* 2(1) (1967): 5–6. R. O. Hall, Rediffusion Broadcast, February 1980.
67. Luk, *A History of Education in Hong Kong*, 92.
68. Hong Kong Government Education Department website, 2010.
69. http://archives.catholic.org.hk/Statistic/ST-Index.htm.
70. Director of Education to R. O. Hall. February 7, 1956. Liu Ming Choi Primary School File. Bishop's House Archive.
71. R. O. Hall to Mrs Lee. April 10, 1957. Ling Oi Primary School File. Bishop's House Archive.
72. R. O. Hall to M. C. Chou. June 11, 1957. Kei Shek Primary School File. Bishop's House Archive.
73. H. L. Chow, Financial Campaign Committee, September 1961, S88, OMS St. Simon's Castle Peak. Bishop's House Archive.
74. R. O. Hall to District Officer, Yuen Long District Office, New Territories, St. Joseph's Primary School. Bishop's House Archive.
75. Kei Sun School, History of HKSKH File. Bishop's House Archive.
76. R. O. Hall, "Sermon on Education Sunday: 'The School and the Community,'" *St. John's Review* (October 1962): 225–27.
77. K. E. Barker, *Change and Continuity: A History of St. Stephen's Girls' College, Hong Kong, 1906–1996* (Hong Kong: St. Stephen's Girls' College, 1996), 198.
78. Fung and Chan-Yeung, *To Serve and to Lead*, 96–97; Luk, *A History of Education in Hong Kong*, 73, 91.

79. There were three types of secondary schools in Hong Kong: academic or grammar, technical, and secondary modern schools (or prevocational schools). HKSKH established academic schools and secondary modern schools.
80. J. Canning, for Director of Education to R. O. Hall. November 1960. St. Basil's Modern Secondary School File. Bishop's House Archive.
81. Director of Education to R. O. Hall. September 27, 1960. St. Basil's Modern Secondary School File. Bishop's House Archive.
82. St. Bennedict School, *St. John's Review* (June 1965): 130.
83. R. O. Hall to J. Leigh. March 12, 1964. Lee Kau Yan Memorial School File. Bishop's House Archive.
84. R. O. Hall, "Notes on Meeting with Education Department Development Section on January 22, 1965." Bishop's House Archive.
85. Y. W. Penn to Director of Education. September 19, 1963. Choi Hung Twin Schools File. Bishop's House Archive.
86. Interview of Lee Hei Man by the author in Vancouver, B.C. June 7, 2010.
87. G. Goodban Letter to D. M. Paton. Not dated. Chung Chi Divinity School Archive.
88. R. O. Hall to N. Hall. August 24, 1953. Hall Family Archive (George She as headmaster of DBS).
89. R. O. Hall to N. Hall. November 27, 1953. Hall Family Archive (Goodban on appointment of George She).
90. DBS Headmaster Report, "Schoolboys Treated Cantonese Dialect with Fun or Contempt." HKMS 94-1-12. Hong Kong Public Record Office.
91. R. O. Hall to N. Hall. December 5, 1953. Hall Family Archive (Crozier on appointment of George She headmaster of DBS).
92. R. O. Hall to N. Hall. July 4, 1949. Hall Family Archive (Meeting between Grantham and ROH on Workers' Children's School).
93. R. O. Hall to N. Hall. November 17, 1949. Hall Family Archive (Herklots fired by Grantham).
94. R. O. Hall to N. Hall. November 28, 1949. Hall Family Archive (ROH asked Cecil Rogers for Grantham to be replaced).
95. R. O. Hall to N. Hall. April 10, 1950. Hall Family Archive (Grantham invited ROH to a private dinner).
96. Fung and Chan-Yeung, *To Serve and to Lead*, 66–67.
97. R. O. Hall to N. Hall. December 1, 1949. Hall Family Archive (Difficult negotiations over workers' children's schools).
98. R. O. Hall to N. Hall. July 1, 1951. Hall Family Archive (ROH felt sidelined).
99. Interview of Oswald Cheung by D. M. Paton. Not dated. Chung Chi Divinity School Archive.
100. R. O. Hall to N. Hall. October 5, 1949. Hall Family Archive (Dean Rose's comments).
101. Interview of Sir Jack Cater by D. M. Paton. Not dated. Chung Chi Divinity School Archive.
102. R. O. Hall to N. Hall. July 14, 1949. Hall Family Archive.
103. R. O. Hall, Council of Churches of Southeast Asia (CCSEA), 1966, 1–3. Bishop's House Archive. Although Korea is not in Southeast Asia, the diocese in Korea had been invited to join the CCSEA.

104. R. O. Hall to C. Long. May 8, 1960. Chung Chi Divinity School Archive.
105. R. O. Hall to L. Wilson. June 2, 1960. Chung Chi Divinity School Archive.
106. Archbishop M. Ramsey to Bishop of Rangoon. July 6, 1962. CCSEA File. Bishop's House Archive.
107. R. O. Hall to L. Wilson. May 23, 1960. Chung Chi Divinity School Archive.
108. "Professor Michael Goulder: Biblical Scholar." *The Times*. February 11, 2010.
109. R. Howard to D. M. Paton. June 24, 1976. Chung Chi Divinity School Archive.
110. R. O. Hall, "The Church in Hong Kong 1932–1957." Manuscript sent to the *Church Times* at the editor's request and published on September 25, 1957. HKMS 96-1-29. Hong Kong Public Records Office.
111. A. S. Abbott, "HK's Future Bishop: Letter to the Editor," *South China Morning Post*. HKMS 94-1-13. Hong Kong Public Records Office.
112. R. O. Hall to J. Wong. August 10, 1965. HKMS 94-1-15. Record of Episcopate of Bishop Ronald Owen Hall, Vol. 6, 1963–66. Hong Kong Public Records Office.
113. "Method of Electing New Hong Kong Bishop Praised." Special Report. *South China Morning Post*, January 10, 1966. Record of Episcopate of Bishop Ronald Owen Hall, Vol 6, 1963–66. HKMS 94-1-13. Hong Kong Public Records Office.
114. Attachment of the Diocesan Synod Minutes of Meeting Book. Record of Ballot for January 6, 1966 election. Bishop's House Archive.
115. K. G. Bergin and R. B. Scott, "Medical Certificate Certifying Bishop Joost de Blank's Inability to Take up Position as Bishop of Hong Kong." Attachment to Minutes of Meeting of Diocesan Synod. Bishop's House Archive.
116. The Joint Nomination Committee meeting. August 15, 1966. Minute Book of the Synod of the Diocese of Hong Kong. Bishop's House Archive.
117. Interview of the Reverend Paul Tong by the author. St. John's College. October 24, 2011.
118. Interview of Archdeacon Pang Wing Cheong and Mrs. James Pong by the author. In their residence. Hong Kong. April 14, 2010.
119. G. Baker to Archbishop M. Ramsey. Ramsey Papers 294. Lambeth Palace Archive. London, England.
120. R. O. Hall to Archbishop M. Ramsey. August 26, 1964. Ramsey Papers 227. Lambeth Palace Library Archive. London, England.
121. *Oxford Dictionary of National Biography*. http://www.oxforddnb.com.
122. R. O. Hall, "Address on Behalf of Himself and Sir Lindsay Ride on the Occasion of Being Conferred the Honorary Doctorate from the University of Hong Kong," *University of Hong Kong Gazette* XIII (2) (November 18, 1965): 15.
123. R. O. Hall, "A Farewell Message from the Bishop," *St. John's Review* (November 1966): 216.

Chapter 7
His Humanity and His Legacies in Hong Kong

> Wherefore seeing we also are compassed about with so great a cloud of witnesses, let us lay aside every weight, and the sin which doth so easily beset us, and let us run with patience the race that is set before us,
>   Looking unto Jesus the author and finisher of our faith; who for the joy that was set before him endured the cross, despising the shame, and is set down at the right hand of the throne of God.
>
> Hebrews 12:1–2[1]

ROH retired to Home Farm, Lewknor, in Oxfordshire, where he and Nora settled and lived among the villagers, who welcomed them warmly. He was, in a sense, returning to his roots, the country of his forebears. Many visitors came from Hong Kong, not only to Home Farm but also to the village church, where they left gifts of gratitude. However, his retirement in England was also, for him, the natural preparation for his end.

His retirement was economically comfortable. The pension for a colonial bishop in England at that time was no more than that for an average country parson, but his 300,000-square-foot property in Sha Tin was sold in 1970 for HK $5.55 million. ROH, who had been so frugal throughout his life as he struggled to save for the university education of his children, would never have thought that one day he would become a Hong Kong millionaire. He asked Edward Johnson to return the money to those who donated to the "M. W. Ho Fund" for his retirement, but the donors rejected the idea of refunds. He then set about sharing his undreamed-of windfall for charitable purposes.[2]

ROH's health began to deteriorate. The "upset tummy" he had for many years, particularly at times of stress and anxiety, began to bother him more. During the summer of 1967 he had episodes of abdominal cramping pain and diarrhea and a particularly bad one in November, following a fatty meal of roast duck. When Judith went to see him around Christmas he was definitely unwell, very pale, with swollen legs and apathy. She was certain that he was suffering from malabsorption. He was seen at the Radcliffe Infirmary in Oxford in mid-January 1968, and was found to be severely anemic and deficient in protein, vitamins, and essential minerals. He had a bone marrow biopsy which confirmed that his anemia was partly due to B_{12} deficiency and partly to iron deficiency. He was given an injection of vitamin B_{12}.[3]

Two days later, although still pale, he was sitting up, alert, and asking for books to read. His anemia took longer to correct, and he spent six weeks in hospital to have various deficiencies replenished, and his general health improved. He continued to receive vitamin B_{12} regularly for the rest of his life.[4]

In early 1969, his voice became hoarse. It worsened, and he had various tests and examinations, leading to a preoperative diagnosis of cancer of the larynx, a very rare occurrence in a non-smoker. An exploratory operation was performed in August, and a cyst was found and removed. He recovered reasonably well, but his voice was never normal again. As this type of problem is usually found among trumpeters, ROH jested that the only trumpet he ever blew was his own!

In November 1974, he and Nora went to Jersey for the winter. ROH caught a cold at Christmas, and his breathing became difficult, presumably from obstruction due to the narrowing of his airway from the previous operation. A tracheostomy (tube into his windpipe in the neck) was carried out to relieve his labored breathing. When they returned to England in early April 1975, ROH was depressed. He had not been able to speak since January 20 and the tracheostomy tube that he could not do without required a lot of attention. He had hoped that the medical expertise at Oxford would be able to help, but before he was seen by a specialist, he developed acute urinary obstruction. He died in his sleep a few hours after being admitted to hospital, mourned by many in Hong Kong and in the Anglican Communion. Unlike most of his predecessors who were buried at Westminster Abbey, his ashes were interred in the sanctuary of the church in Lewknor. A humble man to the very end, ROH claimed nothing special for himself. Nora survived him, feeling purposeless and neglected, until she died in December 1982, having spent her last days in a nursing home at Theydon Bois.

ROH had dictated the beginnings of what he intended to be a book summing up the central themes of Christian faith and of his own life, but his poor health did not allow him to finish it. On the tape, his son Christopher would later find the words of Sydney Carter's poem "The Present Tense," adapted with the author's permission for his epitaph: "He showed us how the Christ he talked about is living now." The tape recording has been transcribed and can be found in Appendix 1.

His Humanity

Summing up a life and a legacy of a person as complex as ROH can seem a rather presumptuous endeavor, but ROH's extensive letters to his family and sermons provide a rich lode of source material. In the desire to get a sense of ROH not only as a bishop but also as a man, I have studied his letters to Nora between 1941 and 1954, kindly released by Canon Christopher Hall to me, as well as the letters between 1954 and 1958 to Christopher himself, donated to the Chung Chi Divinity School Archive. I have also examined letters sent to

Figures 7.1 (Upper) Memorial plaque in Lewknor Church with epitaph: "He showed us how the Christ he talked about is living now," and (lower) the slate tile in the floor nearby, under which ROH's and Nora's ashes were interred (Hall Family Archive).

David Paton by his friends and colleagues when he was writing ROH's biography. These letters reveal a passionate man whose wife and family mattered more to him than anything else, except his love for God and Jesus Christ. ROH was a man of great charisma, spirituality, and love, who in turn was loved by the people he served. Like any human being, however, he had his personal struggles, especially in his marriage, and his personal flaws. Many considered him too impetuous, not careful or thorough enough in his rush to get things accomplished. Those who painted him as the "Red Bishop" thought he was politically naïve and even sentimental about the poor and the destitute. His financial acumen was viewed at times with great suspicion, and his charitableness in dealing with the foibles of others was often seen as excessive softness, perhaps to some as moral weakness.

As a Husband and a Father

In deference to Nora, who was still alive when he was preparing the manuscript of ROH's biography, David Paton did not write about the troubles in ROH's marriage. Although they dearly loved each other and were affectionate parents, ROH and Nora were incompatible in many ways. ROH was an intellectual bishop who devoted his life to God and his work. Nora was extremely domestic and had no interest in intellectual pursuits. Their marriage was further complicated by Nora's demanding and possessive mother, the major reason for their prolonged separation after the war, as well as the prime source of Nora's anxiety and unhappiness.

There is no doubt of ROH's affection and love for Nora even after many years of marriage. He remained faithful and devoted to her despite the prolonged separation and the continuing depression Nora developed after their son's untimely death. He was kind, supportive, and looked after her to make life as comfortable as possible. Much as he loved her, however, he had ordained Li Tim Oi, knowing full well that it would eliminate all chance of becoming a bishop in England, and he would not give up his job as bishop of Hong Kong to become a parish priest. He would rather leave her in England and visit her every two years while he carried on with his work in Hong Kong.

Did he ever regret marrying her? Once he commented in his letter that he had no regret about the marriage, and then added "perhaps a little bit, that it has led to tension in the character of life of you children." ROH also praised Madeline and Geoffrey Allen (Christopher's surrogate parents during and after his time at college), for offering "the sort of background we could have given you and never have." As soon as he approached criticism of Nora, however, he immediately pointed the finger back at himself, saying, "It is as much my fault and failure, for I am no better."[5] He empathized with her struggle as a person, wife, and mother, and he blamed himself for being impatient with her.

It is rather doubtful that Nora would have been happier if he had retired earlier, as Nora could be hard to please. Judith told her brother that, when she was in Hong Kong, she could not win: if she delayed visiting her mother, she was greeted with "Hello Stranger"; if she came again soon, it was "Couldn't you keep away?"

Despite ROH's steadfast love for Nora, he realized that she had, in fact, turned into another Mrs. Baron, demanding and possessive not only of him but also of their children. Shortly before he died in 1975, he wrote two private notes to his children, probably out of his love for them, urging them to release themselves from the physical and emotional burden of living with their mother. To Judith, he wrote, "Mother must never come and live with you—she will eat you up." And for Christopher he wrote, "Christopher must be himself."[6]

It is all too easy to question ROH's judgment in his choice of spouse. He committed himself to marriage with the same concentrated seriousness as he did his vocation, but he could never place his commitment to Nora above his commitment to his flock and his God. It is also hard not to sympathize with Nora, whose mother kept intruding in their lives, and who must have felt left behind, isolated, and inadequate, when Judith became a medical doctor and Christopher a priest.[7]

ROH did his best as a father, but the long separations from his children exacted a toll. ROH tried to compensate by writing frequent letters, but a sign-off he often used as "the absentee father" suggests no small measure of guilt or regret. Still, he made financial sacrifices to support their education and often sent checks in letters to Nora for their children's birthdays or holidays. The prayer by William Bright below, which, according to Christopher, must have been his father's prayer at every Eucharist in all the years he was separated from his family, showed his profound love for his family and his trust in God.

> And then for those, our dearest and our best,
>   By this prevailing presence we appeal.
> O fold them closer to thy mercy's breast,
>   O do thine utmost for their soul's true weal.

ROH hoped that his oldest child would carry on the family lineage by becoming a priest. But he worried that Joc, who had left Hong Kong when he was 13 to continue his schooling in England, could have some misunderstanding of Christianity. Just as legend has it that shoemakers' children supposedly are badly shod, ROH had accompanied his own father on Sundays to church, but when he had a church of his own, Joc was too young to share Sundays with him. Wanting to share what he thought and knew about God, he wrote letters to him that were really a "primer" on Christian belief.[8] They laid out the Christian beliefs that ROH held closest to his heart in relatively simple terms. When Joc chose the career of a scientist, ROH was disappointed but wisely supported the decision. He had always believed that every individual should follow his or her own heart, but sadly, Joc died too young to fulfill his potential.

Far ahead of his time in his thinking about the emancipation of women, ROH wanted Judith to have a profession, and he worked hard to support her through medical school. A student of Diocesan Girls' School, Judith left Hong Kong with Nora and Christopher in 1940. ROH was immensely proud of his daughter, who took what was an unusual step for a woman at the time, going to medical school. In March 1953, ROH sent her a cable of congratulations on her winning the prize for obstetrics and gynecology from St. Bartholomew's

Hospital, which read: "Dearest, Congratulations. Double omen. Finals success and later grandchildren. Father." He had to wait for twenty years for grandchildren from her. When Judith joined her parents in Hong Kong in 1957, she worked simultaneously as a doctor in the medical clinics in St. James' Settlement and St. Thomas' and as a warden for female students at St. John's College.[9]

Christopher, who had been born in Hong Kong in 1935, left for England with Nora in 1940 and was separated from his father, except when ROH was on leave. ROH's great affection for his son can be inferred from the following passage about Christopher's birth. The letter, written a few days before Christopher's twenty-first birthday, looked back on the sense of pride and joy ROH felt when Christopher was born:

> So we caught the last ferry—and by 7:30 am you were safely in sight. And you don't seem to have changed basically since then! Joc was first black haired—Judith so ugly that the nurse had to comfort us that this meant good looks later—but you were complete from the start and have only developed, not changed.[10]

On December 10, 1936, the occasion of Christopher's first birthday, while the whole family was crossing the Indian Ocean on their passage back to Hong Kong from England, ROH wrote an eight-verse ballad that suggested both his playfulness and perhaps a wistfulness about his role as a father:

> Alfred Christopher Hall,
> Was given a lovely ball,
> he present was nurse's,
> Joc's present was horses,
> But Daddy gave nothing at all.
>
> Alfred Christopher Hall,
> Was given a lovely ball,
> And Judith gave blocks
> Each shaped like a box,
> But Daddy gave nothing at all . . .
>
> . . .
>
> Alfred Christopher Hall,
> Was given a lovely ball,
> And his Mum from Colombo
> Brought a cake, not a jumbo,
> And gave him a crumb–O.
> But Daddy paid for it all.

This ditty might suggest questions about what exactly he as a father is offering to his son ("nothing at all"?), and the answer, in the final line, provides a sense of resolution and relief: he has provided the opportunity for others to give to his son. The poem itself is an offering of time, care, and a spirit of playfulness, yet it is also serious.

ROH shared his love of books and literacy with his son and encouraged him to read as widely as possible, introducing him to a number of books that were either classics or that he felt might otherwise be helpful to his son. When Christopher told him that he was considering the path of priesthood, ROH was ecstatic that one of his sons was to carry on the family tradition.

By the time ROH retired, Christopher had already embarked on his own life and career and had little contact with his father except through correspondence. When Christopher told this to the Reverend P. Y. Cheung, Christopher's son exclaimed: "How horrible!" To this P. Y. responded: "It is not horrible at all. It is for Christ and his Kingdom!"

As a Pastor and a Person

ROH was remembered for "his ringing voice and the way in which he presented Christ, always with a freshness, challenging our conventional ideas, leading us to a new level of devotion, a new appreciation of God's creation and his will to care for all his children." He often expressed a sense of the immediacy of Christ to his people in the disarray and poverty of postwar Hong Kong.[11] Having been a highly successful preacher in his younger days at Newcastle, ROH was able to draw on a wealth of intellectual, practical, and prayerful experiences, and used his gift of eloquence in sermons, addresses, lectures, and talks, to call an audience or congregation to a deeper spirituality.

He had fans who went to the church at which he was preaching each Sunday. ROH himself noted, with some discomfort, that, whenever he was preaching, the cathedral or the church, would usually be quite full.[12] In 1948, he wrote to Nora that, despite his excitement over a well-received sermon, he needed to keep remembering to turn all credit and glory over to God, recognizing that God is the author of all talents: "There is something of me in it—something that has come from trying to do God's will and yet again could I have done that . . . unless God had given me the difference. So it all should end in humility and recognition of how much better I could be if I were more obedient to God."[13]

He often found inspiration for his sermons in Lin Yin Tai. Once he confided to Nora the sense of awe and inspiration he received while he was taking the goats out to Stonecutters Bottom (a stream running through Tao Fong Shan) to let them across the stream: "and then I took the goats out and I sat on a stone and watched them and got my sermon on Sunday and also it was then God seemed to say to me—that He is the Giver and when I wrote the words of the collect,[14] I realize they *are* there—'God's bountiful goodness' and that the way He deals with our sin is to give us things: so that our hearts have power to give love back to Him. It's that I want to say on Sunday at the Church of Our Saviour trying to make it the story of two debtors . . . And the overwhelming and unsuspected answer this morning is that God has given me, you and the children Home Farm in Lewknor and Lin Yin Tai in Sha Tin to help us to fight sin—by stirring our hearts continually to love him: only love is stronger than sin."[15]

ROH realized that as a bishop he was in fact a parson's parson, and that he should use his gift of speaking not only to help laypeople but also to help the pastors who needed spiritual renewal. To prepare the sermons he spent long hours working and praying so that he would be able to express what God wanted. Some nights, exhausted, he might collapse into bed, seemingly defeated by the requirements of yet another sermon. Then, waking up in the morning to the rustle of bamboo outside the window, he knelt down to pray, and the sermon "came."[16]

If he sensed that his sermons fell short in some way, ROH could be a stern self-critic. Once he delivered a sermon that he thought he had spoiled with a note of "arrogance," or "self-righteousness," or "a chip on his shoulder" in it. He struggled to understand where this false note came from. His memories took him back to 1914, to an army camp near Nora's home, where boys from Rugby and Cheltenham Schools had a "kind of hearty self-assurance—a sort of natural arrogance" and wore the "right" kind of clothes while he, a son from a relatively poor clergy family, having to make do with very, very little, was wearing an old suit handed down from a cousin. ROH thought that he had never really accepted poverty and that his deliberate refusal to live for money or position was what made him so "arrogant" and so prickly with other people. He reflected that the sermon had probably irritated those who did not believe, and puzzled those who did believe. He wrote to Nora: "So I was praying—for the future, this week, next week, the years ahead that I may somehow let God deal with this seemingly incurable sinfulness."[17]

Like many leaders who have the innate ability to inspire, ROH embodied a simple and unpretentious humility. His complete surrender to the life of service connected him to others but also set him apart. Mollie Higgs, wife of James Higgs, vicar of St. Andrew's Church between 1934 and 1939,[18] wrote: "But RO was always a little apart—not only because of his office but breathing a more rarefied air, perhaps than the rest of us: lonelier, sadder, 'above' us in disciplined dedication. In church he created an atmosphere of what one can only call holiness . . . There was a sense of profound reverence in the way he repeated the familiar words; and his preaching, though uneven, often created that utter stillness which I suppose only the best speakers and preachers occasionally know."

Despite his status as a bishop, "there was nothing stuffy about him," as Goodban put it. A highly experienced school headmaster and an ever-keen observer of human behavior, he commented that ROH was long-suffering, patient, and humble to a remarkable degree for a man whose basic nature was impatient and impulsive: "There can rarely have been a bishop as free from pomposity and self-importance as he was. More than once he sent to me, totally unqualified as I was, the text of a sermon he had delivered, asking for it to be scrupulously criticized."[19]

Unconcerned about the physical appearance he made on the streets of Hong Kong, ROH, a man of medium height and a full head of hair that he kept neatly trimmed, commonly went around in his signature garb: a blue aertex short-sleeved shirt and khaki shorts. Sometimes he used an old necktie as a belt. Although he had several leather belts of very good quality, a friend gave him a rubber belt of little worth, which he wore for many years. He also wore a suit of clothes that had been given to him by a friend, eschewing newer ones that were of better quality and made by well-known tailors. Edward Johnson, who worked as an accountant in the bishop's office, wrote:

> The Bishop did not care much what he wore, nor what he ate; he was truly a very simple and humble man. He would very much prefer to sit on a wooden bench with a friend in a roadside tea shop, sipping Chinese tea, than to eat in a big and well-furnished restaurant![20]

ROH had no patience with the expatriates' assumed superiority when he first arrived in Hong Kong. By asking a Chinese bishop to baptize his own son, he sent an important message that, in the eyes of God, all people are equal. He was ahead of his time for decades on matters of race, social conscience, and gender. Sir Oswald Cheung, an eminent barrister in Hong Kong, was particularly impressed by the bishop's successive appointments of George She and James Lowcock, both Eurasians, to be headmaster of Diocesan Boys' School at a time when such positions were in the domain of the white Anglo-Saxon.[21] But it was the ordination of a woman to the priesthood that rocked the Anglican Communion and confirmed that he was also far ahead of his time on the issue of gender equality.

He often worked more than 14 hours each day during the postwar years, on his many projects to promote the well-being of people in Hong Kong, and stayed up well past midnight writing his correspondence. Close friends found his sacrificial disregard of self and the strain he put on his faculties heartbreaking.[22]

ROH's special concern for the most desperate and marginalized in society seems one of the most remarkable things about him. This was reflected not only in the social welfare projects that he founded in Hong Kong but in his practical day-to-day life. No one who came to see ROH with problems went away empty-handed. In Free China he was constantly giving away his clothing and other material possessions. He lived frugally, saving money to put his children through university, or giving it away to those who needed it. ROH even opened the basement of the Bishop's House to homeless people and vagrants.[23]

Denham Crary, an ex-prisoner of war without any theological training, was ordained by ROH for priesthood.[24] ROH sent him to administer to those "at the bottom of the barrel"—the juveniles. They were drawn to Crary not only by his very interesting and passionate sermons but also by his genuine love. ROH must have realized that Crary, who had been humbled by life, no doubt communicated the kind of compassion and depth of soul that many such holy people carry with them. ROH eventually sent him to Birmingham, England for further training.[25]

ROH's close friend, Bishop Leonard Wilson, bishop of Birmingham, testified to ROH's care for the broken and cast-off:

> I remember listening to a sermon of his in Christ Church, Shamian, where he used the daring metaphor that our Lord was the Beloved Tinker. The greatness of the tinker is that he throws nothing away. However battered, however worn, however used up is the kettle, however often it had been mended before, the tinker does not despair. Unshocked, unshockable, always cheerful, with a song on his lips, with the unconcern of the man who is never beaten, he takes the battered, worn-out thing into his hands and makes it fit again for service.
>
> RO's deep insight into the heart and mind of God has always made him sensitive about conditions which might mar the development of the soul. That is why he is so constantly immersed in social plans. His real interest has always been in people in order that he might try to present them faultless before the Throne of God . . . Like His Master, he too, is a beloved tinker, who can think in terms of the individual broken life as well as share some of the Master's concern for the redemption of the world.[26]

Once, when ROH saw a Chinese man pushing a heavily laden cart up a steep incline, he stopped what he was doing and helped him push it.[27] When the Reverend Kenneth Fung accompanied ROH to the leper colony in Hong Kong, he was moved beyond words to see ROH sharing a chalice with the lepers during Holy Communion.[28] Even though it was known then that transmission of leprosy occurs only through prolonged contact, most would have cringed at the thought of such close contact with supposed untouchables.

Those who met him found a deeply devout Christian and felt cheered, encouraged, and invigorated by this man who radiated such love and joy. Those who came to him in trouble would feel at once that he cared for them in a deeply personal way. Goodban said, "This love drew him especially to the weak, the oppressed, the exploited, and even the harmful. His love was shown in forgiveness and renewed trust—he was never afraid of taking risks. Sometimes it led him into too charitable judgment, a reluctance to perceive evil or ill-will where it existed. I never heard him utter a bitter remark about anyone, and if he did occasionally permit himself a criticism, it would be followed by his characteristic 'bless him.'"

ROH had charisma and leadership skills yet always carried with him a sense of open air and a quality of youthfulness. He was someone whom people would gladly serve—a reason for his success in the reconstruction of the diocese after the war. Even in his school days, ROH was a born leader with great magnetism who inspired many by his utter dedication and love. His curates, who felt it was a privilege to work under him, were devoted to him and felt loved and cared for in return.[29] When David Paton wrote that ROH mirrored for him the way Jesus had treated his disciples, he echoed the sentiments of others:

> He was a magical person, and some of the magic remained with him all his life . . . It is not surprising that he drew many of us to China, to our lasting benefit. The long list of RO's boys included Bishop Leonard Wilson of Birmingham, Bishop Geoffrey Allen of Derby and the present Bishop of Hong Kong [Gilbert Baker]. The only answer I have ever been able to give to the question "Why did you go to China?" was "RO asked me." He called us; but he didn't tie us to himself.
>
> It wasn't only charm, insight and imagination that drew us. A profound and passionate devotion to our Lord enabled him to see many of us dynamically—not as we were but as we were meant to be . . .
>
> Of course we often failed to respond, and then others said: "RO has bad judgment of people." And he made mistakes, I suppose, of his own. But I would have to testify for myself that I felt that he came nearer than anyone else I have known to treating me as I suppose the Lord treated his disciples; and I doubt if I am the only person in whose private picture of Christ there are a good many RO-ish touches.[30]

With his personal warmth and his unselfconscious spirituality, ROH deeply touched the lives of people around him, helping to transform the lives of many, including his friends from the Student Christian Movement who responded to his call to be missionaries in China. He had the ability to help people to see greater, brighter possibilities in their own lives. The Reverend Percy Smith, vicar of Christ Church, Hong Kong, told the story of how his life was changed completely during his first meeting with ROH:

> Some months later, having left Oxford to work in the Rescue Service in Paddington, I received out of the blue a letter addressed to "Percy the Fireman." It was from RO to whom Joan had spoken about me. He had forgotten my surname, but somehow remembered my address . . . So there took place the fateful meeting that was to alter the whole course of my life. He proposed that I should go to Westcott House as soon as possible where his friend Billy Greer had been appointed Principal. He planned my coming out to Hong Kong immediately after the war. He urged me to marry Gaynor without delay. And it all happened—just like that!
>
> What can I say of the initial, powerful impact that his personality made upon me—an impact that was to deepen with the years. Here was someone who could get me on my knees anywhere at any time without

embarrassment! And he has remained the only person. Here was someone who at this first encounter seemed to believe utterly, to love God utterly and who longed to serve his fellow men and women utterly. For this reason I came away from meeting him, believing that I had met a saint—a belief that has never died.[31]

The spirituality that so many people have remarked upon came from ROH's disciplined hours of prayer and meditation daily. ROH was committed to the belief that all people can use prayer to communicate directly and personally with God. All who saw him on his knees could not help but be awed by the passionate concentration that absorbed his whole being as he offered his heart and mind and will to God on behalf of those for whom he prayed. Because of prayers, he believed that he had almost continuous awareness of Christ. He questioned whether this awareness of Christ was not self-cultivated:

> I believe it comes more from obedience—even from the dark night of the soul—than from my own experience of such frequent almost continual awareness of Christ. I can do no other than I have done because of this; and it is easy for me because of this almost continual awareness. I have to be 'ware lest I self-cultivate it and self-produce it.

ROH believed that one must be praying *with* God rather than *to* God. He clarified this: "To pray with God is to lay one's heart beside His, taking up the cross, being willing to be lifted up with Him, to draw all men not to ourselves but to Him."[32] He seldom prayed for his own or his family's safety. On one occasion telling Christopher, "When Joc was in Royal Air Force, I could not pray for his safety, only for courage and efficiency and patience in his job. So with you and Judith now, I cannot pray that you may be kept from harm but that whatever the bowling the bat may be straight, the eye clear and the heart fearless. And you can guess how eagerly I am examining myself and asking that I may be shown how best to help my heart's love here."[33]

Of course, despite his spirituality, warmth, and self-giving nature, ROH, like any human, had ordinary human weaknesses, some of which had been identified before his appointment as bishop of Victoria. He was said to be a poor judge of character. His own headmaster, R. G. Routh, used to say that, as a schoolboy, ROH had one fault: through sheer goodness, he was too ready to understand and therefore too prone to forgive the badness of a malefactor. If this be a fault, it remained with him all his life, enabling him to see people not only as they were (and he was not blind to people's faults) but also as they were meant to be.[34]

This optimistic view of people had caused him at times to send people to jobs that were completely unsuitable, to Wittenbach when he was working in Zengcheng[35] and to Goodban, who said that ROH had sent him individuals unqualified to teach. ROH also wasted time and money when he sent Wittenbach to South China without sufficient reflection. Could it have been that ROH imagined, like a thoughtful and hopeful teacher, that these people would rise to the occasion if they were given positions of responsibility?

ROH sometimes judged a person or a situation a little too quickly and would sometimes scold his clergy wrongly. When he realized that he had made a mistake, he immediately phoned or wrote to apologize and ask for forgiveness. He kept to the principle of "Always apologize: never defend."[36]

His impatience with the long, drawn-out processes of bureaucracy led him to cut corners, sometimes to unfortunate ends. He could be a nightmare to administrators and to his superiors. We saw earlier that he completed his own ordination document. When he was in the Student Christian Movement, he had at times done things without first seeking permission. Tissington Tatlow, his chief at the Student Christian Movement, observed that ROH was "a really good man but that he had this unaccountable streak in him and one could never be sure that he would not take some line of his own."[37] This tendency to take control and bypass regulations persisted throughout his episcopate. Some even said that ROH's indifference to bureaucratic rules made him devious. On one occasion he had embarked on a project after it was voted down by the Church Missionary Society committee. Many saw his ordination of a woman priest as another such presumption.

His impetuous nature often led him to acts which he probably regretted later. When the University of Hong Kong announced its intention to drop Scripture from its matriculation syllabus, he fired off a letter to the vice-chancellor, threatening to appeal to the governor, which rendered any hope of a compromise impossible. When he heard that Dean Barry Till had marital problems, he asked for his resignation but later expressed regret over this rush to judgment.

In the late 1950s some people accused ROH of being autocratic. His overriding of objections from almost all members of the school committee to appoint George She as headmaster of Diocesan Boys' School was such an example. ROH was not a strategist who consulted his colleagues on all the issues before coming to a decision, a process that would be painfully slow and inefficient from his perspective. This tendency to make executive decisions without consulting others seems common among spiritual leaders who share the habit of spending hours on prayer and meditation each day. When Archbishop Desmond Tutu appeared to have acted on instinct and inspiration without consulting others,[38] friends said that "he [Tutu] talks only to God, and his word is final."[39] Such leaders seem to have the clarity of mind to deal with difficult issues, a tendency that no doubt also contributes to efficacy. As Sir Kenneth Grubb remarked, "This is a weakness of dictators but for all I know it may be a strength to bishops."[40]

ROH's acknowledgement of his own weaknesses reveals just how tough he could be on himself. Despite being able to glimpse his own blind spots at times, he confessed to Nora his inability to overcome his faults: "I don't realize enough my own sinfulness—pride, self-will. I'm not disciplined enough in my life. I like comfort and easy ways too much and I don't feel the holiness of God."[41] He struggled to find a balance between the tendency to push ahead into extroverted action and a patient receptivity to God's will: "I am not very pleased with myself, still talking too much and not listening enough. God help me to be more saintly and not just dynamic."[42] His prayers for God's grace to be more saintly, so that he could do more spiritual work for the people in the diocese, shows how he struggled constantly to resist complacency and reach higher.

June Li, who has worked decades with various charitable organizations, especially St. James' Settlement, wrote, "Bishop Hall was one of the most exceptional and inspired individuals I have ever known. He was compassionate, loving, humble and considerate—an outstanding leader and a loving and caring shepherd of his disparate and scattered flocks. Bishop Hall was truly a Saint." June Li was expressing not only her own feelings but also those who had worked closely with ROH.

Wittenbach once said "RO is a saint—and like all saints very exasperating at times."[43] Goodban provides the conclusion:

> But a saint is not to be defined as a man without faults (What price St. Peter?), nor is he to be faulted by lesser man; but in terms of holiness and devotion and the power to reflect living Presence of Christ as a Reality. It was this which made RO different from those who just talk about Christ; it was this which drew people of so many different kinds to him. A dedicated and unswerving loyalty to his Lord and the power to impart an actual reflection and sense of His presence—that was RO's 'Hall-mark' . . .
> It is always easier to describe in words a man's failings than his strengths. In RO's case though the former are not to be ignored, they must be seen against the gigantic stature of the man and all that was heroic, saintly, and lovable in his character. His critics, grumble though they might from time to time, never lost their sense of admiration and devotion towards him or the deep affection in which they held him.[44]

Whether a saint or not, there is no doubt that ROH was a great man, if a man's greatness is seen in his creativity in the lives of others. Upon hearing the news of ROH's death, Sir Kenneth Grubb, president of Church Missionary Society and chairman, Commission of the Churches on International Affairs at the United Nations, gave a fitting eulogy for this complicated man whose light guided many:[45]

> Yet, altho' forewarned, when I heard of his death I felt that something had gone from the world of my own active career and interests, some freshness, a deal of vision, some rising of the summer sun, some brightness of the evening star. A little quarter of one's life grew suddenly dim and dull. And my thoughts and prayers leapt suddenly forward to that "far-off divine event", the Communion of Saints, the forgiveness of sins and the life everlasting.

His Legacies

Contributions to the Anglican Church

Anticipating that Hong Kong would be part of China no later than 1997, ROH planned thoughtfully in the postwar years to have a sustainable indigenous church with capable Chinese clergy and strong parish-school-social welfare center connections. ROH's insistence on the indigenization of the Church by Chinese clergy, along with the political changes in China, contributed greatly to the rapid expansion of the Chinese Church after the war. ROH wanted to see the Chinese Church so deeply rooted that it would not only survive but also flourish in an uncertain future. During his episcopacy he expanded the Church by building 16 new Chinese churches, three times the number of Chinese churches existing at the time that he became bishop of Hong Kong, but only one English church, moving it from one location (St. Peter's) to another and changing its name (Christ Church).

After the separation of the Diocese of Hong Kong and Macao from Chung Hua Sheng Kung Hui, ROH set about to ensure the Church in Hong Kong to be a "Three-Self" church. In order to make the Church self-propagating, he trained Chinese clergy, ordaining a total of 77 Chinese priests or deacons. Following the war, Hong Kong Sheng Kung Hui received little support from Church Missionary Society, which progressively transferred its properties to the schools or to the local churches, leaving these increased numbers of churches with Chinese clergy to be entirely self-supporting. Although the three English-speaking churches chose to remain under the direct metropolitical authority of the archbishop of Canterbury,[46] ROH ended the influence of Canterbury over the Chinese churches, the archbishop of Canterbury finally relinquishing responsibility for the Diocese of Hong Kong to the Council of Churches of Southeast Asia. He also initiated the process of liberating the dioceses in Southeast Asia from the control of Canterbury and were able to elect their own bishops, a process of decolonization and democratization. For the first time, the Church in Hong Kong had become totally self-governing, an ROH legacy to Hong Kong Sheng Kung Hui.

However, ROH was unable to make Christianity indigenous for the Chinese in Hong Kong in a way that integrated Chinese spiritual traditions and practices while maintaining a link with the historical Western church. Before the war he had been very interested in the work of the Chinese Christian Literature Society founded by T. C. Chao, who wrote Chinese hymns and songs. ROH tried to build on this work after the war, but without someone as spiritual and motivated as Chao to take charge, little was accomplished in this area. He was also unable to amalgamate the administration of the English churches and the Chinese churches, despite setting up a committee to investigate this in the 1960s.

One legacy that has lasted was ROH's pragmatic idea of coordinating people's educational, social, and spiritual development through having schools and social welfare centers in proximity to the parish church. This approach allows chaplains and priests to more readily identify and follow through cases that require pastoral care. Such programs foster a community where the various aspects of one's life are harmonized and backed by effective support systems when needed. As Anglicans have typically had a low-key approach to overt evangelism, such an approach continues to give visibility of the Church in a community where education and social services are increasingly secularized.

Many view ROH's ordination of the first Anglican female priest during World War II as his greatest legacy to the Anglican Communion. His reason for the ordination was the pastoral needs of the community, but this challenge to the Anglican Church, despite causing dissension in the Anglican Communion at the time, helped prepare the ground for the Church's eventual acceptance of women as equals. In this sense his contribution to the Church has reached far beyond Hong Kong.

Contributions to Social Justice

During the first two postwar decades, ROH and a number of social activists and reformers worked tirelessly to provide social welfare for the refugees and the poor in Hong Kong. ROH, the most prominent of all these reformers, seized every opportunity to stimulate the conscience of the Hong Kong government. ROH was a significant influence on the Hong Kong government's movement away from the strict *laissez-faire* attitude toward social services that it had practiced both before and after the war.

ROH made an incalculable number of contributions to social welfare in Hong Kong, founding many social welfare organizations directly under Hong Kong Sheng Kung Hui to improve the lives of deprived children—orphans, juveniles, and other marginalized young people—when the government was unable to do so.[47] He laid the foundations of several Anglican churches with adjacent social service centers.[48]

The diverse social welfare institutions ROH established under Hong Kong Sheng Kung Hui showed his creativity in tapping into people's potential to become agents in their own lives. He trained young people to make their own living, teaching young people farming in Tai Po Orphanage, and offering practical courses in carpentry, printing, and mechanics in St. James' Settlement and Holy Carpenter Practical Training Centre. These and other novel and practical ideas such as providing rooftop social services and Sunday schools became models for other voluntary organizations to help underprivileged young people in Hong Kong.

He created the Hong Kong Council of Social Service, to coordinate the diverse voluntary organizations that had sprung up to deal with the problems of refugees, the Hong Kong Housing Society, and the Boys' and Girls' Club Association, and he inspired people to work in them. These organizations, which served the needs of the people in Hong Kong during the postwar years, are still robust, surviving their founder by decades.

His voice was the "voice of social conscience." He repeatedly called on the government to increase the tax rates to raise money for social welfare in Hong Kong[49] even though the business community objected strenuously to this proposal every time it was raised. From the pulpit of St. John's Cathedral or through public broadcast over the radio, he would thunder against the "me-ism" of the Hong Kong majority and exhort the virtue of giving:[50]

> The saddest thing of all about Hong Kong is the lack of a sense of responsibility in its citizens. We love Hong Kong, we are proud of it, we enjoy all its good things, but most of us are not willing to give spare time, still less spare money for the well-being of the City.

In an attempt to move people away from the self-preoccupation of unfettered individualism, he asked people to nail to the cross their "me-centered" outlook and to pray that the "me-centeredness" might die.[51] As he called the people of Hong Kong to be loyal to their city, he drew on the language of Confucian filial piety:[52]

> We need to awaken the city-loyalty which now is dormant in our hearts. God is calling us now in this great city of Hong Kong to recognize our city as a mother, a mother who has adopted us and made us her own children and to acknowledge that to her we owe our loyalty, our love, our most unselfish service.

Most importantly, ROH demonstrated through his work and his life that direct participation in caring for less fortunate people carries its own sense of fulfillment and creates a more vibrant, engaged citizenry. According to the secretary for home affairs, who was interviewed by David Paton in 1976, ROH insisted very early on that the government needed a more humane approach and that the voices of economically disadvantaged people should be heard. When he retired from Hong Kong, the secretary remarked on the great loss for Hong Kong and noted that, if ROH had left in the early 1950s, the consequences would have been very serious.[53] Sir Jack Cater, the founding commissioner of the Independent Commission Against Corruption, Hong Kong, commented in 1976 on ROH's singular contribution to Hong Kong, "In the enormous evolution of Hong Kong, RO was a factor."[54]

ROH, who instituted the Hong Kong Housing Society and guided it along in its early stages of development, was largely responsible for its success in low-cost housing as a prototype for the Hong Kong Housing Authority. His vision of a coordinated program of schools and social service in housing estates, followed closely by the Housing Authority, had helped foster the social stability needed for the economic take-off in Hong Kong in the late 1960s and early 1970s.

ROH's contributions to education in Hong Kong are among his most significant legacies. A follower of F. D. Maurice, who believed in education as a means of advancing the kingdom of Christ in this world, ROH played a major role in expanding education in cooperation with the Education Department, establishing a range of educational facilities from primary schools to a college. He promoted education for the sake of education rather than as evangelism, advocated the use of Chinese language as the medium of instruction, urged parents to teach their children Chinese culture and Chinese history to retain their Chinese heritage, and appealed to the teachers and students to reach out in their neighborhood. He also pressed the government for free primary education. It was not until 1971, five years after his retirement, that free primary education was available and the policy of compulsory education for children aged 6 to 12 was adopted. The children of working-class parents became healthier, happier, and better educated. Many were able to move up socially because of their education and became professionals and important members of the society. The Anglican secondary schools—particularly the Anglo-Chinese bilingual schools—have produced graduates that have become leaders in many fields, both locally and internationally.

Low-cost public housing, inexpensive primary and secondary education, and social welfare provided the ingredients for economic growth in Hong Kong in the 1960s and 1970s. The increasing number in the workforce with tertiary education, and efficient public services in the late 1970s and 1980s, further helped lead Hong Kong to emerge as a modern international city with a vibrant local economy, solid industrial base, state-of-the-art telecommunications, and a modern international banking system. By providing the ingredients needed for economic growth, ROH, together with other activists and reformers, spurred Hong Kong's economic and social development as it was emerging as a global city.

Though a complicated man, ROH was single-minded in pursuing the social theology of Maurice, seeking to manifest the kingdom of God on earth. Because of his position and his charisma, he and his supporters and followers were able to translate this theology of love-in-action into practical terms, playing a major role in Hong Kong's economic and social evolution that is so much his Hong Kong legacy. In accomplishing all this, ROH retained the spirit of a true missionary: one of scaffolding. He was non-possessive of his creations, the social welfare organizations or schools, passing on their management to other people once they had been founded, and giving credit to them. He was the right person at the right time in the right place, contributing enormously to Hong Kong's postwar reconstruction and development, guiding the city, and affecting its destiny.

ROH's faith in God and his vision of Christ had a profound effect on him and his apostolic mission. His belief in God's self-giving love, which is like the warmth of the sun, given freely to all, and love-in-action, left a lasting imprint on Hong Kong society.

He lived a life of self-sacrifice, simplicity, humility, and love, caring for all, especially the meek, the lowly and the marginalized, in grateful obedience to God's will. His total trust in God, together with his hours of prayers and meditation, provided the spirituality and the power to constantly reflect the living presence of Christ.

As we go about in our labors in our homes, workplaces, organizations, and cities, we may recall his epitaph:[55]

> He showed us how the Christ he talked about is living now.

Notes

1. Quoted by Bishop Hall in his message to the Diocese of Hong Kong on its 125th anniversary.
2. E. C. C. Johnson to R. O. Hall. April 9, 1973. Chung Chi Divinity School Archive.
3. J. Hall to D. M. Paton. June 22, 1984. Chung Chi Divinity School Archive.
4. The diagnosis was pernicious anemia due to vitamin B_{12} deficiency since ROH had a classical response to treatment. Pernicious anemia in turn could lead to bacterial overgrowth because of achlorhydria (lack of acid secretion by the stomach as part of the disease process), leading to other deficiencies. Achlorhydria could cause steatorrhea, which presents as "upset tummy" and diarrhea or frequent loose bowel movement.
5. R. O. Hall to A. C. Hall. October 13, 1957. Chung Chi Divinity School Archive.
6. Personal communication from Canon Christopher Hall.
7. R. O. Hall to A. C. Hall. October 23, 1957. Chung Chi Divinity School Archive.
8. R. O. Hall. Letters to Joc, I–VIII. Chung Chi Divinity School Archive.
9. *Outpost* (September 1960): 25 (Dr. Judith Hall).
10. R. O. Hall to A. C. Hall. December 5, 1956. Chung Chi Divinity School Archive (Christopher Hall's 21st birthday).
11. Church Information Office. Diocese of Hong Kong and Macao. *Newsletter* (April/May 1975). News of Death of Bishop Hall.
12. R. O. Hall to N. Hall. April 19, 1948. Hall Family Archive (Preaching at St. John's Cathedral).
13. R. O. Hall to N. Hall. March 23, 1948. Hall Family Archive (Preaching at St. Andrew's Church).
14. Collect of that week was "Through thy bountiful goodness we may all be delivered from the hands of those sins which by our frailty we have committed."
15. R. O. Hall to N. Hall. November 18, 1947. Hall Family Archive (Sermon: God is the giver).
16. R. O. Hall to N. Hall. March 3, 1950. Hall Family Archive (Prayer and sermon).

17. R. O. Hall to N. Hall. November 16, 1951. Hall Family Archive (Critical of his own sermon).
18. M. C. Higg to G. Baker. November 20, 1976. Chung Chi Divinity School.
19. G. Goodban on R. O. Hall. Not dated. Chung Chi Divinity School Archive.
20. E. C. C. Johnson on R. O. Hall. Not dated. Chung Chi Divinity School Archive.
21. Interview of Sir Oswald Cheung by D. M. Paton. 1976. Chung Chi Divinity School Archive.
22. M. C. Higgs to D. M. Paton. December 29, 1976. Chung Chi Divinity School Archive.
23. Paton, R. O.: *The Life and Times of Bishop R. O. Hall*, 163.
24. Ibid., 225–26 (Denham Crary).
25. *Fragrant Stream* (June 1953): 3.
26. L. Wilson, *Outpost* (February 1957): 18.
27. T. Wheeler to D. M. Paton. June 17, 1976. Chung Chi Divinity School Archive.
28. Interview of the Reverend Kenneth Fung by the author. Hong Kong. November 4, 2010.
29. W. Greer, *Outpost* (February 1957): 23.
30. D. M. Paton on R. O. Hall. Not dated, probably about 1976. Chung Chi Divinity School Archive.
31. Paton, R. O.: *The Life and Times of Bishop R. O. Hall*, 226–27 (Percy Smith).
32. R. O. Hall, "On Praying with God." Not dated. Hall Family Archive.
33. R. O. Hall to A. C. Hall. Prayer. May 21, 1955. Chung Chi Divinity School Archive.
34. P. Smith, "Sermon Preached at Memorial Service of Bishop Hall on St. Barnabas' Day 1975 at St. Martin-in-the-Fields." Chung Chi Divinity School Archive.
35. H. Wittenbach to D. M. Paton. July 5, 1976. Chung Chi Divinity School Archive.
36. Paton, R. O.: *The Life and Times of Bishop R. O. Hall*, 88 (James Pong).
37. T. Tatlow to Archibishop G. Fisher. October 15, 1945. Chung Chi Divinity School Archive.
38. A. Sparks and M. Tutu, *Tutu* (Auckland, New Zealand: Harper One, 2011).
39. Archbishop Desmond Tutu led the blacks in South Africa to fight against apartheid when Nelson Mandela was in jail. Tutu's vital role was in guiding the country during the period of transition by chairing the Truth and Reconciliation Commission peacefully with no bloodshed.
40. K. Grubb to D. M. Paton. Not dated. Chung Chi Divinity School Archive.
41. R. O. Hall to N. Hall. February 10, 1943. Hall Family Archive (ROH "confessed" his sinfulness).
42. R. O. Hall to N. Hall. November 11, 1945. Hall Family Archive (ROH "confessed" to talking too much).
43. See note 35.
44. See note 19.
45. See note 40.
46. R. O. Hall. CCSEA 1966, 1–3. Bishop's House Archive.
47. P. R. Webb, "Voluntary Social Welfare Services. 1951–1976." A Quarter-Century of Hong Kong Chung Chi College, 25th Anniversary Symposium. Chung Chi College, the Chinese University of Hong Kong, 1977.

48. For example, St. Barnabas' Church in Kwun Tong, Calvary Church in Wong Tai Sin, and the Church of the Crown of Thorns in Tsuen Wan.
49. Staff Correspondent, "Bishop Hall Wants More Taxation," *South China Morning Post*, May 19, 1958.
50. R. O. Hall, "Rediffusion Broadcast, February 1950," in Paton, *R. O.: The Life and Times of Bishop R. O. Hall*, 276–78.
51. R. O. Hall, "Sermon Preached on the Centenary of St. John's Cathedral, April 29, 1949," *St. John's Revew* (1949): 237–44.
52. R. O. Hall, "Jesus Christ: Citizen." Preached on Commonwealth Sunday in Hong Kong, June 2, 1957. *St. John's Review* (July 1957): 172–75.
53. Interview of D. Bray by D. M. Paton. Not dated. Chung Chi Divinity School Archive.
54. Interview of Sir Jack Cater by D. M. Paton. Not dated. Chung Chi Divinity School Archive.
55. The words on ROH's memorial tablet were adopted from a poem by Sydney Carter that ROH quoted in a recording that he made for a book after his retirement: "The living truth is what I long to see; I cannot lean upon what used to be. So shut the Bible up and show me how the Christ you talk about is living now."

Appendix 1
Transcript of Bishop R. O. Hall's Tape Recordings Made after His Retirement

I shall have to begin by telling you in what sense I understand the Christian revelation and the New Testament. I shall have to go on to talk about the meaning of authority, of power, of ministry and the various other words used in the New Testament.

First of all, then, about how I understand and use the New Testament. My understanding is that what made the New Testament and has made it possible for us to know Christ and for the New Testament to be written and for us indeed to know anything of the Old Testament is the strange experiences that happened after the Resurrection.

It is this that convinced the disciples that this was indeed God who had been amongst them. And from this began the new life which created the New Testament.

Now remember that the New Testament is written in language that was coined to describe experiences *before* the revelation of God in Christ. In other words, they are rather like the early carmakers who had to use the old carriage, as a horseless carriage they called it, to carry the new engine they had developed. Now of course the new engine has adapted the vehicle which carries it, so that it is more suitable to the engine.

We have not yet begun hardly to adapt the language of the New Testament, which is all they had to use, to the new experience they were trying to describe.

This is particularly true in the basic concept of God. You will find how God and Christ and Holy Spirit seem somehow to get very much tangled up when St. Paul is trying what he was living with and going through. Similarly, they had to speak to Jews and to the Jews, in order that they might be convinced that these men were not godless heretics. They were in fact fulfilling all the promises which the Jews had learned in the past: they kept quoting from the Old Testament in order to convince the Jews that they were indeed not disloyal.

It is interesting though in 1 Corinthians 15 to find that when he describes what the resurrection means, he says that He died according to scriptures, He rose again the third day according to scriptures. He then goes on to describe the really vivid experiences which created and changed the Christian Church and changed their whole way of life without any reference to the scriptures, because this was in fact quite unexpected and could not be proved from scripture.

Similarly in Athens, when he speaks to the Greeks, he was using the Greek language; he also referred to the Greek poets. But of course when he speaks of the Resurrection, this made them feel he was talking nonsense, just as it did the Jews. 'To the Jews, a scandal; to the Greeks, foolishness.' That's what it meant to claim that Christ was the power of God and the wisdom of God.

Similarly, the word Logos was the best they could find to describe both in the New Testament, and later what this astonishing experience of God living with them, companying with them, unfolding how God had always been with them, to describe this in terms of anything but the Logos, there was no other word.

It is possible that in fact the Chinese word *Tao* may prove to be in the end a better word to carry this astonishing experience of Christ, which has been the life, and is now the ongoing life, of the Christian Church. The Living Christ, manifested not only himself but God, the whole Godhead as it were, in his short life on earth, revealing that God had always been a 'with-dweller-with-men'. This heart of God has always been beating amongst them and it had to wait for the fullness of time before the veil could be lifted and the mystery could be unveiled in a human life.

This applies also to phrases like: 'God sent His son', 'His holy servant Jesus'. And finally perhaps St. Paul finds words which really described his experience: It was God that was in Christ. It is God that is in Christ; and we only really know what God is by what Christ has shown him to be.

Similarly the phrase, 'God sent His Son' had to be used because it was so difficult to use any other. But it does imply, which was not what they meant, that the Son was in any sense inferior to the Father, or that God was not himself present fully in the sending, in the coming. But here experience was too much for language and these phrases had to be used. Perhaps they still have to be used, I am not sure; we may be able to find better.

Our Lord was similarly limited to the phrases available for God. He used the word Father, Abba Father, describing of course the intimacy of God's presence, and of his relationship with all humanity. But in his parables, and perhaps still more in his living and dying, he showed the kind of father God is and the word 'father' just isn't big enough. Experience of human fatherhood is so totally different in many ways that we cannot easily use it.

I have noticed even famous church leaders using the phrase 'Self-giver' for God, rather than our loving heavenly Father. I remember the horror with which I heard a bright young man straight out of a seminary talking about Abba as Daddy—God was in a sense like a Daddy. This is not the picture that is revealed on the cross. It is not the picture of the Prodigal father—the father who gave all he could to the younger son and let him go free with it, and then ran out to welcome him home. He had given all the rest that he had to his elder son, sharing completely with him, keeping nothing to himself, giving himself completely away. He goes out and pleads with the elder son to come in and join them but he would not. The father had to go with a very heavy heart.

This is not fatherhood as we know it except the fatherhood of folly, and we know that the folly of God is wiser than men. To give to utterly untrustworthy what you know they are not to be trusted with is the height of folly. But this is the relationship God the Self-giver has with creation. 'While we were yet in our sins, Christ died for us', and still that is true. In a sense, biblical theology has set the clock back especially as it filtered down from the theologians to the pew. That is why I got permission to print at the beginning of this chapter Sydney Carter's poem. It finishes up:

'So shut the Bible up and show me how the Christ you talk about is living now.'

That is what St. Paul did, but he had to use the Bible when he was trying to persuade his fellow countrymen that the way he was living, the person in whose presence he was living was indeed the living God. He had to show these book-minded people that what he was doing was not contrary to the book even though 'the Word had be made flesh and dwelt among us.'

In my judgment the recent remarkable book written on the Holy Communion is, as a matter of fact, spoiled by its backward-lookingness of it. It describes the New Covenant of his Body and his Blood. It then goes on though to pick up all the little bits of similarities and foretastes of it that there are in the Old Testament. Surely the emphasis is not on the covenant but the word 'new'. And in fact though the word 'covenant' was used to describe this remarkable bread-breaking ceremony, it was used because there was no other word to use. But it was basically not a covenant. A covenant means two parties who agree to certain conditions and to accept certain conditions: 'I give you this if you do something in return.'

But this is not what our Lord did—'While we were yet in our sins, he died for us.' He gave himself utterly for all the world without any question of making any conditions or making a covenant.

This was the new thing: God letting the world he had made break Him; God present in the brokenness; God redeeming through the acceptance of brokenness and all the power of love which he pours out all the time. Those who notice and respond and use it become indeed His priests, His representatives, whoever they may be.

Perhaps the sun is the best illustration of what this means. The sun after all is one of God's great servants in creation. Without the sun, there could be no human life. God could not have appeared among us, there would have been no us to come to, no us to love, no us to love Him.

The whole nature of the sun is like our Lord's death upon the cross, an utter self-giving, an utter giving of all that is himself pouring it out from without any thought or question as to who is going to be the receiver at the other end. He is giving it for all men, pouring it out, so that it is available to those who like the earth have accepted the warmth of the sun on that side which is turned towards it. From that accepted warmth, life grows. And so man's response to God's self-giving makes possible the fulfillment of God's creation in the life and work of God and man as fellow workers together.

You will see I am not shutting the Bible up, but I shall be interpreting it, as is my way, in terms of the experience which created the first Christians who wrote the epistles and wrote the gospels and the extraordinary intertwining, for example, of the gospel phrase 'the Son of Man came not to be ministered unto but to minister; and to give his life a ransom for many', with 2 Corinthians 6, in which ministry and reconciliation—the presence of God, the activity of Christ and the activity of the Holy Spirit, our acceptance of suffering, our endurance, our patience—all these things are tangled up, as it were, in words which try to describe a similar experience. In other words, the writers of the gospel like the writers of the epistles, were putting into words a living experience. And again the words they have to use are charged with the meaning that Christ gives to them and are attempts to describe what Christ does mean.

The word 'minister' is perhaps as misleading as the word 'priest'. In Paul (though convinced of what he called his Apostleship as he had been sent and called of God to do certain specific things in His name, while other people were given other parts of the same ministry), there is no separation here of the minister or the priest from the rest of the Christian family. He has the opportunity, calling perhaps he believes, to do certain things which, though they are different, they are part of the same total ministry.

Now I must at this point add that another weakness to me of the Biblical Theology movement has been the emphasis on what I call 'people of Godism' and the idea of 'Servant Church'. It is only through carrying from the Old Testament into the New the sense of a chosen people. It is true of course that, in trying to describe the calling of the Christian family, the *old* words were used by New Testament writers. But the whole attitude, the whole belongingness to everybody, which was part of their very being, was so different from the exclusiveness of the Jews.

Similarly when people talk about the Servant Church, they are not using the word Servant in the sense and with the meaning that Christ used it. How can you, for example, be a servant—that is a slave obeying orders—if in fact the person you are serving does not give you orders? You try to do for them what you think they need.

And this, as those of us who have been responsible for dealing with relief and refugee problems know very well, this very often means doing what we think is best for people, and, strangely enough, it often leads to much unhappiness, jealousy and resentment.

When St. Paul said that Jesus took the form of a slave, he did not mean slave in the sense that we use the word 'servant'. He meant the absolutely lowest, least powerful, least independent of men, which in the end was exemplified by his dying a slave's death on the cross, powerless to establish justice for himself, utterly dependent on what other people do with him. This is what being 'a servant' means. Now this is work and the life of every individual Christian. But in a sense it cannot be of the organized Christian family. Christian organization, though it must be minimal, exists really to stimulate and develop individual Christian living, and the attempt to create corporate service by the church is, I think, very mistaken. On the other hand, the Church should be active in encouraging its members to take an active share in community life and to give themselves without stint as individuals in the life of the community so that they become salt as it were spread out amongst the food.

You will see I am not really 'shutting the Bible up', but I am using it only where it puts into words the impression that Jesus' living made upon those amongst whom he lived, and the echoes there must be of some of the things he said, certainly words describing what he was,

He that has seen me has seen the father.
My father worketh hitherto, and I work.
No man hath seen God at anytime; the only begotten son, he has revealed him

All these phrases showed that what has been demonstrated was a totally new conception of God's power. It is the power of complete self-giving, the power of a slave who gives himself, who has to give himself utterly to the needs for others without any thought of himself, the power of the powerless man on the cross, nailed by the hands and feet. This is the picture of the power of God.

It is also the picture of his authority. And here it is most important for those of us who are being ordained, not to think in terms of any authority that may be given to us because authority can only be influence and the influence must in fact be the influence of love. We have a charge from Christ to be lovers, to be self-givers. This is how he would have us open our hearts to him in order that he may dwell in us and shine out of us to others. There is no other authority of God. There is only authority of men.

© Canon Christopher Hall 2012

Appendix 2
Bishop R. O. Hall's Life Events

Date	Life Events	Church Events	China and World Events
1895	July 22: ROH is born		
1898		Joseph Charles Hoare as 4th bishop of Victoria	Death of Queen Victoria
1899			Boxer Rebellion
1907		Gerald Heath Lander as 5th bishop of Victoria	
1909	Enters Bromsgrove School		
1911			Establishment of Republic of China
1912		Establishment of Chung Hua Sheng Kung Hui	Sun Yat-sen becomes first president, then steps down in favor of Yuan Shikai
1914	Leaves school; in September, joins army		World War I starts
1915		2nd Chung Hua Sheng Kung Hui Conference	Japan's 21 demands
1916			Yuan dies; China fragmented
1918	Awarded Military Cross with Bar	3rd Chung Hua Sheng Kung Hui Conference	May 4th movement; Guomindang founded
1919	Demobilized; enters Oxford University		

Date	Life Events	Church Events	China and World Events
1920	Summer term at Cuddesdon; ordained on September 26; becomes intercollegiate secretary of Student Christian Movement	Charles Ridley Duppuy as 6th bishop of Victoria	
1921		4th Chung Hua Sheng Kung Hui Conference	Chinese Communist Party founded
1922	Arrives in China for the first time to attend World Student Christian Federation Conference in April in Beijing and National Christian Council Conference in May in Shanghai	World Student Christian Federation Conference in Beijing; National Christian Council Conference in Shanghai	Anti-Christian Movement
1923	April 24: marries Nora		
1925	June 1: Joc is born; November: leaves for Shanghai		Death of Sun Yat-sen; May 30 incident
1926	September: returns to England		General Strike in England
1927	Publishes *China and Britain*; installed as vicar of St. Luke's Church, Newcastle		Guomindang Northern Expedition
1928		6th Chung Hua Sheng Kung Hui Conference; Cosmos Lang becomes archbishop of Canterbury	Chiang Kai-shek becomes president; capital in Nanjing
1929	January 13: Judith is born		Great Depression
1930		Chung Hua Sheng Kung Hui recognized by Lambeth Conference	
1931		7th Chung Hua Sheng Kung Hui Conference	Japanese invade Manchuria

Appendix 2   215

Date	Life Events	Church Events	China and World Events
1932	October 28: consecrated; December 30: enthroned as bishop of Victoria		
1934			Chinese Communist Party's Long March to Yan'an
1935	December 10: Christopher is born	ROH consecrates Mok Sau Tsang as assistant bishop	
1936	Family on leave in Britain; purchase Home Farm in Lewknor, Oxfordshire		Xi'an Incident
1937			Lugouqiao Incident; Sino-Japanese War begins
1938	Relief work in South China. Joc leaves for England to further his schooling	ROH consecrates Christopher Sargent assistant bishop of Foochow	Guomindang government moves to Chongqing; establishment of Gong He; fall of Guangzhou
1939	Becomes chairman of International Committee for Promotion of Chinese Industrial Cooperatives or Gong He		
1940	December: Nora, Judith, and Christopher leave for England via Singapore on *Anchises*		
1941	Decorated with Order of the Brilliant Star by Guomindang government; in the fall, lecture tour in the US	ROH consecrates Y. Y. Tsu assistant bishop of Yunnan-Guizhou district	Pearl Harbor; World War II begins; fall of Hong Kong
1942	January: returns to England; publishes *Art of the Missionary*; in UK raising funds; October: returns to Free China	William Temple becomes archbishop of Canterbury	

Date	Life Events	Church Events	China and World Events
1943	Publishes *China's Fight for Freedom*; travels to different parts of Free China	Bishop Mok, William Paton, and Bishop Sargent die	
1944	Ordains Li Tim Oi as priest	Archbishop William Temple dies	
1945	May: returns to England on leave; September: leaves for Hong Kong. Nora and children remain in England	Geoffrey Fisher becomes archbishop of Canterbury	May: end of European War; August: Japan surrenders; end of World War II
1946	Reconstruction of postwar Hong Kong and south China; Li Tim Oi gives up license to practice as a priest; ROH on leave in England, December 1946–June 1947	Forward Movement by Chung Hua Sheng Kung Hui ROH consecrates Quentin Huang as bishop of Yunnan-Guizhou district	Civil war begins between Guomindang and Chinese Communist Party in China
1947		10th Chung Hua Sheng Kung Hui Annual Meeting in Shanghai	
1948	Decorated with Order of the Brilliant Star again by Guomindang government; attends Lambeth Conference	Lambeth Conference rules against ordination of women to priesthood	
1949		Centenary celebration of the Dioceses of Victoria and South China	Establishment of the People's Republic of China
1950	Publishes *T. Z. Koo: Chinese Christianity Speaks to the West*	Three-Self Movement in China	Korean War starts and United Nations launches embargo

Appendix 2

Date	Life Events	Church Events	China and World Events
1951		Mo-Yung In consecrated as bishop of Canton; Diocese of Hong Kong and Macao separate from Chung Hua Sheng Kung Hui	
1954	Nora returns to Hong Kong		
1955	May 6: Joc dies in motorcycle accident		
1956	Visits Japan and China with Nora		Hundred Flowers Campaign
1957	Jubilee celebration; Judith in Hong Kong		Anti-Rightist Movement; Great Leap Forward
1958	Attends Lambeth Conference		
1960		Kuching Conference; consecration of James C. L. Wong as bishop of Jesselton	
1961		Rangoon Conference; Archbishop Fisher retires; succeeded by Michael Ramsey	
1962		Establishment of the Council of Churches of Southeast Asia; Roland Koh consecrated as assistant bishop of Malaysia	
1966	Retires in Lewknor, Oxfordshire	Gilbert Baker elected as ROH's successor	Beginning of Cultural Revolution
1967			Leftist-inspired riots in Hong Kong
1975	April 22: ROH dies in England		End of Vietnam War

Appendix 3
Bishops Consecrated, Deans Installed, Archdeacons Appointed, and Clergy Ordained by Bishop R. O. Hall

The following tables are compiled from various sources: *St. John's Review, Outpost, South China, Fragrant Stream*, and others. The author apologizes for possible omissions and mistakes.

Table A3.1: Bishops Consecrated, Archdeacons, and Deans Appointed by Year

Year	Bishop	See
1935	Mok Sau Tsang	Guangzhou
1940	Andrew Y. Y. Tsu	Yunnan-Guizhou
1946	Quentin Huang	Yunnan-Guizhou
1946	Nelson Victor Halward	Guangzhou
1950	Mo-Yung In	Guangzhou
1960	James C. L. Wong	Jesselton in 1960; Taiwan in 1965
Year	Archdeacon	Jurisdiction
1946	Lee Kau Yan	Hong Kong
1946	Tsang Kei Ngok	Beihai
1949	Mo-Yung In	Beihai
1965	Chung Yan Laap, John	Hong Kong
Year	Dean of St. John's Cathedral	
1938	John Leonard Wilson	
1941	Alaric Pearson Rose	
1953	Frederick Temple	
1958	Barry Till	
1963	John Foster	

Roland Koh became assistant bishop of Malaysia in 1962 (consecrated in England) and bishop of Sabah in 1965. James Pong was consecrated as bishop of Taiwan in 1971. John Chou Meng Chou became archdeacon in 1973.

In the Anglican Church, the dean is the chief cleric of a cathedral and the head of the chapter of canons.

Table A3.2: Chinese Clergy Ordained by Year

Year	Name	Year	Name
1930	Chung Yan Laap, John	1955	Chung Yang Yun
1934	Peter Mak	1955	Wong Nai Hon, Stephen
1935 (D)	Yip Chor Sang	1955	Samuel Wu
1937	Philip Wong	1956	Walter Hsi
1938 (D)	Leung Ching Wah	1956	Loong Gon
1939 (D)	Kong Hon Cheung	1956	Mak Kwok Fai, Timothy
1940 (D)	Ko Shiu Hung	1957	Ho Sai Ming, Simon
1940 (D)	Loong Shiu-Kei, John	1957 (D)	Peter Kao
1940	James C. L. Wong	1957	Lo Ping Leung, Luther
1941	T. C. Chao	1957	Tsang Ping Sun, Richard
1941	Roland Koh	1958 (D)	Jane Huang (priested 1971)
1943	Cheung Siu Kwei	1959	Cheung Siu Pui, Peter
1943	Wu Sheng To	NA	Paul Doh
1943	Yip Yat Ching	NA	Richard Yao
1943 (D)	Peter Baung	1961	Chiu Lin Chun
1944	Cheung Luk Heung, Luke	NA	Stephen Ko
1944	Chou Meng Chou, John	NA	Fang Wing Cheung
1944	Lau Kin Shun	1961	Frank Lin
1944	Li Tim Oi, Florence	1962	Chan Chor Choi, Alan
1944	John Tsang	1962	Edmund Der
1944	Tsai Yung Chun	1963	David Leigh
1945	Jack Wen	1963	Lau Wan, Baldwin
1946	Cheung Wing Ngok	1964	Chung Bak Him, Abel
1946	George She	1964 (D)	Lee Siu Ying
1946	Wong Po Lam, Daniel	1964	Yip King-wei, Paul
1947	Ngan Kwok-Hung	1965	Chan Sik Fai, Stephen
1947 (D)	Hui Kung Shiu	1965	Chu Kwong Chung, Bernard
1949 (D)	Chan Pak Chung	1965	Liu Yik Hin, Alfred
1950 (D)	James Leslie Chow	1966	Kwong Kong Kit, Peter
1951	Denham Crary	1966	Pao Suen Yui, Benjamin
1952	Chow Fok Hing, James	1966	Pau Pei Tak, Peter
1952	Kwok Hei Leung, Henry	1966	Tsang Kwok Wai
1952	Lau Kin Chi, Thomas	1966 (D)	Cheung Pui Yeung (priested 1967)
1952	Pong Tak Ming, James	1966 (D)	Chu Che Wen, James (priested 1967)

Appendix 3

Year	Name	Year	Name
1952	Pun Siu Wah, James	1966 (D)	Ho Hin Ming, Allan (priested 1967)
1953	Pak Chun Chan	1966 (D)	Leung Chi Ling, Andrew (priested 1967)
1953	Pang Yan Cheong, Peter	1966 (D)	Tong Hin Sum, Paul (priested 1967)
1954	Pang Wing Cheong, Andrew	1966 (D)	Lee Tung Cheng (priested 1968)
1954	Lee Shiu Keung		

(D) = year ordained as deacon, year of being priested not found; NA = year of ordination not available but likely around the time listed in the table. Lee Siu Ying was priested in 1965 at St. Paul's Cathedral, London.

Table A3.3: European Clergy Ordained by Year

Year	Name	Year	Name
1934 (D)	William Arthur Molyneux	1952 (D)	Molly Rudd
1935 (D)	Gilbert Russel	1955 (D)	Kenneth Uttley
1935	Christopher Sargent	1956	Timothy Beaumont
1936	Gilbert Baker	1957	Wally Andrews
1938	Arthur Charman	1957	Albert Barton
1938	Osmund Peskett	1959	E. W. Fisher
1941	David Paton	1960	Douglas Lancashire
1941	Murray Rogers	NA	Theodore Evans
1944	E. J. B. Matchett	1961	James Gray Bates
1946	John Ogilvie	1961	Stephen Sidebotham
1946	Eli Ernest Low	1962 (D)	Joyce Bennett (priested in 1971)
1947	Percy Smith	1963	Noel Alfred Stone
1948 (D)	Charles Harth	1965	Michael Corbett-Jones
1951	Michael Goulder	1965	Karl Christine Misso
1952	Rex Howe	1965	Stephen Sturton
1952	Eric Kvan	1965	Barry Simmons
1952	James Proud	1965	James Wall
1952	Geoffrey Speak	1966 (D)	Horace Dutton

(D) = year ordained as deacon, year of being priested not found; NA = year of ordination not available but likely around the time listed in the table.

Appendix 4
Churches and Schools in Hong Kong during Bishop R. O. Hall's Episcopate

Table A4.1: Churches in the Diocese According to Year of Establishment up to 1968

Year	Church	Current Site
Before ROH's episcopacy		
1847[2]	*St. John's Cathedral	Central, Hong Kong
1865[2]	St. Stephen's Church Hollywood Road; moved to Pok Fu Lam Road in 1888; rebuilt in 1965	Near the University of Hong Kong, Hong Kong
1872[2]	St. Peter's Church, West Point (closed in 1933)	Sai Ying Pun, Hong Kong
1889[2]	Holy Trinity Church; rebuilt in 1938	Kowloon City, Kowloon
1891[1]	All Saints' Church; rebuilt in 1928	Mong Kok, Kowloon
1904[2]	*St. Andrew's Church	Tsim Sha Tsui, Kowloon
1911[2]	St. Paul's Church	Glenealy, Hong Kong
1920[1]	St. Mary' Church, built in 1936	Causeway Bay, Hong Kong
1930[1]	St. Peter's Church, Castle Peak; rebuilt in 1955	Castle Peak, New Territories
During ROH's episcopacy		
1933[1]	*Christ Church	Mong Kok, Kowloon
1937	St. Mark's Church in Macao	Macao
1939[1]	St. Matthias' Church; rebuilt in 1960	Yuen Long, New Territories
1949[1]	St. Matthew's Church; rebuilt in 1968	Hollywood Road, Central, Hong Kong
1950[1]	St. James' Church in St. James' Settlement, proper church built in 1962	Wan Chai, Hong Kong
1951[1]	St. Luke's Church in St. Luke's Settlement; in Liu Ming Choi Primary School in 1959	Kennedy Town, Hong Kong
1950[1]	St. Thomas' Church in a Nissen hut; new church in 1965	Shek Kip Mei, Kowloon
1954[1]	St. Joseph's Church	Kam Tin, New Territories
1955[2]	**Church of the Good Shepherd	Hung Hom, Kowloon
1956[2]	The Holy Carpenter Church	Hung Hom, Kowloon

Year	Church	Current Site
1960[1]	Calvary Church	Wong Tai Sin, Kowloon
1961[1]	St. Barnabas' Church	Kwun Tong, Kowloon
1961[1]	St. Mark's Church	Hung Hom, Kowloon
1961[2]	St. Peter's Church, North Point	North Point, Hong Kong
1961[2]	Kei Oi Church	Li Cheng Uk, Hong Kong
1964[2]	The Crown of Thorns Church	Tsuen Wan, New Territories

*English-language church; **Mandarin; churches built before 1932 are included because almost all were rebuilt during the episcopacy of ROH, with the exception of St. John's Cathedral, St. Andrew's Church, and St. Paul's Church. Christ Church was started in 1933, and the founding stone was laid in 1936. 1: The year that the church was started with a congregation; 2: The year of laying foundation stone or consecration. All information was derived from the History of Hong Kong Sheng Kung Hui File, Bishop's House Archive.

Table A4.2: Social Welfare Organizations during Bishop R. O. Hall's Administration by Year of Founding

Year	Organization	Function or Services Provided
1933	Street Sleepers' Association	Temporary shelter for refugees
1935	Tai Po Rural Orphanage renamed St. Christopher's Home in 1954	Home for orphans, to provide primary education and practical life skills
1935	Hong Kong School for the Deaf[1]	Training deaf children to lip-read and to speak
1936	Boys' and Girls' Clubs Association	Provided basic primary education, games, and character building; the association carried out fundraising and other activities
1938	Hong Kong Refugee and Social Welfare Council; renamed Hong Kong Council of Social Service in 1949	Coordinated voluntary organizations; social welfare centers
1948	Hong Kong Housing Society	Built rental housing for low-income families
1949	Juvenile Care Centre	Provided temporary shelter for juvenile delinquents for placement; clubs for boys and girls
1949	St. James' Settlement	Provides a range of social services to children, young people, adults, elderly people, and those with disabilities; trains young people in practical skills; primary school; church; medical and dental clinics
1951	St. Luke's Settlement	Primary school, church, clubs for boys and girls, medical clinics
1951	St. Thomas' School, Clinic, and Church	Primary school, church, medical clinic, hostel for young workers
1954	Holy Carpenter Church and Hostel and Youth Centre	Hostel, church, youth center, practical training center, day nursery
1954	St. Simon's Hostel, Castle Peak	Church, hostel, primary school, medical clinic
1959	Hong Kong Sea School	Residential school, training for seafarers
1960	Children's Meals Society	Provided one meal each school day to schoolchildren at low cost
1987	Bishop Ho Ming Hua Chinese Centre	Community center in St. Martin-in-the-Fields Church, in London for Chinese immigrants

[1] The first Hong Kong School for the Deaf was founded by three CMS missionaries. Ms. Lee Luk Wah was the first principal of the school.

Table A4.3: Housing Estates Completed before 1970 by the Hong Kong Housing Society*

Year	Name of Estate	Site	Number of Units	Special Features	Outcome
1950	Ma Tau Chung	Ma Tau Chung	180	Cottages	
1952	Sheung Li Uk	Sham Shui Po	360 in 5 blocks	Community center	Rebuilt in 1995
1956	Hung Hom Chuen	Hung Hom	NA	NA	Rebuilt in 1987 as Ka Wai Chuen
1962	Ming Wah	Shau Kei Wan	3,169 in 13 blocks	–	Renovated in 2006
1962	Yue Kwong	Aberdeen	1,175 in 5 blocks	–	Renovated in 1980 and in 2008
1964	Mun Lok	Shau Kei Wan	947 in 4 blocks	Community center	Renovated in 2003
1965	Chun Sin Mei	Kowloon City	1,037 in 3 blocks	–	Renovated in 2003 with addition of elevators
1965	Healthy Village	North Point	(1) For rent: 1,191 in 9 blocks (2) For sale: 1,048 in 5 blocks	89 for elderly people; elevators	Ownership scheme in 1990 after renovation
1965	Kwun Tong Garden	Kwun Tong, Ngau Tau Kok	4,926 in 9 blocks	117 for elderly people; elevators	
1968	Kwun Loong	Kennedy Town	2,317 in 8 blocks	Elevators	Phase 1: rebuilt in 2008 Phase 2: rebuilt in 2010
1970	Lok Man	To Kwa Wan	3,676 in 9 blocks	10 units for elderly people; elevators	

*Information in this table was derived from annual reports of the Hong Kong Housing Society, Bishop's House Archive, and from 香港房屋協會：《房協60樓影集》(香港：香港房屋協會, 2008). NA = Not available.

Table A4.4: Primary Schools during Bishop R. O. Hall's Episcopate by Type and Year of Founding

Type	Name	Year Founded	Site
CMS day schools	St. Matthew's	1876	Hollywood Road; rebuilt at New Street in 1938
	St. Peter's	1884	West Point; new school at Hill Road built in 1955
	Stanley Village (D)	1881	Stanley
	St. Timothy's	1887	To Kwa Wan; rebuilt in 1957 and again in 2007
	St. Michael's	1919	King's Road; new school at North Point in 1962
	St. Thomas'	1924	Cheung Sha Wan Road; new school at Berwick Street in 1952
	St. Stephen's College Preparatory	1938	Stanley
Church schools	Holy Trinity Church	1952	Kowloon City
	St. Stephen's Church	1956	Bonham Road
	St. Mary's Church	1958	Causeway Bay
	Church of the Good Shepherd	1963	Hung Hom
New primary schools	Diocesan Preparatory	1950	Kowloon Tong
	St. Joseph's	1954	Kam Tin
	Kei Yan	1955	Hollywood Road, Central
	Kei Shek (D)	1957	Tai Po St. Christopher's Home
	Chi Nam	1957	Wong Chuk Hang+
	Ling Oi	1934	A private school in 1934, transferred to SKH in 1958
	Kei Oi	1958	Li Cheng Uk
	St. Simon's Primary School (D)	1958	Castle Peak
	Liu Ming Choi	1960	Kennedy Town
	St. James'	1961	Wan Chai
	Kei Tak	1962	Wong Tai Sin
	St. Philip's (D)	1964	Mount Butler
	Yat Sau	1965	Choi Hung
	Ching Shan	1965	Choi Hung
	*Kei Wing	1968	Lai Chi Kwok Road

Type	Name	Year Founded	Site
Resettlement estate schools	Kei Sun (D)	1959	Wong Tai Sin, Block U/V
	Chu Yan	1961	Tai Wo Hau, Tsuen Wan, Block S
	St. Barnabas (D)	1961	Kwun Tong, Block W
	Kei Sum (D)	1963	Wang Tau Hom, Block J
	*Yeuk Wing (D)	1968	Tse Wan Shan
	*Chu Oi	1968	Kwai Chung, Block 8
	*Kei Hin	1968	Ngau Tau Kok

CMS = Church Missionary Society; (D) = discontinued; *1968 schools included because planning and building of schools took a long time. All resettlement schools no longer exist except Chu Yan. + Chi Nam was originally in Wong Chuk Hang but was moved to the resettlement estate in Tin Wan and again to Chi Fu Fa Yuen.

Table A4.5: Secondary Schools during Bishop R. O. Hall's Episcopate by Type and Year of Founding

Type	Name	Year	Site
Established school with primary division*	St. Paul's College	1849	Glenealy before World War II; reopened in Bonham Road in 1950
	Diocesan Girls' School	1860	Bonham Road, then Caine Road in 1900; Jordan Road, Kowloon in 1913
	Diocesan Boys' School	1869	Bonham Road, then moved to Mong Kok in 1926
	St. Stephen's Boys' College	1903	Bonham Road, then moved to Stanley
	St. Stephen's Girls' College	1906	Lyttelton Road
	St. Paul's Girls' College renamed St. Paul's Co-educational College in 1953	1915	MacDonnell Road
	Heep Yunn School	1936	Kowloon City, combining Fairlea and Victoria Home
New secondary schools	St. Mark's School	1949	Glenealy, then moved to Shau Kei Wan in 1956
	Bishop Hall Jubilee School	1961	Kowloon Tong
	SKH Tang Siu Kin Secondary School	1962	Founded in 1962; new campus in Morrison Hill in 1970
	Lee Kau Yan Memorial School	1964	San Po Kong
	SKH Lam Woo Memorial Secondary School**	1970	Kwai Chung
Church schools	All Saints' Middle School	1951	Ho Man Tin
	St. Mary's Church Mok Hing Yiu College	1963	Causeway Bay
	St. Stephen's Church College**	1968	Bonham Road
Modern schools	St. Basil's Modern Secondary (D)	1965	Shau Kei Wan
	St. Benedict's Modern Secondary (D)	1965	Choi Hung

Type	Name	Year	Site
Vocational training	Holy Carpenter Vocational Training Centre (D)	1965	Hung Hom

*The primary division partial or full; **included because planning took place in the 1960s; (D) = discontinued.

Appendix 5
Names of Places, People, and Terms in English and Chinese

In this book, Hanyu Pinyin is used for names of places, people, and terms with exception of those whose names in Wade-Giles romanization are more readily recognized because of their exclusive use in the past.

Table A5.1: Names of Places

Pinyin	Wade-Giles or Original	Simplified Chinese	Traditional Chinese
Baoshan	Paoshan	保山	保山
Beihai	Pakhoi	北海	北海
Beijing	Peking	北京	北京
Beidaihe	Pei Tai Ho	北戴河	北戴河
	Castle Peak	青山	青山
	Causeway Bay	铜锣湾	銅鑼灣
Chengdu	Chengtu	成都	成都
Chongqing	Chungking	重庆	重慶
Cuiheng	Chuihang	翠亨	翠亨
Ding Xian	Ting-Hsien	定县	定縣
Fujian	Fukien	福建	福建
Fuzhou	Foochow (Fuchou)	福州	福州
Guangzhou	Canton	广州	廣州
Guangdong	Kwangtung	广东	廣東
Guangxi	Kwangsi	广西	廣西
Guiyang	Kweiyang	贵阳	貴陽
Guizhou	Kweichow	贵州	貴州
Guilin	Kweilin	桂林	桂林
Hankou	Hankow	汉口	漢口
Hangzhou	Hangchow (Hangchou)	杭州	杭州
Hepu	(formerly) Limchow	合浦	合浦
Jinan	Tsinan	济南	濟南
Jiangmen	Kongmoon	江门	江門
	Kam Tin	锦田	錦田
	Kowloon Tong	九龙塘	九龍塘

Pinyin	Wade-Giles or Original	Simplified Chinese	Traditional Chinese
Kunming	Kunming	昆明	昆明
	Kwun Tong	观塘；官塘	觀塘；官塘
	Li Cheng Uk	李郑屋	李鄭屋
Lashio	Lashio	腊戍	臘戍
	Lin Yin Tai	灵荫台	靈蔭台
Lugouqiao	Lukou Bridge (Marco Polo Bridge)	卢沟桥	盧溝橋
	Macau (Macao)	澳门	澳門
	Mong Kok	旺角	旺角
Nanjing	Nanking	南京	南京
	Pak Hok Tung	白鹤洞	白鶴洞
	Pek-taam	派潭	派潭
Pingshi	Ping Shek	坪石	坪石
Qufu	Chufu	曲阜	曲阜
Qujiang	Kukong (Chu Chiang)	曲江	曲江
Qujing	Kutsing (Chuching/Chutsing)	曲靖	曲靖
Shamian	Shameen	沙面	沙面
	Sham Shui Po	深水埗	深水埗
Shandong	Shantung	山东	山東
Shanghai	Shanghai	上海	上海
	Sha Tin	沙田	沙田
	Shek Kip Mei	石硤尾	石硤尾
Shiqi	Shekki	石岐	石岐
Shenyang	Shenyang (formerly Mukden)	沈阳（盛京）	瀋陽（盛京）
Shenzhen	Shum Chun	深圳	深圳
	South China Athletic Stadium	南华球场	南華球場
	Tai Po	大埔	大埔
	Tao Fong Shan	道风山	道風山
Tianjin	Tientsin	天津	天津
	Tsuen Wan	荃湾	荃灣
	Wan Chai	湾仔	灣仔
	West Point	西环	西環
	Wong Tai Sin	黄大仙	黃大仙
Wuchang	Wuchang	武昌	武昌
Wuhan	Wuhan	武汉	武漢
Xi'an	Sian	西安	西安
Xiaodong	Siu Tung	小董	小董

Appendix 5

Pinyin	Wade-Giles or Original	Simplified Chinese	Traditional Chinese
Yan'an	Yenan	延安	延安
	Yuen Long (Un Long)	元朗	元朗
Yinkeng	Ngunhang	银坑	銀坑
Yunnan	Yunnan	云南	雲南
Zengcheng	Tsang Shing (Tseng Cheng)	增城	增城
Zhejiang	Chekiang	浙江	浙江
Zhangzhou	Tsangchow (Tsangchou)	漳州	漳州
Zhaoqing	Shiu Hing	肇庆	肇慶

Table A5.2: Names of People

English	Wade-Giles	Simplified Chinese	Traditional Chinese
	Confucius	孔子	孔子
Deng Yingchao	Teng Yingchau	邓颖超	鄧穎超
Gong Peng	Kung Peng	龚澎	龔澎
	Alexander Grantham	葛量洪	葛量洪
Gu Ziren	Koo T. Z. (Koo Tz-Zung or Koo Tzu Jen)	顾子仁	顧子仁
	Cecil Harcourt	夏悫	夏愨
	Ho Ming Hua	何明华	何明華
	Huang K. Y., Quentin	黄奎元	黃奎元
Jiang Jieshi	Chiang Kai-shek	蒋介石／蒋中正	蔣介石／蔣中正
Kong Xiangxi	Kung Hsiang-Hsi	孔祥熙	孔祥熙
Liu Tingfang	Lew Ting Fang, Timothy	刘廷芳	劉廷芳
Mao Zedong	Mao Tze Tung	毛泽东	毛澤東
	Mok Sau Tsang	莫寿增	莫壽增
Emperor Puyi	Emperor Puyi	溥仪	溥儀
	Sun Yat-sen	孙逸仙／孙中山	孫逸仙／孫中山
	Tsu Yu Yu, Andrew	朱友渔	朱友漁
Qiao Guanhua	Chiao Kuanghua	乔冠华	喬冠華
Wu Yaozong	Wu Yao Tsung	吴耀宗	吳耀宗
Yan Yangchu, James	Yen Yang Chu, James	晏阳初	晏陽初
	Mark Young	杨慕琦	楊慕琦
Yu Rizhang, David	Yui Z. T., David Yu Jih Chung	余日章	余日章
Yuan Shikai	Yuan Shi Kai	袁世凯	袁世凱
Zhang Xueliang	Chang Hsueh Liang	张学良	張學良
Zhao Zichen	Chao Tzu Chen	赵紫宸	趙紫宸
Zhou Enlai	Chou En Lai	周恩来	周恩來

Appendix 5

Table A5.3: Some Terms

Wade-Giles or English (Original)	Traditional Chinese
Chinese Industrial Cooperatives, Gong He	工業合作社／工合
Yenching University	燕京大學
Wen Lin Tang (Church in the Forest of Learning)	文林堂
Hundred Flowers Campaign	百花齊放
The Word Was Made Flesh ("Dao Shing Yuk San")	道成肉身
tong fai	堂費

Appendix 6
Sources of Information

Primary Sources

Archives

Hall Family Archive
Bishop's House Archive
Chung Chi Divinity School Archive
Hong Kong Public Record's Office
Church Missionary Society Archive
The National Archives, London
Lambeth Palace Library, London

Private Letters of Bishop Hall to His Wife, Nora, and Sons, Joc and Christopher Hall

Bishop Hall's Publications

An Overwhelming Experience and Attempted Interpretation. Private circulation only, 1956.
China and Britain. London: Edinburgh House Press, 1927.
China: Anno Domini 1950. An Attempt at Theological Interpretation. CSCA, Chung Hua Sheng Kung Hui Source Documents. http://www.ttc.edu.sg/csca/skh/index.html, 1950.
China's Fight for Freedom. CSCA, Chung Hua Sheng Kung Hui Source Documents. http://www.ttc.edu.sg/csca/skh/index.html, 1943.
Hong Kong: What of the Church? London: Edinburgh House Press, Morrison and Bibb Ltd., 1952.
T. Z. Koo: Christianity Speaks to the West. London: SCM Press, 1950.
The Art of the Missionary. London: International Missionary Council, 1942.
"The Development of Social Conscience in Modern China." In *The Christian Movement in China in a Period of National Transition*, 33–42. Mysore City: Wesley Press and Publishing House, 1938.
"The New Church Order." The 27th Annual Hale Memorial Sermon. Delivered on November 14, 1941, Seabury-Western Theological Seminary. Evanston, IL (CHDS), 1941, 65.
"What Happens in Hong Kong." In *Part-Time Priests? A Discussion*, edited by Robin Denniston. London: SPCK, 1960.

Secondary Sources
Periodicals

Chung Chi College Bulletins 1961–66
Diocesan Echo 1997
Fragrant Stream 1953, 1954, 1959, 1960
Outpost 1930–67
South China 1937, 1939, 1949, 1950–52
St. John's Review 1930–67
The Chinese Recorder 1941
University of Hong Kong Gazette 1965

Government Publications

Colonial Office CO 129
Hong Kong Blue Books 1935–40

Books

呂大樂：《凝聚力量：香港非政府機構發展軌跡》。香港：三聯書店（香港）有限公司，2010。
刑福增、劉紹麟：《天國、龍城：香港聖公會聖三一堂史 1890–2009》。香港：基督教中國宗教文化研究社，2010。
Atherton, J. *Social Christianity: A Reader*. London: SPCK, 1994.
Barker, K. *Change and Continuity: A History of St. Stephen's Girls' College, Hong Kong (1906–1996)*. Hong Kong: St. Stephen's Girls' College, 1996.
Bennett, J. *Hasten Slowly*. Chichester, West Sussex, UK: Little London Associates Publishing, 1991.
Bennett, Joyce. *This God Business*. Hong Kong: Religious Education Resource Centre, 2003.
Bosch, D. J. *Transforming Mission: Paradigm Shifts in Theology of Mission*. Maryknoll, NY: Orbis Books, 2010.
Boyd, R. *The Witness of the Student Christian Movement: Church Ahead of the Church*. London: SPCK, 2007.
Brown, D. *The Anglican Church in Hong Kong and the Challenge of Transition (1949–1993)*. Seminar, September 22–24, 1993. Hong Kong: Centre of Asian Studies, The University of Hong Kong, 1993.
Carpenter, J. *Gore: A Study in Liberal Catholic Thought*. London: The Faith Press, 1960.
Chen, J. "The Communist Movement 1927–1937." In *The Cambridge History of China, Volume 13: Republican China 1912–1949, Part 2*, edited by J. Fairbank and A. Feuerwerker, 226–29. Cambridge: Cambridge University Press, 1986.
Cheng, J. Y. S. *Hong Kong in Transition*. Hong Kong: Oxford University Press, 1986.

Chow, N. *Social Welfare in Hong Kong*. Prepared by Hong Kong Organizing Committee for the 20th International Conference on Social Welfare, Hong Kong, July 16–22, 1980.
Doggett, R. E. *Ridley Duppuy: Friend and Bishop*. London: CMS Press, 1946.
Eitel, E. J. *Europe in China: The History of Hong Kong from the Beginning to the Year 1882*. Reprinted with an introduction by H. J. Lethbridge. Hong Kong: Oxford University Press, 1983.
Endacott, G. B. *Government and People in Hong Kong 1841–1962: A Constitutional History*. Hong Kong: Hong Kong University Press, 1964.
———. *A History of Hong Kong*. Second Edition. Hong Kong: Oxford University Press, 1973.
Endacott, G. B., and D. She. *The Diocese of Victoria, Hong Kong: A Hundred Years of Church History*. Hong Kong: Messrs Kelly and Walsh Ltd., 1949.
English, J. *Citizen of the World: The Life of Pierre Elliott Trudeau, Volume 1: 1919–1968*. Toronto, ON: Vintage Canada, 2006.
Fairbank, J. K., ed. *The Cambridge History of China, Volume 12: Republican China, 1912–1949, Part 1*. Cambridge: Cambridge University Press, 1983.
Fairbank, J. K., and A. Feuerwerker, ed. *The Cambridge History of China, Volume 13: Republican China, 1912–1949, Part 2*. Cambridge: Cambridge University Press, 1986.
Faure, D. *A Reader in Social History*, edited by David Faure. Hong Kong: Oxford University Press, 2003.
Fung, Y. W., and M. Chan-Yeung. *To Serve and to Lead: A History of the Diocesan Boys' School*. Hong Kong: Hong Kong University Press, 2009.
Hanson, E. *Catholic Politics in China and Korea*. Maryknoll, NY: Orbis Books, 1980.
Harrison, T. *Much Beloved Daughter: The Story of Florence Li Tim-Oi*. Toronto: Morehouse-Barlow, 1985.
Hayford, C. W. *To the People: James Yen and Village China*. New York: Columbia University Press, 1990.
Ho, S. Y. "Public Housing." In *Hong Kong in Transition*, edited by Joseph Y. S. Cheng, 331–48. Hong Kong: Oxford University Press, 1986.
Hutcheon, R. *High Rise Society*. Hong Kong: Hong Kong Housing Society, 1998.
Jarman, R. *Hong Kong Annual Administrative Report 1841–1949, Volume 5, 1931–1939*, 539–42.
Leung, B., and John D. Young, eds. *Christianity in China: Foundations for Dialogue*. Hong Kong: Centre of Asian Studies, The University of Hong Kong, 1993.
Luk, B. H. K. *A History of Education in Hong Kong: Report Submitted to Lord Wilson Heritage Trust*, 2000.
Lutz, J. G. *China and Christian Colleges (1850–1950)*. Ithaca, NY: Cornell University Press, 1971.
———. *Chinese Politics and Christian Missions: The Anti-Christian Movement of 1920–1928*. Notre Dame, IN: Cross Cultural Publications, Cross Roads Books, 1988.
MacQuarrie, L. *The Development of Social Services in Hong Kong*. Hong Kong: School of Social Work, Hong Kong Polytechnic, 1984.
Morris, J. *To Build Christ's Kingdom: F. D. Maurice and His Writings*. Norwich, UK: Canterbury Press, 2007.

Orens, J. R. "Politics and the Kingdom: The Legacy of the Anglican Left," *Anglican Theological Review* ATR/LXIII.I: 21–41.
Paton, D. M. *Christian Missions and the Judgment of God*. London: SCM Press, 1952.
———. R. O.: *The Life and Times of Bishop Ronald Hall of Hong Kong*. Hong Kong: The Diocese of Hong Kong and Macao and the Hong Kong Diocesan Association, 1985.
Pepper, S. "KMT-CCP Conflict 1945–1949." In *The Cambridge History of China, Volume 13, Republic China 1912–1949, Part 2*, 723–88. Cambridge: Cambridge University Press, 1986.
Potter, P., and T. Wieser. *Seeking and Serving the Truth: The First Hundred Years of the World Student Christian Federation*. Geneva: WCC Publications, 1977.
Ramsey, M. *An Era in Anglican Theology. From Gore to Temple: The Development of Anglican Theology between Lux Mundi and Second World War 1889–1939* (Hale Lectures, 1959). Eugene, OR: Wipf and Stock, 1960.
Smart, A. *The Shek Kip Mei Myth: Squatters, Fires, and Colonial Rule in Hong Kong 1950–1963*. Hong Kong: Hong Kong University Press, 2006.
Snow, P. *The Fall of Hong Kong*. New Haven, CT: Yale University Press, 2004.
Sparks, A., and M. Tutu. *Tutu*. Auckland, New Zealand: Harper One, 2011.
Spence, J. *The Search for Modern China*. New York: W. W. Norton and Company, 1990.
Sun, York Siu. *The Evolution of Public Housing in Hong Kong*. Ann Arbor, MI: UMI, 1993.
Sweeting, A. *Education in Hong Kong 1941–2001: Visions and Revisions*. Hong Kong: Hong Kong University Press, 2004.
Tsang, S. *A Modern History of Hong Kong*. Hong Kong: Hong Kong University Press, 2004.
Webb, P. R. *Voluntary Social Welfare Services, 1951–1976*. A Quarter-Century of Hong Kong Chung Chi College, 25th Anniversary Symposium. Chung Chi College, The Chinese University of Hong Kong, 1977.
Weil, S. *Gravity and Grace*. London: Routledge and Kegan Paul, 1947.
West, P. *Yenching University and Sino-Western Relations, 1916–1952*. Cambridge, MA: Harvard University Press, 1976.
Wilbur, C. M. "The Nationalist Revolution: From Canton to Nanking, 1923–28." In *The Cambridge History of China: Volume 12, Republican China, Part 1*, 527–52. Cambridge: Cambridge University Press, 1983.
Wickeri, P. *Reconstructing Christianity in China: K. H. Ting and the Chinese Church*. Maryknoll, NY: Orbis Books, 2007.
Wilding, P., A. S. Huque, and J. P. Tao-Lai. *Social Policy in Hong Kong*. Cheltenham, UK: Edward Elgar, 1997.
Yip, N. M., and K. Y. Lau. "Housing." In *Social Policy in Hong Kong*, edited by P. Wilding, A. Huque, and J. P. Tao-Lai, 39–54. Cheltenham: Edward Elgar, 1997.

Theses

Hong, Zhou. "The Origins of Government Social Protection Policy in Hong Kong: 1842–1941." PhD thesis, University of Michigan, 1992.

Lam, C. W. "Where East Meets West: A Comparison of Social Work Values between Britain and Hong Kong." PhD thesis, University of Birmingham, 1997.

Wu, Qing. "A Study of Bishop R. O. Hall and His Relationship with China (1922–1966)." PhD thesis, Chinese University of Hong Kong, 2008.

Online Resources

http://archwebs.mh.sinica.edu.tw
http://special.lib.umn.edu/findaid/html/ymca
http://www.tbtsf.org.tw
http://www.ttc.edu.sg/csca/skh
http://tupian.hudong.com
http://www.cnki.net
http://www.womenpriests.org
http://www.anglicancommunion.org
http://www.franciscans.org.uk
http://archives.catholic.org.hk/Statistic
http://www.oxforddnb.com

Interviews by the Author

Dr. and Mrs. Samuel Lam in Hong Kong. April 5, 2010.
Archdeacon Pang Wing Cheong and Mrs. James Pong in Hong Kong. April 14, 2010.
Mr. Timothy Ha in Hong Kong. April 19, 2010.
Canon Alan Chan in Sha Tin. April 28 and April 30, 2010.
Mr. Wong Kwok To (黃國度) and Mr. Leung Sze Woon (梁士瑗) accompanied by the Reverend Lewis Leung in Holy Carpenter Church, Hung Hom, Hong Kong. May 1, 2010.
Dr. Wong Siu Tak (Luke) and Mrs. Wong Chor Heng in Vancouver. May 29, 2010.
Ms. Lee Hei Man in Vancouver. June 7, 2010.
Canon Christopher Hall in Banbury, UK, June 25, 2010, and in Hong Kong, October 26, 2011.
Professor Ma Ho Kei in England. June 27, 2010.
Mr. Michael Lai in St. James' Settlement. August 11, 2010.
The Reverend Kenneth Fung in Hong Kong. November 4, 2010.
The Reverend Paul Tong at St. John's College, Hong Kong. October 24, 2011.

Index

All Saints' Church 55, 73, 168
Allen, Geoffrey 25, 54, 188, 195
Alley, Rewi 63, 71
Archbishop of Canterbury 31, 35, 68, 75, 76, 77, 78, 91, 104, 106, 138, 151, 155, 171, 174, 175, 199
Art of the Missionary, The 67

Baines, Harry 25, 56, 173
Baker, Gilbert 25, 54, 55, 61, 77, 176, 195
Barker, Kay 166
Barth, Karl 36
Beihai 53, 55, 61, 71, 102
Beijing 2, 3, 4, 6, 7, 8, 10, 25, 35, 48, 49, 55, 134, 140
Bennett, Joyce 77
Bernacchi, Brook 92, 128
Bilbrough, Harold 33
Boys' and Girls' Clubs Association 57, 92, 93, 96, 98, 117, 118
Brasenose College 20–23
Brittain, Donald 113
Buddhism 51, 53, 162, 164
Burrough, Paul 176

Calcutta 69, 98
Calvary Church 155, 160, 168
Cambridge 23, 31, 125, 128
Canada 13, 53, 77, 84, 137, 155, 164
Canton Union Theological College 54, 73, 91, 112, 136, 176
Carlile, Prebendary 68
Carr, Canon 22
Carter, Sydney 186
Cater, Jack 172, 201
Chakkravarti, Manu 6
Chan, Alan 24, 173
Chang, Michael 135

Chao, T. C. 9, 35, 61, 199
Chen, Jitang 47, 55
Cheung, Oswald 164, 193
Cheung, P. Y. 163, 191
Cheung, Wing Ngok 54, 176
Chiang, Kai-shek 13, 47, 64, 85
Children's Meals Society 155, 163–64
China
  civil war in 47, 85, 89, 93, 100, 101
  culture of 47, 51, 56, 58, 136, 158, 162, 202
  Free China 61, 64, 69–71, 86, 99
  People's Republic of 85, 90, 100, 102, 104, 105, 134, 136, 139
China and Britain 13–14, 54
Chinese clergy 54, 56, 72, 97, 111, 113, 151, 154, 159, 176, 177, 199
Chinese Communist Party 1, 10, 13, 47, 64, 85, 89, 104, 134
Chinese Industrial Cooperatives 63, 65
Chongqing 53, 61, 71, 102, 135
Chou, Meng Chou 54, 71
Christ Church 36, 199
Christian Buddhist Institute 51
Christian Socialism 37, 38, 102
Christian Study Centre in Chinese Religion 162
Chung Chi College 126, 127, 128, 158, 160, 162, 164, 166, 171, 203
Chung Chi Theological Seminary 160
Chung Hua Sheng Kung Hui 31–33, 53, 54, 73–76, 88, 91, 99, 100, 104, 105, 106, 123, 149, 153–59, 165, 167, 168, 172, 174, 175, 199, 200
Chung, Yan Laap 54, 99, 100, 203
Church Guest House 96
Church of Good Shepherd 113, 114, 115
Church Missionary Society 32, 34, 57, 58, 99, 102, 128, 153, 198

Church Missionary Society Day School Council 99, 158
Church Missionary Society Day Schools 95, 98, 123, 165
Church Times 74, 75, 77, 175
Clarke, H. H. 155
colonialism 4, 6, 8, 13, 31, 34, 48, 51, 68, 133, 138, 142, 171, 185
communism 29, 38, 64, 71, 101, 102, 116, 138, 139, 141
Confucius (Confucianism) 7, 12, 39, 51, 53, 162, 201
Council of Churches of Southeast Asia 155, 173, 174, 175, 199
Crary, Denham 119, 120, 127, 194
Cromwell, Oliver 19
Crowe, C. T. 137, 138
Crown of Thorn Church 160
Crozier, D. J. S. 123, 170, 172
Cultural Revolution 139, 142

de Blank, Joost 176
de Chardin, Teilhard 36, 40
Denunciation Movement 104, 105, 134, 140
Diocesan Boys' School 56, 58, 98, 127, 128, 139, 170, 193, 197
Diocesan Education Committee 99, 158, 163
Diocesan Girls' School 58, 139, 190
Duppuy Fund 89, 97, 99
Duppuy, Ridley C. 31, 33, 35, 89, 96, 97, 99

Elliott, Elsie 90
evangelism 31, 53, 88, 156, 168, 200, 202

Fairlea 58
Faulkner, C. J. W. 92
Featherstone, W. T. 32
Fisher, Geoffrey 75, 76, 77, 155, 173, 174
Fisher, Michael 152
Forward Movement 88, 91, 114
Foster, John 158, 200, 201
France 8, 21, 35

Gollancz, Victor 41
Gong He 63, 64, 68, 71, 101
Gong, Peng 71, 135
Goodban, Gerald 25, 128, 170
Gore, Charles 24, 37, 38, 101
Goulder, Michael 175
Grantham, Alexander 63, 85, 90, 96, 115, 125, 126, 127, 134, 138, 153
Great Leap Forward 137, 138
Grubb, Kenneth 125, 197, 198
Guangdong 31, 47, 48, 55, 61, 89, 105, 106, 115, 142
Guangzhou 6, 13, 49, 53, 54, 56, 60, 61, 64, 72, 88, 91, 100, 102, 105, 118, 134, 138, 146
Guiyang 53, 61, 71
Guizhou 31, 48, 61
Guomindang 13, 47, 64, 85, 89, 100, 101, 102, 171

Hall, (Alfred) Christopher 27, 54, 65, 86, 127, 130, 132, 150, 186, 189, 190, 191, 196
Hall, Gallopine, Cecil 19, 20
Hall, Giles 35, 48
Hall, Jocelyn Baron Owen (Joc) 3, 27, 36, 41, 60, 65, 66, 71, 75, 86, 132, 149, 189, 190, 196
Hall, Judith Marion 27, 65, 86, 132, 150, 154, 185, 188, 189, 190, 196
Hall, Noel 13, 20, 68, 136, 137, 179
Hall, Nora 3, 4, 23, 26, 27, 33, 34, 41, 51, 59, 60, 65, 66, 69, 71, 75, 86–90, 98, 114, 116, 129–34, 140, 149, 150, 153, 154, 155, 170, 174, 177, 185–92, 197
Hall, Ronald Owen
 activism of 149
 army 20–26, 192
 birth of 19
 criticism of 33, 59, 77, 134, 172, 198
 death of 186
 education 6, 24, 29, 38, 40, 56–61, 87, 91, 95, 97, 112, 115, 116, 119–23, 125, 126, 127, 134, 153, 156, 158, 163–72, 185, 189, 200, 202

Index

enthronement 49–50
episcopacy of 37, 53, 98, 149, 155, 168, 199
evangelism 31, 53, 88, 156, 168, 200, 202
faith 6, 21, 29, 36, 37, 40, 42, 49, 100, 101, 111, 132, 138, 153, 154, 164, 169, 177, 203
fundraising 58, 61, 68, 88, 96, 119, 128, 151, 155
Ho Ming Hua 49, 57, 185
Ho, M. W. Fund 99, 185
marriage and family 26, 27, 34, 50, 59, 113, 129–34, 150, 154, 187, 188, 189
"Pink or Red Bishop" 115, 139, 149, 188
religion and society 6, 12, 13, 24, 28–43, 53, 71, 102, 104, 105, 132, 137, 138, 162
retirement of 99, 155, 167, 168, 175, 177, 185, 202
silver jubilee of 100, 149, 150, 151, 152, 154
social justice 20, 68, 86, 115–18, 127, 200–203
travels 4, 11, 35, 36, 48, 60, 66, 68, 71, 86
workers' rights and living conditions 1, 2, 28, 38, 48, 61, 98, 115–22, 127, 128, 135, 169, 171, 172
Halward, Victor 56, 57, 88, 99, 105
Hammarskjöld, Dag 162
Harcourt, Cecil 85, 94
Harth, Charles 98, 99
Higgs, Mollie 59, 192
Hinduism 4, 6, 162
Holy Carpenter Church 117, 119, 120, 127, 160, 169, 200
Holy Trinity Church 55, 56, 168
Hong Kong
British rule 1, 2, 4, 11, 13, 14, 48, 51, 68, 85, 90, 94, 105, 136, 142, 177
fall of 67
government 90, 95, 111, 136, 177, 200

housing 57, 93–94, 121–22, 201
refugees 48, 56, 57, 61, 62, 63, 89, 90, 93, 102, 111, 121, 122, 200, 201
relief efforts 56, 60, 63–65, 90, 92–93, 111, 122
welfare (social welfare) 56, 61, 63, 88, 90, 97, 100, 116, 118, 122, 127, 137, 140, 152, 153, 155, 158, 159, 160, 163, 164, 165, 168, 172, 193, 199, 201, 202
Hong Kong Council of Social Service 63, 92, 93, 94, 200
Hong Kong Housing Society 94, 121–22, 165, 201
Hong Kong Sheng Kung Hui (Diocese of Hong Kong) 49, 55–59, 72–75, 89, 100, 105, 106, 123, 149, 153, 155, 156, 158, 165, 167, 172, 174, 175, 199, 200
Hong Kong Sheng Kung Hui Diocesan Welfare Council 158
Hong Kong Sheng Kung Hui primary schools 165–67
Hong Kong Sheng Kung Hui Primary School Council 158
Hong Kong Sheng Kung Hui secondary schools 167–68, 202
Hong Kong Union Theological College 112, 159–60, 173, 174
Huang, Jane 77
Huang, Quentin 61, 62, 102, 104
"Hundred Flowers Campaign" 134, 141
Hunter, Leslie 28, 33

imperialism 1, 3, 6, 13, 101, 104, 116
India 4, 25
Islam 162

Japan 31, 47, 57, 60, 61, 63, 64, 66, 68, 86, 89, 93, 95, 176
Johnson, Edward C. C. 98, 99, 185, 193
Juvenile Care Center 117

Kam Tin 114, 165
Kei Oi Church/School 98, 155, 160, 163

Kierkegaard, Søren 36
Kingsley, Charles 38
Koh, Roland 99, 159, 176, 177
Kong, Xiangxi 63
Koo, T. Z. 3, 7, 9, 10, 11, 27, 49, 61
Korean War 90, 104, 111, 123, 134
Kunming 32, 53, 61, 69, 71
Kvan, Eric 125
Kwong, Peter 173

Lambeth Conference 76, 77, 86, 154
Lam, Chik Ho 100
Lam, Chik Suen 100
Lam, Woo 100
Lang, Cosmo Gordon 32, 68
Lee, Edward Y. P. 54, 56, 91, 114
Lee, Hei Man 118, 128, 164
Lee, Kau Yan 53, 54, 56, 99, 151, 167, 168, 173
Lewknor 60, 66, 99, 130, 131, 154, 185, 186, 192
Lew, Timothy Tingfang 9
Li, Fook Wo 99, 100
Li, Tim Oi 54, 73, 74, 76, 77, 134, 188
Lian Da (National Southwest Associated University) 61
Lin Yin Tai 51, 55, 86, 87, 88, 99, 191, 192
Long, Charles 113, 151
Loong, S. K. 99
Ludlow, John 38
Lux Mundi 37, 40

MacDougall, David 171
Mao, Zedong 47, 63, 64, 85, 101, 104, 141, 142
Martin, E. W. L. 99, 112, 154
Marxism 29, 38
Maurice, F. D. 24, 36, 37, 38, 39, 64, 116, 140, 162, 202
May 30 incident 2, 14
Ming Hua College 91, 112
missionaries 3, 6, 7, 8, 9, 14, 25, 26, 31, 35, 39, 51, 53, 54, 61, 66, 67, 72, 88, 95, 97, 104, 105, 111, 140, 156, 173, 175, 195, 197, 198, 199, 202

Mohammedanism 71
Mok, Sau Tsang 49, 53, 54, 60, 105
Mo-Yung, In 61, 105, 134, 179

Nanjing 1, 6, 47, 134, 135
National Christian Council 8–10, 39, 88, 161
New Zealand 19, 77, 151, 155, 173
Niebuhr, Reinhold 67
Niebuhr, Ursula 67, 69, 72

Octavia Hill's principle 28, 121
O'Neill, Con D. W. 136, 138
ordination of female priest 43, 54, 72, 76, 77, 78, 200

Paton, David 11, 24, 27, 175, 187, 188, 195
Peill, Arthur 54
Penn, Y. W. 100
Pope, Beatrice 58, 128

Qiao, Guanhua 135
Qufu 12, 14

Ramsey, Michael 77, 174, 176, 177
resettlement estate schools 165–67
"Resolution 28" 77
Roman Catholic Church 3, 37, 63, 111, 161, 164, 165
Rose, Alaric 112
Ryan, T. F. 63, 90, 121

Sargent, Christopher 56, 72
secondary schools, academic 167
secondary schools, modern 167
She, George 57, 76, 87, 91, 92, 95–99, 109, 112, 113, 115, 123, 125, 128, 170, 171, 193, 197
Shenyang (Mukden) 12, 14
Sino-Japanese War 53, 60–62, 64–65
Smith, Percy 195
Snow, Edgar 63
St. Andrew's Church 55, 65, 174, 192
St. Barnabas' Church 160
St. Christopher's Home (Tai Po Rural Orphanage) 57, 119, 120, 165

Index

St. James' Settlement 100, 117–18, 127–28, 155, 163–65, 169, 190, 198, 200
St. John's Cathedral 22, 48, 56, 63, 87, 98, 105, 113, 118, 119, 126, 151, 154, 158, 171
St. John's College (Hall) 98, 112, 123–25, 127, 129, 151, 158, 190
St. Luke's Church (Kennedy Town) 114, 155
St. Luke's Church, Newcastle 27–30, 39, 49, 91
St. Luke's Settlement (Kennedy Town) 165
St. Mark's Church 160
St. Mary's Church 55, 56
St. Matthew's Church 114
St. Paul's Church 55, 96, 97, 100
St. Paul's Coeducational College (St. Paul's Girls' School) 6, 58, 99, 100, 126
St. Paul's College 6, 61, 96, 97, 98
St. Peter's Church (North Point) 155, 160, 173
St. Peter's Church (West Point) 55, 57
St. Simon's Hostel 165
St. Stephen's Boys' College 6, 58
St. Stephen's Church 55, 86, 176, 201
St. Stephen's Girls' College 58, 158, 164, 166
St. Thomas' Church 155, 169
Stanton House (Central Hospital) 95–97, 98
Stewart, Arthur 32, 35
Street Sleepers Society 57
Student Christian Movement 2, 3, 4, 8–11, 23–28, 31, 33, 39, 54, 61, 175, 195, 197
Swann, Alfred 48, 49
Synod 33, 53, 72, 73, 76, 87, 100, 101, 147, 151, 156, 175, 176

Taiping Rebellion 56, 102
Taiwan 85, 139, 142, 159, 163

Tatlow, Tissington 25, 33, 197
Temple, William 39, 72, 74, 73, 75, 77, 91, 116
"Three-Self" Church 9, 104
Till, Barry 113, 197
Tin Kwok School 57
Tractarianism 19, 37, 38, 42
Trudeau, Pierre Elliott 137
Tsang, Kei Ngor 56
Tso, Paul S. F. 56, 99, 150, 173
Tyneside 27–29, 31, 33, 49, 63

Victoria Diocesan Association 34, 35, 58, 61, 88
Victoria Home 57, 58

Wan Chai 55, 114, 118, 119, 155, 165
Weil, Simone 36, 71, 116
Westcott House 31, 195
Westminster 176, 186
Westminster Abbey 84, 186
Wilson, Leonard 25, 31, 63, 66, 67, 176, 194, 195
Wittenbach, Harry 55, 89, 196, 198
Wong, James C. L. 92, 112, 159, 175
Workers' Children's School 115, 171
World Student Christian Federation Conference 3, 6–8, 10, 39, 161
Wu, Y. T. (Wu Yaotsung) 9, 104

Yan, Yangchu, James (James Y. C. Yen) 55
Yenching University 9, 61
Yingchao, Deng 135
Yip, Francis 120
YMCA 2, 3, 6, 9, 14, 56, 112
Yui, David 2, 3, 10
Yunnan-Guizhou 62, 89, 102, 104
YWCA 2, 3, 90, 92

Zengcheng 53, 54, 55, 57, 89, 196
Zhou, Enlai 71, 102, 104, 135, 136, 138, 141
Zhu, Y. Y. 61, 62